Geoff Armstrong wrote *A Century of Summers*, the centenary book of the Sheffield Shield, in 1992. Ten years later, he produced *ESPN's Legends of Cricket*, which profiles 25 of the game's greatest players. In between, he was the co-author of *The People's Game*, a history of Australia in one-day international cricket, *Whiticisms*, a book with Mike Whitney, *Winning Attitudes*, featuring interviews with Australian Olympic Gold medallists, *Hands & Heals*, the autobiography of Ian Healy, and *Phar Lap*, the definitive biography of Australia's greatest racehorse. He has also collaborated with Steve Waugh on each of the Australian Test captain's 10 best-selling books.

Ian Russell has compiled the records sections that appear in the autobiographies of a number of Australian Test players of the last two decades, including those of Geoff Lawson, Mike Whitney, David Boon, Mark Taylor and Ian Healy. Russell has also provided the statistics for Steve Waugh's tour diaries, *A Century of Summers*, *The People's Game*, and helped produce the questions (and researched the answers) for *David Hookes' Cricket Trivia Challenge*. In all, he has been involved in the making of more than 30 cricket books.

TOP 10s OF AUSTRALIAN TEST CRICKET

GEOFF ARMSTRONG & IAN RUSSELL

ABC
Books

Front Cover Photographs

The cricketers featured on the cover of *Top 10s of Australian Test Cricket* are the men nominated in this book as Australia's all time Top 10 (see page 5 of the introduction — The Greatest Ever Australian Cricket Team: A Short History — where the reasons for the players' selections are outlined).

Left column, top to bottom: Sir Donald Bradman, Shane Warne, Victor Trumper, Adam Gilchrist; Middle column: Allan Border, Dennis Lillee, Charlie Macartney; Right column: Fred Spofforth, Alan Davidson, Keith Miller.

All the photographs on the front cover are from the magnificent Getty Images library. As always, the authors are extremely grateful for the support, patience and friendship from all at Getty Images, especially from James Nicholls and Ruth Gray.

Published by ABC Books for the
AUSTRALIAN BROADCASTING CORPORATION
GPO Box 9994 Sydney NSW 2001

Copyright © Geoff Armstrong and Ian Russell 2003

First published November 2003

ISBN 0 7333 1354 X.

Set in 10pt Minion
Cover design by NinehundredVC
Produced by Geoff Armstrong
Prepress by Colorwize Studio, Adelaide
Printed in Australia by Griffin Press, Adelaide

5 4 3 2 1

CONTENTS

CHAPTER TWO: THE BOWLERS

CHAPTER THREE: WICKETKEEPERS AND FIELDSMEN

CHAPTER FOUR: THE ALLROUNDERS

CHAPTER FIVE: THE CAPTAINS

CHAPTER SIX: THE TEAMS

CHAPTER SEVEN: AROUND THE GROUNDS

CHAPTER EIGHT: AROUND THE WORLD

CHAPTER NINE: YOUNGEST AND OLDEST

CHAPTER TEN: EXTRAS

MATTHEW HAYDEN'S NEW WORLD RECORD!

On October 9–10, 2003, while this book was at the printers, Matthew Hayden broke the world record for the highest score made in a Test match. Against Zimbabwe at the WACA Ground in Perth, Hayden smashed 380 from 437 balls, in a sensational display of hitting that featured 38 fours and 11 sixes. In the process, he also did some damage to a few of the Top 10s in this book.

Among the Top 10s Hayden's amazing achievement changed are:

10 Highest Scores (page 16): Hayden is now No. 1.

10 Highest Match Aggregates (page 18): Hayden, with 380 runs, is now equal second.

Highest Score by an Opener (page 18): Hayden is now No. 1.

10 Batsmen with the Most Hundreds (page 24): Hayden, with 15, is now equal 10th.

10 Batsmen with the Highest Percentage of Innings as Centuries (page 27): Hayden stays second, now averaging a century every five times he goes out to bat.

10 Highest Scores in First Innings (page 29): Hayden is now No. 1.

10 Batsmen Who Hit the Most Fours in an Innings (page 33): Hayden is now No. 3. His 11 sixes is the most hit by an Australian in a Test innings.

10 Batsmen Who Scored the Most Runs in an Innings from Boundaries (page 37): Hayden's 218 runs from boundaries puts him at No. 1.

10 Longest Innings (page 45): Hayden batted for 622 minutes, the sixth longest innings by an Australian in Tests.

Hayden's innings boosted his career Test batting average to 56.75, moving him to third all-time (page 15). Every one of Hayden's Test innings have been as an opening batsman, which means he is now second on the 'Best Batting Averages for an Opener' Top 10 (page 48). His score is now also, of course, the highest Test innings made at the WACA (page 168) and the highest innings by an Australian against Zimbabwe (page 178).

Also of note from the Test: Adam Gilchrist's unbeaten 113 took his career Test average to 61.06, second highest among all batsmen with 30 Test innings (see especially pages 15 and 111) … Australia's 6–735 declared is now No. 2 on the 'Top 10 Highest Innings Totals by Australia' (page 127) … the partnerships of 207 between Hayden and Steve Waugh for the fourth wicket and 233 by Hayden and Gilchrist for the sixth wicket are Australian Test records for the WACA (page 170).

ACKNOWLEDGMENTS

The statistics featured in this book come from a wide variety of sources. Inevitably, most stats are derived from published scorecards of Test matches, so we are extremely grateful for the work of Bill Frindall, whose three-volume *The Wisden Book of Test Cricket* records the scores of every Test match from 1877 to 2000. As far as Tests played in Australia, the two volumes of *First-Class Cricket in Australia*, by Ray Webster and Allan Miller, which cover exhaustively every first-class match played in Australia from 1850–51 to 1976–77, were similarly valuable. Elsewhere, the quality of published cricket stats ranges from superb to ordinary. We found two websites — *howstat.com.au* and *cricinfo.com* — to be fantastic resources for checking information, while many of the Association of Cricket Statisticians publications are excellent. A full list of sources consulted during the compiling of this book is listed in 'Further Cricket Reading'.

We are extremely grateful for the support of many individuals who helped get this book to the printer. Our thanks go the terrific cricket people who contributed Top 10s — Gerry Collins, Merv Hughes, Terry Jenner, Dean Jones, Justin Langer, Geoff Lawson, Dan Lonergan, Jim Maxwell, Glenn Mitchell, Peter Newlinds, Paul Reiffel, Steve Waugh and Roger Wills. Also, in the course of putting the words and stats together a number of experts we talked to were very helpful, most notably Mike Coward and Neil Marks, whose knowledge and friendship is much appreciated. Thanks also to Ian Heads, Phil Jennings, Robert Joske, Peter Longman, Sarah Shrubb and Peter Thompson for their support and good humour; to Chris Magus for his work on the cover; and to Stuart Neal, Jo Mackay, Brigitta Doyle and Lindsay Somerville at ABC Books, who are a joy to work with.

INTRODUCTION

THE GREATEST EVER AUSTRALIAN CRICKET TEAM: A SHORT HISTORY

There was a time in Australian cricket when any attempt to compare current champions with the giants of the past was met with close to derision. In sports where you could precisely measure improvements, competitors were faster and stronger, but in cricket the modern stars had apparently gone backwards. In the summers after World War II, for example, most pundits would argue that Australia's greatest ever side was either Joe Darling's 1902 side or Warwick Armstrong's 1921 combination. Those with a real eye for history might mention the 1882 side. The best Bradman's '48 team could do was third.

The respected English cricket writer Ronald Mason, in his 1971 book *Warwick Armstrong's Australians*, provides an example of this thinking:

The image of Armstrong's Australians, for reasons which are not easy to define, looms over a half-century's distance with an unusual, I might almost say magnetic, impressiveness; they are monolithic, indestructible, awesome. There has been nothing to compare with them since.

This last curt generalisation may seem to do no sort of justice to Bradman's superb combination of 1948, whose record was better and who, unlike the earlier destroyers, were never defeated, no not ever. Yet somehow they seem to stand out less in relief against a universal mediocrity than their gigantic predecessors, constitute in historical perspective less of a severely traumatic experience …

Nostalgia was king. Armstrong himself once said that 'the 1902 side could play 22 of my [1921] chaps and give them a beating'. He was on his first tour in 1902, his fourth when captain nearly two decades later. The Test batsman and acclaimed author Jack Fingleton even claimed in 1949 that Bill Woodfull's 1930 team was superior to Bradman's '48 side, which presumably meant that he thought that Woodfull's bowling line-up of Clarrie Grimmett, Tim Wall, Alan Fairfax and one of Percy Hornibrook or Ted A'Beckett was at least close to Ray Lindwall, Keith Miller, Bill Johnston and Ernie Toshack. Despite all The Don's runs, Fingleton also always firmly believed that Victor Trumper was the greater batsman, even though he was just seven years old when Trumper died in 1915 and consequently must have based his opinion on what he was grandly told by Trumper's contemporaries. Monty Noble, Australia's Test captain from 1903 to 1909, said on ABC Radio in 1936 that he had 'no hesitation giving the palm to Victor Trumper as the world's greatest batsman'. By this time, Bradman had played 28 Tests and scored seven centuries, six double centuries and two triple centuries, and was averaging almost 100 in Test cricket, to Trumper's final career figure of 39.05.

Naturally, given this affection for Trumper, you'd reckon that in his day, everyone would have agreed that he was the best ever. You'd be wrong. In 1921, Jack Blackham, the famous 19th century wicketkeeper, told the Melbourne weekly, *The Australasian*, 'Not even Trumper, Giffen, Hill, Darling, Graham or Gregory ever quite reached Bannerman's standard.'

Blackham was talking about Charlie Bannerman, scorer in 1877 of cricket's first Test century.

Adding to this mix, JC Davis, the long-time editor of Sydney's greatest ever sporting newspaper, *The Referee*, a man who started on that paper in 1886 as a junior cricket and rugby reporter, wrote in November 1935 that, 'His Australian contemporaries who lived to see Victor Trumper were loath to agree that Victor was greater.' Davis was writing about Billy Murdoch, Australian captain from 1880 to 1884, and again in 1890, a batsman whom WG Grace described in 1899, the year of Trumper's debut Test, as being the best Australia ever produced.

In his book *Cricket Between Two Wars*, Sir Pelham Warner — a pillar of the cricket establishment in England — wrote of a train trip across the Nullarbor in 1932, when he was manager of Jardine's touring team to Australia, of how to pass the time he and his travelling companions selected best ever England and Australian XIs. Their Australian combination was: Monty Noble (captain), Victor Trumper, Charlie

Macartney, Don Bradman, Clem Hill, George Giffen, Warwick Armstrong, Jack Gregory, Bert Oldfield, Fred Spofforth and Charlie Turner. The team does seem short of a batsman to go in first with Trumper, so the absence of at least one of Bannerman or Murdoch is surprising. Why weren't they preferred to Armstrong, who in this team would bat at No. 7 and only get a bowl after Spofforth, Turner, Gregory, Noble, Macartney and Giffen? Warner was born in 1873, a decade after JC Davis and two decades after Jack Blackham. For cricket watchers in the 1930s aged less than 60, the memories of champions from long-gone days were very distant, if at all. That the 'Demon' Spofforth did make Warner's side, having played his final Test in January 1887, is in fact a tribute to his greatness.

Here were the first signs of a trend. When a retired player starts losing his champions, the fans who saw him in his prime, from that time his relative greatness begins to fade.

In Jack Pollard's wonderful work *Cricket The Australian Way*, first published in 1961 and reprinted through the 1960s and into the '70s, Arthur Mailey selected his best-ever Australian XI. First, the former Test legspinner chose a best Australian team since World War I, which was dominated by men who played their best cricket between the Great Wars: Bill Ponsford, Warren Bardsley, Charlie Macartney, Don Bradman (captain), Archie Jackson, Neil Harvey, Keith Miller, Jack Gregory, Bert Oldfield, Bill O'Reilly and Clarrie Grimmett. Then Mailey held his breath and nominated his greatest ever Australian team: Victor Trumper, Bill Ponsford, Charlie Macartney, Don Bradman, Archie Jackson, Keith Miller, Monty Noble (captain), Jack Gregory, Bert Oldfield, Bill O'Reilly and Hugh Trumble.

In Mailey's opinion, published four decades ago, only one man who made his Test debut after 1932 was good enough to make Australia's best ever team. But Trumble, who debuted in 1890, was the oldest player chosen. Fast forward to 1987, when for his book *The Top 100 and the 1st XI*, Philip Derriman asked six eminent cricket men to select their all-time Australia XIs. Bill O'Reilly and Alan McGilvray both found room for Greg Chappell; otherwise all their team had retired from Test cricket by the end of 1960. The former Test man Hunter 'Stork' Hendry didn't even pick Chappell; his most 'modern' player was Alan Davidson (last Test, 1963). Dennis Lillee was the only member of Jack Pollard's XI to appear in a Test after 1956. Victor Trumper made every team, bar that of the former Australian selector Phil Ridings, whose oldest players were Bradman and O'Reilly. Don Tallon had totally superseded Oldfield as the greatest keeper. No one picked Bannerman, Murdoch, Giffen or Turner, and only one, Cliff Winning, the NSW Cricket Association archivist, went for Spofforth. Still, the current-day players missed out too. Allan Border didn't get a vote, neither did Rod Marsh; Lillee received two and a half votes (Ridings bracketing him and Bill Johnston for the last fast bowling place), Greg Chappell got three. Preferences were still strongly towards the old, though some players, it appeared, had been retired too long.

Just 13 years after Derriman's book was published, an Australian 'Team of the Century' was announced in early 2000 and though all of Mailey's XI were eligible for selection, only Ponsford, Bradman, Miller and O'Reilly made the side. This time, five of those selected made their Test debuts in 1970 or later. What was a trend was now a revolution. No longer were they automatically better in the good old days; without eyewitnesses to support them and with marketeers and blanket television coverage highlighting the enormous skills of the modern players, the heroes of the grand old days had been largely forgotten. Trumper was cast aside. Bradman and his Invincibles seem an exception to the rule.

The Team of the Century was: Arthur Morris, Bill Ponsford, Don Bradman, Neil Harvey, Greg Chappell, Keith Miller, Ian Healy, Ray Lindwall, Shane Warne, Dennis Lillee, Bill O'Reilly and Allan Border (12th man).

Soon after, the 2000 *Wisden* included a feature piece on its cricketers of the century, and seemed to strike a better balance between past and present. The Almanack's method was to invite 100 experts to each nominate the five players who in their view had contributed most to the game's 20th century. The Australians to receive votes were Sir Donald Bradman (at No. 1), Shane Warne (4), Dennis Lillee (6=), Bill O'Reilly (15), Ray Lindwall (17=), Richie Benaud (20=), Victor Trumper (23=), Clarrie Grimmett (29=), Allan Border, Ian Chappell and Stan McCabe (all 33=).

Eighteen months later, the giant American sports network ESPN formed a committee of eminent cricketers and cricket people to select the 50 'Legends of Cricket', for what became a very well-received documentary series. Among those recognised were 14 Australians: Sir Donald Bradman (at No. 1), Shane Warne (4), Dennis Lillee (6), Keith Miller (13), Greg Chappell (17), Steve Waugh (23), Allan Border (25), Bill O'Reilly (30), Richie Benaud (36), Glenn McGrath (41), Clarrie Grimmett (43), Ray Lindwall (45), Victor Trumper (46) and Alan Davidson (49).

No one had given a thought to Billy Murdoch or Charlie Bannerman. The Demon hardly got a vote. Bradman was the only Australian in the Top 25 to have played Tests before World War II. If there once had been a clear and unfair bias towards the old, now punditry seems too much tilted in favour of the new. The correct answer, surely, lies somewhere in between.

❖   ❖   ❖

In seeking to address the need to find a balance between new and nostalgia, the method we've adopted to identify Australia's top 10 all-time cricketers works around the quite logical and oft-stated theory that a champion cricketer in one era would be a champion cricketer in any era. If Fred Spofforth was around today, this logic implies, he'd be a great bowler — different from the one who terrorised batsmen in the 1870s and 1880s, sure, but still a great one; his dedication, natural talent and highly competitive spirit would see to that. We have divided Australia's Test history into 10 eras — 1877–1895, 1896–1912, 1920–1929, 1930–1939, 1946–1956, 1957–1969, 1970–1979, 1980–1989, 1990–1999, 2000–2003 — and nominated the best player of each era, to create an all-time Top 10 of Australian Test cricket. The sheer number of Test matches played these days, and the number of times the Australian Test team has won under Steve Waugh's leadership, is sufficient reason, we believe, to have the most modern of these eras running to just four years. The only rule we have applied in our selections is that while a player can be eligible for selection in more than one era, he is judged purely by what he does in the specific era. Thus, for example, Rod Marsh is eligible to be chosen as the cricketer of the 1980s, but in picking the best players of this decade he is measured purely on what he did between 1980 and his final Test in early 1984.

Our nominations are as follows:

Era	Player	Runner-up
1877–1895	Fred Spofforth	Jack Blackham
1896–1912	Victor Trumper	Clem Hill
1920–1929	Charlie Macartney	Jack Gregory
1930–1939	Don Bradman	Bill O'Reilly
1946–1956	Keith Miller	Neil Harvey
1957–1969	Alan Davidson	Richie Benaud
1970–1979	Dennis Lillee	Greg Chappell
1980–1989	Allan Border	Rod Marsh
1990–1999	Shane Warne	Steve Waugh
2000–2003	Adam Gilchrist	Glenn McGrath

To us, most of these selections seem at least reasonably clearcut. Spofforth and Blackham was a toss-up, but the Demon's extraordinary ability to win Tests on his own, most notably in the 'Ashes' Test of 1882, worked in his favour. Miller's all-round skills pushed him ahead of Harvey and Ray Lindwall for the 1946–56 decade, and we had little trouble rating Davidson and Benaud so highly for the second post-World War II era even though they only played for half the 13 years from 1957. (Although the 1960s featured a bevy of outstanding Australian cricketers, including Bob

Simpson, Bill Lawry, Norm O'Neill, Graham McKenzie, Wally Grout, Doug Walters and Ian Chappell, none of these players were what we consider to be truly great.) Similarly, the 1980s lacked a great Australian cricketer apart from Border; the careers of men such as Lillee, Greg Chappell, Marsh and Jeff Thomson were winding down; those of future stars such as Steve Waugh, Dean Jones, Ian Healy, Craig McDermott and Merv Hughes were still evolving; bowlers such as Geoff Lawson and Terry Alderman were excellent but not elite.

A MUCH HARDER TASK is to rank these champions in order, but this we have done as follows:

1. Don Bradman
2. Dennis Lillee
3. Shane Warne
4. Victor Trumper
5. Adam Gilchrist
6. Keith Miller
7. Fred Spofforth
8. Allan Border
9. Charlie Macartney
10. Alan Davidson

A second 10 might look this way:

11. Greg Chappell
12. Steve Waugh
13. Clem Hill
14. Glenn McGrath
15. Bill O'Reilly
16. Neil Harvey
17. Jack Blackham
18. Richie Benaud
19. Jack Gregory
20. Rod Marsh

There is nothing new in putting Sir Donald Bradman at No. 1, but his statistics are so far ahead of everyone else that he must be ranked there. Not one of his famous teammates — not Woodfull or Ponsford, McCabe or Morris, Harvey or Hassett — averaged even half as much as Bradman's career average of 99.94. Across all countries four other batsmen have averaged 60 in Tests, but none has averaged better than Graeme Pollock's 60.97. At 10 September 2003, 27 batsmen from all countries had batted 30 times or more in Tests and achieved a Test career average of between 50 and 61. It is as if Sir Donald wins the Melbourne Cup by a furlong, with the rest of the field dashing across the line, well beaten and all together. No other cricketer, no other Australian sports champions bar maybe Heather McKay and Walter Lindrum in the relatively obscure sports of squash and billiards respectively, comes near him.

Dennis Lillee's greatness is beyond dispute; the way most of his contemporaries rank him above all of the great West Indian fast men of the 1970s and '80s is proof of this. The courage he showed to fight back from an injury that would have ended 99 per cent of careers in our view adds considerably to his lustre, as does the manner in which he was brilliantly successful bowling both lightning fast and later in his career at fast medium. The only thing that shakes our firm belief that he was the game's finest paceman is the fact that Alan Davidson reckons that Ray Lindwall was 'the greatest bowler he ever saw'. Alan Davidson is as certain of this as we all are that the Gabba is in Brisbane, and Alan Davidson — definitely the best left-arm bowler, fast or slow, Australia has had — knows a lot about cricket.

Shane Warne is ranked third because of the way he made spin bowling fashionable again in the early 1990s. Warne was an especially phenomenal bowler between 1993 and 1998, when he took his first 300 Test wickets — it seems such a long time ago when most experts (including most of the members of the Australian Test team) thought that spinners were a thing of the past. It was actually the late '80s, when the West Indies fast bowlers were winning everything and experts were writing books arguing that the rules had to change. Now most kids want to bowl just like Warney. O'Reilly was a different sort of legspinner, so it's hard to compare the two, but him aside it is impossible to believe that Australia, no, make that world cricket, has had a leggie to come close to Warne — a slow bowler who even the quickest batsmen can't get down the wicket to, who could spin a ball around the legs of the most accomplished pro, who could land the ball on the proverbial sixpence, could humiliate world-class batsmen with a devastating flipper, and who did it all without ever having to resort to the wrong 'un.

At numbers four, five and six in our Top 10 are three cricketers — Victor Trumper, Adam Gilchrist and Keith Miller — who were surely cut from the same cloth. We imagine many observers will sneer at Gilchrist being as high as No. 5, but our strong view is that this about right. Yes, we know his career is still to be played out, but even so, how many Australian batsmen since 1877 have played as many game-turning innings as Adam Gilchrist has in his first 45 Tests? He's done so in Hobart, in Mumbai, Birmingham,

Johannesburg and Cape Town. Think of the first week of 2003, at the Sydney Cricket Ground, when he played another gem — not a matchwinner in this instance — in which he decisively outscored Steve Waugh at a time when the Aussie captain was playing one of finest innings of his life. Waugh finished with 102 runs from 135 deliveries; Gilchrist 133 from 121. Clem Hill was many times fantastic, so was Neil Harvey, so was Greg Chappell, but did any of these three great champions turn any more games than has Gilchrist? Allan Border and Steve Waugh have produced a range of courageous backs-to-the-wall efforts, Border's in the '80s being especially notable because so often he had to fight a lone hand. But think of the times when Gilchrist has come out and quickly changed the game to Australia's clear advantage; he must be the best No. 7 in history, better even than Ian Botham. His Test batting average after the July 2003 Tests against Bangladesh was 58.80, second best among Australians and no flash in the pan, for he has played more than 60 Test innings, scored nearly 3000 Test runs. He averages more than twice as much per innings as Ian Healy or Rod Marsh did, yet both Healy and Marsh were considered in their day to be better-than-average keeper/batsmen.

Gilchrist bats at No. 7, we hear you mutter, so you can't compare him with, say, Charlie Macartney, who made most of his finest hundreds going in at first wicket. In the 1920s the legendary Macartney was known as the 'Governor-General', so regal was his runmaking, a batsman who could reputedly smash a ball back at the bowler's head early on, just to confirm who was in charge. We concede at the beginning of our chapter on batting that purely on batting Gilchrist is still a fraction behind Macartney, and also Border, Greg Chappell, Hill, Steve Waugh and Harvey. However, Gilchrist bats at seven for a reason: he is an allrounder of the highest order, highly skilled in two quite diverse cricket skills. Macartney was an effective left-arm bowler before World War I, a great batsman afterwards, but at Test level he was rarely both at once. Keith Miller's Test batting average is only 36, a reflection of the load he carried as strike bowler as well as key batsman (and also of the fact that he never took the game, or himself, *too* seriously). Keeping all day and scoring hundreds isn't easy; no one else has ever been able to do it anything like what Gilchrist does consistently. Some purists like to knock his glovework, but the fact is that on a dismissal-per-Test basis he is the best Australian keeper of all time. Whatever flaws some try to find in his technique, Adam Gilchrist doesn't miss many. An astonishingly valuable cricketer.

To appreciate the true quality of Keith Miller, talk to just about any Australian cricket fan who today is aged between 55 and 75. To a man and woman they'll say, 'Keith Miller was my hero when I was a kid ...' Was Miller as special as Victor Trumper? When you read the way Trumper's contemporaries — men such as Macartney, Hill, Monty Noble and Warwick Armstrong — spoke of him, he must have been of the absolute highest class. Trumper was like Shane Warne, in that the way he played his cricket changed the game for the better; an evolution caused by one great player refusing to be hamstrung by the signs of the times. 'Victor's wonderful (batting) demonstrations shocked old ideas and brought light out of semi-darkness,' Noble wrote in 1926. 'With his coming, the old order passed for ever.' As Warne has the kids of today spinning leg-breaks, so Victor had the young bats of his day attacking the bowlers from the start, attempting brilliant strokes to all parts of the ground. No more pad play, of 'barnacle' batsmen wearing bowlers out, taking no risks. Those who change the game are the types who must be rated at the pinnacle of any Top 10 of Australian Cricket.

In the pages that follow we will provide a broad selection of Top 10s. We have included the more traditional categories, such as most runs and wickets, best averages, highest partnerships, and also analysed some of these stats to try to make more sense of them. Sometimes we have gone out on the proverbial limb, to offer our view as to the best of all time. We acknowledge that this is in some ways quite outlandish, but we do so purely to generate thought and discussion, never believing or intending to offer *definitive* answers to questions such what has been the great Test innings played by an Australian batsman, the greatest shot ever struck, the greatest ball ever delivered by an Australian bowler, the greatest catch ever taken by an Australian fieldsman. Forget their batting, and who do you think was Australia's greatest ever wicketkeeper? You'll discover why we have ranked the men listed above from No. 1 all the way to No. 20, and a whole lot more, including what we think is Australia's cricket's greatest song, most memorable quote, biggest controversy, strangest off-field occupation. If you're naming your son, we'll tell you what is the best name to choose if you want the boy to play for Australia. Who were Australia's best and worst No. 11s? At times, we'll make you think; at times, you'll disagree with us. Most of all, we hope to start a debate or two.

A couple of things to remember: one, statistics can lie, we all know that. David Hookes averaged 111 when batting in the fourth innings of Tests (four innings, two not outs, runs 222, highest score 68 not out), but that probably doesn't mean you'd want him batting for your life on the last day if Allan Border (career fourth-innings average 34.40) was also available. David Hookes was a good cricketer on his day, but as a batsman he was no Allan Border. However, statistics can also tell the truth. They support the case for many players' greatness, while sometimes casting doubt on the reputations of others. In studying the Top 10s that follow, please consider that it was harder to score runs before World War I — the leading career averages up to that time were around the 40 mark, while after the war the best, Bradman apart, climbed to near 50. Similarly, pre-World War I bowlers had things better than their postwar comrades, maybe by around four or five runs a wicket. In this instance, the stats are simply reflecting the fact that wickets improved after 1920, batting techniques got tighter, batsmen's appetites grew, the game became more professional.

And the second thing? Some cynics like to say that you can't compare eras. Don't listen to these people, they're spoilsports. And just because you didn't see a bloke play doesn't mean you can't have an opinion as to how good he might or might not have been. As long as your prime objective is to have some fun — and throughout this book ours always is — comparing players, teams and contests from different eras is one of the most interesting things a sports fan can do. Cricket enthusiasts young and old have been doing it for years.

We hope you enjoy doing it here.

Geoff Armstrong & Ian Russell
September 2003

PREAMBLE ON GROUNDS

Australia has played Test cricket on 55 grounds (of the 90 used worldwide) in the following countries: Australia (nine grounds), England (seven), India (eight), New Zealand (four), Pakistan (six), South Africa (eight), Sri Lanka (six), United Arab Emirates (one), West Indies (five) and Zimbabwe (one).

Throughout this book, grounds are identified by the city in which they are located, except for the two grounds in London — Lord's and The Oval.

Australia
Brisbane has hosted Tests at two grounds: the Exhibition Ground was the location for the city's first two Tests in 1928–29 and 1930–31; Woolloongabba (known to all as 'The Gabba') hosted its first Test in 1931–32 and has been the location for every Test in Brisbane since.

The other Australian grounds to host Test matches are the Adelaide Oval, Bundaberg Rum Stadium (Cairns), Marrara Oval (Darwin), Bellerive Oval (Hobart), the Melbourne Cricket Ground, the WACA Ground (Perth), and the Sydney Cricket Ground.

England
Grounds in England that have hosted Ashes Tests are Lord's and The Oval (both London), Bramall Lane (Sheffield), Edgbaston (Birmingham), Headingley (Leeds), Old Trafford (Manchester) and Trent Bridge (Nottingham).

South Africa

Two South African cities have hosted Australia in Test cricket at more than one ground. Three Johannesburg grounds have done so (Old Wanderers 1902 to 1935–36, Ellis Park in 1949–50 and New Wanderers since 1957–58), and two in Durban (Lord's in 1921 and Kingsmead since 1935–36).

India

Two Indian cities have hosted Australia in Test cricket at more than one ground. At Bombay (now Mumbai), Brabourne Stadium was the site for Tests until 1969; since 1979 it has been Wankhede Stadium. At Madras (now Chennai), there have been two grounds used: Corporation Stadium until 1964 and since 1969 MA Chidambaram Stadium (formally Chepauk).

Between 1995 and 2001, three Indian cities that have hosted Australian Tests adopted new names: Bombay became Mumbai in 1995, Madras became Chennai in 1996 and Calcutta became Kolkata in 2001.

Pakistan

In 1959, Australia played in what was then East Pakistan, at Dacca. That city is now called Dhaka, the capital of Bangladesh. Australia has not played a Test in Bangladesh; for the purpose of this book Dacca is considered a venue in Pakistan.

Sri Lanka

Australia has played Test cricket on three grounds in Colombo: Sinhalese Sports Club in 1992 and 1999, Khettarama Stadium in 1992 and P Saravanamuttu Stadium in 2002.

Neutral venues

Australia has played two series at 'neutral' venues. In England in 1912, in what was known as the Triangular Tournament, Australia played three Tests against England and three against South Africa. In 2002, owing to the military situation in Afghanistan and fears of unrest in Pakistan, a three-Test series against Pakistan was played in Sri Lanka (one Test) and the United Arab Emirates (two Tests).

All statistics and career records in this book are as at 10 September 2003.

CHAPTER ONE

THE BATSMEN

If we use the same method used in the introduction to determine Australia's greatest ever players — that is, split the history of Australian Test cricket into 10 eras and then select the best batsman from each era — it seems to us that you get a Top 10 that is, at the very least, not too far from being about right. Here is our Top 10 Australian batsmen, with the era the batsman represents noted …

Rank	Batsman	Era
1.	Don Bradman	1930–1939
2.	Victor Trumper	1895–1912
3.	Allan Border	1980–1989
4.	Charlie Macartney	1920–1929
5.	Greg Chappell	1970–1979
6.	Steve Waugh	1990–1999
7.	Neil Harvey	1946–1956
8.	Adam Gilchrist	2000–2003
9.	Billy Murdoch	1877–1894
10.	Bob Simpson	1957–1969

A case could be put that some champion batsmen of old — most notably Clem Hill and Stan McCabe — should be in this Top 10 ahead of Billy Murdoch, though the talents of Murdoch, Australia's first consistently productive Test batsman, should not be underestimated. His innings at The Oval in 1880, when he bet WG Grace that he'd outscore him and then went out and scored 153 not out to Grace's 152, was a masterpiece; Murdoch was as responsible as any player in getting from the gentlemen of England the respect Australian cricket needed to make Test cricket a going concern in the 1880s.

The choice of Adam Gilchrist ahead of Matthew Hayden, Justin Langer and especially Ricky Ponting as the 21st century's representative is a tough one, but as we explained in this book's introduction, we believe the manner in which a number of the keeper-batsman's innings have changed Test matches, in a manner almost unique in Australian Test history, puts him in front. This foursome, along with their captain, Steve Waugh, has provided Australia with as dynamic and productive a batting order as any line-up that didn't include Don Bradman.

A number of the Top 10s that follow demonstrate just how good the current Australian team's batsmen are. One example: Gilchrist, Hayden, Ponting and Waugh are all in the Top 10 career batting averages. For all this, however, nothing compares to the dominance throughout this chapter of The Don. As you will see, his batting figures are simply phenomenal.

❖   ❖   ❖

10 LEADING CAREER RUN-SCORERS

Rank	Batsman	Tests	Inns	NO	Runs	HS	100s	50s	Avge
1.	Allan Border	156	265	44	11174	205	27	63	50.56
2.	Steve Waugh	162	251	45	10521	200	32	46	51.07
3.	Mark Waugh	128	209	17	8029	153*	20	47	41.82
4.	Mark Taylor	104	186	13	7525	334*	19	40	43.50
5.	David Boon	107	190	20	7422	200	21	32	43.66
6.	Greg Chappell	87	151	19	7110	247*	24	31	53.86
7.	Don Bradman	52	80	10	6996	334	29	13	99.94
8.	Neil Harvey	79	137	10	6149	205	21	24	48.42
9.	Doug Walters	74	125	14	5357	250	15	33	48.26
10.	Ian Chappell	75	136	10	5345	196	14	26	42.42

As is reflected by some of the batting averages, this table reflects players' longevity and the more concentrated playing schedules of recent decades as much as it does ability. Moving beyond the top 10, the first player on a list of highest Australian career aggregates to have played his career solely before World War II is Clem Hill (1896 to 1912) at No. 23, with 3412 runs from 49 Tests. Victor Trumper (3163 runs) is 25th, Warwick Armstrong (2863) is 30th.

Twelve Australians have scored 5000 Test runs, Michael Slater (5312 runs) and Bill Lawry (5234) being numbers 11 and 12 respectively. Eighteen have scored 4000 runs. Twenty-seven have scored 3000 runs. The leading wicketkeeper is Ian Healy, at No. 18, with 4356 runs from 119 Tests. Rod Marsh, with 3633 runs from 96 matches, is 19th.

Quickly moving up this table are Ricky Ponting, currently 14th with 4856 runs, Justin Langer (16th, 4632), Matthew Hayden (21st, 3536) and Adam Gilchrist (29th, 2940). Damien Martyn, with exactly 2000 Test-match runs, is 46th.

Of the 46 with 2000 or more runs, one averages in the 90s, six in the 50s (four of whom were in the Australian team that played Bangladesh in 2003), 23 in the 40s, 11 in the 30s, four in the 20s and one — Shane Warne (2238 runs in 107 Tests) — averages 16.83.

10 LEADING CAREER BATTING AVERAGES
(Qualification: 30 innings)

Rank	Batsman	Tests	Inns	NO	Runs	HS	100s	50s	Avge
1.	Don Bradman	52	80	10	6996	334	29	13	99.94
2.	Adam Gilchrist	45	62	12	2940	204*	8	16	58.80
3.	Greg Chappell	87	151	19	7110	247*	24	31	53.86
4.	Matthew Hayden	44	74	6	3536	203	14	10	52.00
5.	Jack Ryder	20	32	5	1394	201*	3	9	51.63
6.	Ricky Ponting	69	108	13	4856	206	17	18	51.12
7.	Steve Waugh	162	251	45	10521	200	32	46	51.07
8.	Allan Border	156	265	44	11174	205	27	63	50.56
9.	Neil Harvey	79	137	10	6149	205	21	24	48.42
10.	Doug Walters	74	125	14	5357	250	15	33	48.26

Much has been made over the years of the fact that Don Bradman finished his Test career with a batting average of 99.94. Less publicised is the fact that for much of The Don's Test career his average was below 100; it isn't as if he spent his entire cricket life with a century average, only to have it stolen away by that infamous Eric Hollies googly that bowled him second-ball for a duck in the final Test of 1948.

Over his career, Bradman possessed a century-or-better batting average after 25 of his 80 Test innings. It wasn't until he made 232 at The Oval in 1930 that he first pushed his average over three figures, and it stayed there for just one innings, because he was dismissed for 4 in the first Test of the 1930–31 series at home against the West Indies. A season later, when the South Africans toured, Bradman's 299 not out in the fourth Test in

Adelaide pushed his average from 99.83 to 112.29, the highest it would ever reach. The average remained over 100 for 10 innings, but then didn't get that high again until the second Ashes Test after World War II, in Sydney, when he scored 234.

Had The Don retired after the 1938 England tour, his career average would have been 97.94. Following the war, the average always hovered around the 100 mark, never much over or under. His 173 not out at Leeds in the fourth Test of 1948 pushed it up to 101.39, with just The Oval Test to go. After England were bowled out for 52 and the first Australian wicket didn't fall until 117, the likelihood was that Bradman would bat only once, so he went out needing just a boundary to preserve the hundred average. Unfortunately, Hollies — and many argue the emotion of his farewell innings — got the better of him.

10 HIGHEST SCORES

Rank	Score	Player	Versus	Venue	Series
1=.	334	Don Bradman	England	Leeds	1930
1=.	334*	Mark Taylor	Pakistan	Peshawar	1998
3.	311	Bob Simpson	England	Manchester	1964
4.	307	Bob Cowper	England	Melbourne	1965–66
5.	304	Don Bradman	England	Leeds	1934
6.	299*	Don Bradman	South Africa	Adelaide	1931–32
7.	270	Don Bradman	England	Melbourne	1936–37
8.	268	Graham Yallop	Pakistan	Melbourne	1983–84
9.	266	Bill Ponsford	England	The Oval	1934
10.	254	Don Bradman	England	Lord's	1930

The highest score made by an Australian in the first Test of a series is the 11th highest overall: Doug Walters' 250 against New Zealand in Christchurch in 1977 (Justin Langer also made 250 in a Test, against England in Melbourne in 2002–03). Walters' score is also the highest against New Zealand. Highest scores by Australians against teams not listed above are:

Score	Player	Versus	Venue	Series
242	Doug Walters	West Indies	Sydney	1968–69
223	Justin Langer	India	Sydney	1999–00
219	Michael Slater	Sri Lanka	Perth	1995–96
177	Darren Lehmann	Bangladesh	Cairns	2003
151*	Steve Waugh	Zimbabwe	Harare	1999

THE TOP 10 INNINGS BY AUSTRALIAN BATSMEN

Rank	Batsman	Score	Versus	Venue	Series
1.	Stan McCabe	187	England	Sydney	1932–33
2.	Charles Bannerman	165†	England	Melbourne	1876–77
3.	Kim Hughes	100*	West Indies	Melbourne	1981–82
4.	Don Bradman	334	England	Leeds	1930
5.	Joe Darling	160	England	Sydney	1897–98
6.	Dean Jones	210	India	Madras	1986
7.	Victor Trumper	185*	England	Sydney	1903–04
8.	Steve Waugh	63*	West Indies	Port-of-Spain	1995
9.	Neil Harvey	92*	England	Sydney	1954–55
10.	Adam Gilchrist	204*	South Africa	Johannesburg	2002

† retired hurt

Stan McCabe's masterpiece, in our view the greatest of his three famous Test innings (189 not out at Johannesburg and 232 at Trent Bridge being the others), gets top billing because it was the perfect, classic counterattack, made against Larwood at his fastest, against the full bodyline attack, at a time when Australia could have been overwhelmed by England's shock tactics. Don Bradman missed this Test; what might have happened had he joined McCabe in a successful assault on the bumpers? Might Jardine have changed his method?

The sheer stats of Charlie Bannerman's innings in the first ever Test match, a knock which only ended when he had to retire hurt, are incredible. Next top score in the Australian first innings was 18, in the Test it was 20. Without Bannerman's innings England would have won easily. Kim Hughes on Boxing Day 1981 was also a one-man band; in exhilarating fashion he attacked the great Windies pacemen after coming in at 3–8, scoring his innings out of an innings total of 198, and adding 43 for the last wicket with Terry Alderman.

Of Bradman's many great innings, we went for statistically his greatest. It was an extraordinary exhibition of runmaking, featuring a century before lunch and 309 runs in a day. But perhaps more importantly, it so quickly changed the balance of Ashes cricket: England had thrashed Australia in Australia in 1928–29, and won the opening Test of this series. Then Bradman made a brilliant 254 at Lord's, then this triple century in a day, and Australia was back in the ascendancy, to the point that England was making plans for its bodyline assault before the tour was even over.

Joe Darling's innings was probably the most belligerent exhibition of extended pure hitting Australian Test cricket had seen until Adam Gilchrist slaughtered the South Africans at Johannesburg in 2002. Dean Jones' effort in Madras, which ended with him in hospital connected to a saline drip, was as brave as any marathon effort, while Victor Trumper's in Sydney was the ultimate in grace and brilliance. Trumper reached his century that day in 94 minutes, and as he had at Old Trafford in 1902, he scored a Test century in a session, this time between tea and stumps. Steve Waugh and Neil Harvey may not have reached three figures, but they were classic examples of great batsmen gallantly and successfully standing up to supreme fast bowlers (Waugh to Curtly Ambrose, Harvey to Frank Tyson) in conditions that clearly suited the bowlers. ◾

10 HIGHEST MATCH AGGREGATES

Rank	Aggregate	Batsman	Scores	Versus	Venue	Series
1.	426	Mark Taylor	334* & 92	Pakistan	Peshawar	1998
2.	380	Greg Chappell	247* & 133	New Zealand	Wellington	1974
3.	345	Doug Walters	242 & 103	West Indies	Sydney	1968-69
4.	334	Don Bradman	334	England	Leeds	1930
5.	321	Don Bradman	244 & 77	England	The Oval	1934
6.	315	Bob Simpson	311 & 4*	England	Manchester	1964
7.	307	Bob Cowper	307	England	Melbourne	1965-66
8.	304	Don Bradman	304	England	Leeds	1934
9.	303	Allan Border	150* & 153	Pakistan	Lahore	1980
10.	300	Matthew Hayden	197 & 103	England	Brisbane	2002-03

HIGHEST SCORE FOR EACH BATTING POSITION

Position	Batsman	Score	Versus	Venue	Series
1/2.	Mark Taylor	334*	Pakistan	Peshawar	1998
3.	Don Bradman	334	England	Leeds	1930
4.	Bob Cowper	307	England	Melbourne	1965-66
5.	Don Bradman	304	England	Leeds	1934
6.	Doug Walters	250	New Zealand	Christchurch	1977
7.	Don Bradman	270	England	Melbourne	1936-37
8.	George Bonnor	128	England	Sydney	1884-85
9.	Clem Hill	160	England	Adelaide	1907-08
10.	Reg Duff	104	England	Melbourne	1901-02
11.	Rodney Hogg	52	West Indies	Georgetown	1984

10 HIGHEST SCORES ON DEBUT
(First innings in Test cricket)

Rank	Batsman	Score	Versus	Venue	Series
1.	Charlie Bannerman	165†	England	Melbourne	1876–77
2.	Archie Jackson	164	England	Adelaide	1928–29
3.	Kepler Wessels	162	England	Brisbane	1982–83
4.	Wayne B. Phillips	159	Pakistan	Perth	1983–84
5.	Doug Walters	155	England	Brisbane	1965–66
6.	Mark Waugh	138	England	Adelaide	1990–91
7.	Bill Ponsford	110	England	Sydney	1924–25
8.	Gary Cosier	109	West Indies	Melbourne	1975–76
9.	Greg Chappell	108	England	Perth	1970–71
10.	Harry Graham	107	England	Lord's	1893

† retired hurt

Greg Blewett (102* v England at Adelaide in 1994–95) is the only other Australian to score a century in his maiden Test innings. Reg Duff, Roger Hartigan, Herbert Collins, Jim Burke and Dirk Wellham scored centuries in the second innings of their first Test. Walters, Ponsford and Blewett scored hundreds in each of their first two Tests. Graham also scored a century in his first Test in Australia, while Blewett scored a century in his first Test in South Africa and in England (meaning he'd scored centuries in each of his first three Tests against England).

Wessels, with 208 runs (162 and 46), has scored the most runs for Australia by a player on debut. Jackson (164 and 36) is the only other man to score 200 or more runs on debut. Third highest is 167, by Bruce Laird (92 and 75) against a West Indies bowling attack of Andy Roberts, Michael Holding, Colin Croft and Joel Garner at the Gabba in 1979–80.

The highest innings by an Australian batting in his second Test is Ross Edwards' 170 not out at Trent Bridge in 1972.

---

10 AMUSING QUOTES FROM AUSTRALIAN TEST CRICKET HISTORY

1. 'It's all right, I'll hang on.'
   – A line attributed to Bert Ironmonger's wife, reputedly said after she rang the home dressing room just as Ironmonger was going out to bat during the second Test of the bodyline series. Her husband stayed out in the middle long enough to see Don Bradman to a century.

10 HIGHEST AGGREGATES IN A SERIES

Rank	Batsman	Tests	Inns	NO	Runs	HS	Avge	Versus	Series
1.	Don Bradman	5	7	0	974	334	139.14	England	1930
2.	Mark Taylor	6	11	1	839	219	83.90	England	1989
3.	Neil Harvey	5	9	0	834	205	92.67	South Africa	1952–53
4.	Don Bradman	5	9	0	810	270	90.00	England	1936–37
5.	Don Bradman	5	5	1	806	299*	201.50	South Africa	1931–32
6.	Don Bradman	5	8	0	758	304	94.75	England	1934
7.	Don Bradman	5	6	2	715	201	178.75	India	1947–48
8.	Greg Chappell	6	11	5	702	182*	117.00	West Indies	1975–76
9.	Doug Walters	4	6	0	699	242	116.50	West Indies	1968–69
10.	Arthur Morris	5	9	1	696	196	87.00	England	1948

The record for a four-Test series is the 523 runs Ricky Ponting scored against the West Indies in the Caribbean in 2003. Ponting, who missed the final Test of the series, played five innings, one unbeaten, and averaged 130.75. The record for a three-Test series is Matthew Hayden's 549 runs (six innings, one not out, average 109.80) in India in 2001.

There have been six instances of Australian batsmen scoring four centuries in a series — Don Bradman in 1930, 1931–32 and 1947–48 as above; Neil Harvey in 1949–50 (660 runs at 132.00 v South Africa) and 1952–53 as above; and Doug Walters in 1968–69 as above. In 1931–32, Bradman played in the fifth Test but did not bat due to injury. In 1968–69, Walters missed the first Test but then scored one double century, three centuries and two fifties in his six innings during the remainder of the series.

There have been 22 instances of Australians scoring three centuries in a series. Matthew Hayden against South Africa in 2001–02 is the only man to do so in a three-Test series. Don Bradman (1938 Ashes series, when the fourth Test was abandoned without a ball being bowled) and Ricky Ponting (v West Indies in 2003) are the only batsmen to manage this in a four-Test series. As we have already mentioned, Ponting did not play in the final Test of that series in the Caribbean. Bradman did not bat in the fifth Test in 1938.

Don Bradman scored three double centuries in a series once (in 1930) and two double centuries in a series three times (1931–32, 1934, 1936–37). No other Australian has scored more than one double hundred in any one series.

10 HIGHEST AGGREGATES IN A CALENDAR YEAR

Rank	Player	Year	Tests	Inns	NO	Runs	HS	100s	50s	Avge
1.	Matthew Hayden	2001	14	25	3	1391	203	5	5	63.23
2.	Bob Simpson	1964	14	26	3	1381	311	3	7	60.04
3.	David Boon	1993	16	25	5	1241	164*	4	7	62.05
4.	Mark Taylor	1989	11	20	1	1219	219	4	5	64.16
5.	Matthew Hayden	2002	11	17	1	1160	197	6	3	72.50
6.	Kim Hughes	1979	14	27	3	1152	130*	2	8	48.00
7.	Mark Taylor	1998	12	22	3	1112	334*	3	4	58.53
8.	Mark Taylor	1993	15	23	2	1106	170	4	5	52.67
9=.	Allan Border	1985	11	20	3	1099	196	4	2	64.65
9=.	Dean Jones	1989	11	18	3	1099	216	4	4	73.27

10 BATSMEN TO REACH 1000 RUNS IN THE LEAST NUMBER OF INNINGS

(Statistics are as at the completion of the innings in which 1000 runs were achieved)

Rank	Batsman	Tests	Inns	NO	HS	Avge	100s	50s
1.	Don Bradman	7	13	1	254	99.67	5	2
2.	Neil Harvey	10	14	4	178	103.30	6	2
3.	Sid Barnes	11	17	1	234	63.13	3	4
4=	Herbert Collins	12	18	1	203	63.65	4	4
4=	Doug Walters	11	18	3	155	66.73	2	7
4=	Mark Taylor	10	18	1	219	64.00	3	5
7.	Arthur Morris	12	19	3	155	64.00	5	4
8=	Jack Fingleton	12	20	1	136	54.05	5	3
8=	Norm O'Neill	14	20	5	181	70.47	4	3
8=	Brian Booth	11	20	3	169	62.41	4	5

Don Bradman is also the youngest Australian to score 1000 Test runs, being 21 years and 318 days when he reached the landmark at Headingley in 1930. Harvey and Walters were 22 when they reached 1000 runs, Ricky Ponting, Paul Sheahan, Steve Waugh, Graeme Wood, Norm O'Neill and Stan McCabe were all 23.

The quickest to score 1000 runs (from first Test to 1000th run) is Michael Slater, who took 291 days from his debut in the first Ashes Test of 1993 to reach four figures. The only others to do this in less than one year are Mark Taylor and Allan Border, while Matthew Elliott took a year and five days. Bradman is fifth quickest, taking a year and 224 days.

10 BATSMEN TO REACH 2000 RUNS IN THE LEAST NUMBER OF INNINGS

Rank	Batsman	Tests	Inns	NO	HS	Avge	100s	50s
1.	Don Bradman	15	22	1	334	100.71	9	2
2.	Doug Walters	22	35	4	242	66.61	7	12
3.	Arthur Morris	23	36	3	196	63.06	10	4
4.	Neil Harvey	22	37	4	190	60.73	8	7
5.	Michael Slater	23	40	1	176	51.90	6	8
6.	Adam Gilchrist	30	41	8	204*	61.48	6	10
7.	Bob Cowper	26	43	1	307	47.71	5	10
8=.	Greg Chappell	26	44	6	247*	53.00	7	9
8=.	Mark Taylor	24	44	3	219	50.46	6	13
10=.	Bill Woodfull	30	45	4	161	48.90	7	11
10=.	Norm O'Neill	28	45	5	181	50.38	6	10

Don Bradman (23 years, 92 days) is the youngest Australian to score 2000 Test runs, but only just, Neil Harvey being just five days behind him. Doug Walters, Michael Slater and Ricky Ponting all had 2000 runs before their 25th birthdays. In terms of time, Slater is the quickest to 2000, and at one year, 248 days, the only Australian batsman to do so inside two years. Allan Border, Mark Taylor and Adam Gilchrist and Bradman all did so within three years.

10 BATSMEN TO REACH 3000 RUNS IN THE LEAST NUMBER OF INNINGS

Rank	Batsman	Tests	Inns	NO	HS	Avge	100s	50s
1.	Don Bradman	23	33	3	334	100.67	13	4
2.	Neil Harvey	31	54	5	205	61.80	12	11
3.	Matthew Hayden	37	61	4	203	54.00	12	10
4.	Arthur Morris	37	64	3	206	49.21	10	11
5=.	Bill Lawry	36	65	6	210	50.86	8	16
5=.	Greg Chappell	38	65	10	247*	55.62	12	13
7=.	Doug Walters	39	68	7	242	49.52	10	17
7=.	Mark Taylor	36	68	5	219	47.68	8	17
9.	Michael Slater	40	69	3	219	46.12	8	12
10=.	Bob Simpson	42	74	7	311	45.64	4	20
10=.	Dean Jones	44	74	9	216	46.72	9	11

10 BATSMEN TO REACH 4000 RUNS IN THE LEAST NUMBER OF INNINGS

Rank	Batsman	Tests	Inns	NO	HS	Avge	100s	50s
1.	Don Bradman	31	48	3	334	94.49	16	7
2.	Neil Harvey	46	80	6	205	54.14	15	14
3.	Greg Chappell	49	87	13	247*	54.30	14	20
4=.	Doug Walters	52	89	10	242	50.65	12	25
4=.	Mark Taylor	50	89	6	219	48.72	12	22
6=.	Bob Simpson	51	90	7	311	49.44	8	24
6=.	Bill Lawry	50	90	7	210	49.75	12	20
8.	Justin Langer	58	94	5	250	45.22	13	16
9.	Michael Slater	54	95	4	219	45.57	13	14
10=.	Mark Waugh	60	96	4	140	43.88	10	26
10=.	Ricky Ponting	61	96	12	197	49.13	14	16

10 BATSMEN TO REACH 5000 RUNS IN THE LEAST NUMBER OF INNINGS

Rank	Batsman	Tests	Inns	NO	HS	Avge	100s	50s
1.	Don Bradman	36	56	5	334	99.54	21	8
2.	Neil Harvey	61	105	10	205	52.96	18	18
3.	Greg Chappell	60	106	15	247*	55.03	17	23
4.	Bill Lawry	64	117	11	210	47.50	13	25
5.	Doug Walters	70	118	12	250	47.47	14	31
6.	Mark Taylor	66	119	8	219	45.09	13	30
7=.	Allan Border	68	120	21	196	50.62	13	28
7=.	Michael Slater	68	120	7	219	44.29	14	20
9.	Ian Chappell	68	121	8	196	44.32	14	25
10.	Mark Waugh	76	123	5	140	42.41	13	32

The three tables (fastest to 3000, 4000 and 5000 runs) demonstrate how Don Bradman was able to sustain his wonderful batting average, while others with very impressive numbers early in their international cricket careers — batsmen such as Doug Walters, Neil Harvey and Arthur Morris — gradually came back to the field.

Eight Australian batsmen have scored 6000 Tests runs. Bradman, who took 68 innings (average 98.43), was easily the quickest to reach the mark. Next best is Greg Chappell, who took 129 innings, followed by Neil Harvey (134 innings), Allan Border (140), David Boon (148), Steve and Mark Waugh (both 151), and Mark Taylor (152). With Bradman finishing his Test career with 6996 runs, Greg Chappell takes over as the quickest (of six) to reach 7000, in 151 innings, from Border (159 innings), Taylor (173), Steve Waugh (174), Boon (177) and Mark Waugh (183).

Border is the fastest of three to 8000 runs, taking 184 innings. Steve Waugh took 194 innings, Mark Waugh 206. The great left-hander also beat Steve Waugh to 9000 runs, 207 innings to 216, and to 10,000 runs, 235 to 244, and passed 11,000 runs in his 259th innings, his Test batting average at that point being exactly 51.

10 BATSMEN WITH THE MOST SCORES BETWEEN 50 AND 99

Rank	Batsman	Tests	Inns	50s	100s	Total 50s+
1.	Allan Border	156	265	63	27	90
2.	Mark Waugh	128	209	47	20	67
3.	Steve Waugh	162	251	46	32	78
4.	Mark Taylor	104	186	40	19	59
5.	Doug Walters	74	125	33	15	48
6.	David Boon	107	190	32	21	53
7=.	Greg Chappell	87	151	31	24	55
7=.	Ian Redpath	66	120	31	8	39
9=.	Bill Lawry	67	123	27	13	40
9=.	Bob Simpson	62	111	27	10	37

Don Bradman had 42 scores of 50-plus during his Test career: 29 centuries and 13 fifties. The two other Australians with 40 or more scores of 50-plus, apart from those in the Top 10 above, are Neil Harvey (21 hundreds, 24 fifties) and Ian Chappell (14 hundreds, 26 fifties).

10 BATSMEN WITH THE MOST HUNDREDS

Rank	Batsman	Tests	Inns	100s	200s	300s
1.	Steve Waugh	162	251	32	1	0
2.	Don Bradman	52	80	29	12	2
3.	Allan Border	156	265	27	2	0
4.	Greg Chappell	87	151	24	4	0
5=.	David Boon	107	190	21	1	0
5=.	Neil Harvey	79	137	21	2	0
7.	Mark Waugh	128	209	20	0	0
8.	Mark Taylor	104	186	19	2	1
9.	Ricky Ponting	67	106	17	1	0
10=.	Doug Walters	74	125	15	2	0
10=.	Justin Langer	63	105	15	2	0

In this Top 10, '100s' refers to all scores of 100 or more; '200s' refers to all scores of 200 or more. The opposition against whom this Top 10 made their hundreds are as follows (a zero indicates that the batsman has played against a particular team but never scored a century against them):

Batsman	100s	Ban	Eng	Ind	NZ	Pak	SA	SL	WI	Zim
Steve Waugh	32	2	10	2	2	3	2	3	7	1
Don Bradman	29	–	19	4	–	–	4	–	2	–
Allan Border	27	–	8	4	5	6	0	1	3	–
Greg Chappell	24	–	9	1	3	6	–	0	5	–
David Boon	21	–	7	6	3	1	0	1	3	–
Neil Harvey	21	–	6	4	–	0	8	–	3	–
Mark Waugh	20	–	6	1	1	3	4	1	4	0
Mark Taylor	19	–	6	2	2	4	2	2	1	–
Ricky Ponting	17	0	4	2	1	3	2	1	4	0
Doug Walters	15	–	4	1	3	1	0	–	6	–
Justin Langer	15	0	3	1	3	3	2	0	3	0

The Australian who has scored the most hundreds against each of the Test-playing teams is featured in the table above, with the exception of Darren Lehmann, who like Steve Waugh has scored two centuries against Bangladesh. Don Bradman's 19 hundreds against England is a record for the most made against any one country.

Steve Waugh is the only Australian to score Test centuries against all nine of today's Test-playing teams. Besides Waugh, Taylor (hundreds against seven Test teams), Mark Waugh (seven), Ponting (seven), Border (six), Boon (six) and Walters (five), other Australians with Test hundreds against five or more teams are:

Batsman	100s	Ban	Eng	Ind	NZ	Pak	SA	SL	WI	Zim
Matthew Hayden	14	0	3	2	1	1	4	–	3	–
Adam Gilchrist	8	0	2	1	1	1	2	–	1	–
Bob Simpson	10	–	2	4	–	2	1	–	1	–
Keith Stackpole	7	–	3	1	1	0	1	–	1	–
Ian Chappell	14	–	4	2	2	1	0	–	5	–
Graeme Wood	9	–	3	1	2	1	–	0	2	–
Dean Jones	11	–	3	2	0	2	–	3	1	–
Michael Slater	14	–	7	0	2	3	0	1	1	0

Steve Waugh has scored Test centuries on 20 different grounds, in nine different countries (counting the 'West Indies' as one country), both Australian records. Having now reached three figures in Tests played at Darwin and Cairns, he is also the only man to score Test centuries on seven different Australian grounds. However, with Waugh still to make a Test century in Perth, David Boon, Mark Taylor and Mark Waugh remain the only men to score Test centuries in each of the Australian states. Neil Harvey and Mark Waugh scored Test hundreds on 15 different grounds across the cricketing world, Allan Border, Mark Taylor and Ricky Ponting on 14. Border scored hundreds in seven different countries, Mark Waugh and Ponting in six.

The most Test hundreds scored by one batsman in Australia is 18, by Don Bradman. The record for most hundreds scored in one country outside Australia is 11, by Bradman in England.

10 BATSMEN WITH THE MOST SCORES OF 150 OR MORE

Rank	Batsman	Tests	Inns	150s
1.	Don Bradman	52	80	18
2.	Steve Waugh	162	251	14
3.	Neil Harvey	79	137	9
4=	Greg Chappell	87	151	8
4=	Allan Border	156	265	8
6=	Arthur Morris	46	79	6
6=	Bob Simpson	62	111	6
8=	Bill Lawry	67	123	5
8=	Ian Chappell	75	136	5
8=	Dean Jones	52	89	5
8=	Mark Taylor	104	186	5
8=	Michael Slater	74	131	5

Seven of Steve Waugh's 14 scores of 150 or more have been not outs. In contrast, only two of Bradman's 18 were undefeated. Allan Border and Greg Chappell each have three undefeated scores of 150 or more.

All of Bob Simpson's 10 Test centuries, including the six of more than 150, were made as Australian captain. In the 23 Tests in which he was not the captain Simpson's highest score was 92.

10 AMUSING QUOTES FROM AUSTRALIAN TEST CRICKET HISTORY

2. 'Kanhai, haven't you heard the 11th commandment? Dowe shall not bowl.'
   — from a Jamaican fan after the West Indies captain decided to bring back paceman Uton Dowe late on the opening day of the 1973 Australia– Windies series. Keith Stackpole had smashed the young quick earlier in the day.

10 BATSMEN WITH THE HIGHEST PERCENTAGE OF INNINGS AS CENTURIES *(Qualification: 30 innings)*

Rank	Batsman	Tests	Inns	100s	innings/100*
1.	Don Bradman	52	80	29	2.76
2.	Matthew Hayden	44	74	14	5.29
3.	Greg Chappell	87	151	24	6.29
4.	Ricky Ponting	69	108	17	6.35
5.	Neil Harvey	79	137	21	6.52
6.	Arthur Morris	46	79	12	6.58
7.	Bill Ponsford	29	48	7	6.86
8.	Lindsay Hassett	43	69	10	6.90
9.	Justin Langer	65	107	15	7.13
10.	Adam Gilchrist	45	62	8	7.75

* Signifies how many innings per century. Thus, Bradman scored a Test century every 2.76 times he went out to bat.

The Test careers of Hayden and Ponting did not get off to particularly spectacular starts. However, their respective renaissances have been quite fantastic. Hayden's first 13 Tests, between 1994 and 2001, yielded just 536 runs at 24.36, with one century. His next 29 Tests, from the beginning of the series in India in 2001 to the end of the series in the West Indies in 2003, brought him 2939 runs at 66.80, and featured 13 centuries. That's a century every 3.85 innings. From the time of his Test debut in December 1995 until when he was dropped during the 1998–99 Ashes series, Ponting played 22 Tests, for 1209 runs at 36.64, with two hundreds. Since he was restored to the Australian team during the series in the Caribbean that followed to the end of 2003 Windies tour, he has played 45 Tests, scoring 3578 runs at 59.63 with 13 hundreds — a century every 4.73 innings.

At No. 7, Ponsford's statistics are distorted to some degree by the fact that he scored hundreds in his first two Tests, in 1924–25, and hundreds in his final two Tests, in England in 1934. In between, he played in 27 Tests and scored 1384 runs at 37.40, including three centuries, a hundred every 13.67 innings which is hardly prolific. Those three hundreds actually came in a run of four Tests from the final Test of the 1930 Ashes series to the third Test against the West Indies in 1930–31.

A fair case can be put that Bill Ponsford was not quite the batsman many cricket historians have suggested. He was dropped more than once during his Test career and was considered by some to have been lucky to make the 1930 Ashes tour. *The Sydney Morning Herald*, for one, referring to the controversy over the omission of Jack Ryder, thought the final batting place had come down to a choice between Ryder and Ponsford.

Question marks always existed over his ability against quick bowling. Footage of Ponsford batting against Larwood in Brisbane during the 1928–29 series — on a pitch on which the tourists made 521 in their first innings — clearly shows him backing away as he faces the great English fast man during Australia's reply. This seems more a problem of technique than courage, for four years later, during the bodyline series, Ponsford was very brave, most notably in Adelaide when he made 85 and took a series of blows on his back and chest. But he was dropped twice during that summer, for the second and fifth Tests, as his footwork was consistently shown up by the speed and skill of Larwood and Voce.

❖   ❖   ❖

OPINION
THE TOP 10 EXAMPLES OF AUSTRALIANS SCORING HUNDREDS IN BOTH INNINGS OF A TEST

Rank	Batsman	Scores			Test	Versus	Series
1.	Greg Chappell	123	&	109*	West Indies	Brisbane	1975–76
2.	Steve Waugh	108	&	116	England	Manchester	1997
3.	Doug Walters	242	&	103	West Indies	Sydney	1968–69
4.	Warren Bardsley	136	&	130	England	The Oval	1909
5.	Allan Border	150*	&	153	Pakistan	Lahore	1980
6.	Matthew Hayden	197	&	103	England	Brisbane	2002–03
7.	Greg Chappell	247*	&	133	New Zealand	Wellington	1974
8.	Dean Jones	116	&	121*	Pakistan	Adelaide	1989–90
9.	Don Bradman	132	&	127*	India	Melbourne	1947–48
10.	Jack Moroney	118	&	101*	South Africa	Johannesburg	1949–50

All up, there are 14 instances of Australians achieving this feat, the others being by Arthur Morris (v England, Adelaide, 1946–47), Bob Simpson (v Pakistan, Karachi, 1964), Ian Chappell (v New Zealand, Wellington, 1974) and Allan Border (v New Zealand, Christchurch, 1986).

Greg Chappell's effort at the Gabba in his first Test as Australian captain gets top billing here, mainly because of his second innings masterpiece — with brother Ian he turned what should have been an extremely awkward last-day run chase into a decisive eight-wicket victory. Of Steve Waugh's two centuries at Manchester it was the first, when he bravely and skilfully withstood the English bowlers on a tricky opening-day pitch and in the process justified Mark Taylor's surprising decision to bat first, that stands out.

Doug Walters was the first man to score a double century and a single century in one Test match, and he did so against an attack that featured

Wes Hall, Charlie Griffith, Garry Sobers and Lance Gibbs, and after Australia had slipped to 3–51 after being sent into bat. Warren Bardsley was the first to score twin hundreds in a Test and Border the first to score 150 in both innings of the same Test. Don Bradman and Jack Moroney offer the only instances of Australians scoring hundreds in both innings of a Test against India and South Africa respectively. For Moroney, the feat was a clear highlight of a brief international career. Having made his debut at the start of the series in South Africa as Arthur Morris' new opening partner, he made 7 in his only innings of the fifth Test, then a pair in the first Ashes Test of the following Australian season, and was promptly dropped. ■

10 HIGHEST SCORES IN FIRST INNINGS

Rank	Score	Batsman	Versus	Venue	Series
1=	334	Don Bradman	England	Leeds	1930
1=	334*	Mark Taylor	Pakistan	Peshawar	1998
3.	311	Bob Simpson	England	Manchester	1964
4.	266	Bill Ponsford	England	The Oval	1934
5=	250	Doug Walters	New Zealand	Christchurch	1977
5=	250	Justin Langer	England	Melbourne	2002-03
7.	247*	Greg Chappell	New Zealand	Wellington	1974
8.	244	Don Bradman	England	The Oval	1934
9.	242	Doug Walters	West Indies	Sydney	1968-69
10.	235	Greg Chappell	Pakistan	Faisalabad	1980

10 HIGHEST SCORES IN SECOND INNINGS

Rank	Score	Batsman	Versus	Venue	Series
1.	307	Bob Cowper	England	Melbourne	1965-66
2.	304	Don Bradman	England	Leeds	1934
3.	299*	Don Bradman	South Africa	Adelaide	1931-32
4.	268	Graham Yallop	Pakistan	Melbourne	1983-84
5.	254	Don Bradman	England	Lord's	1930
6=	234	Don Bradman	England	Sydney	1946-47
6=	234	Sid Barnes	England	Sydney	1946-47
8=	232	Don Bradman	England	The Oval	1930
8=	232	Stan McCabe	England	Nottingham	1938
10.	225	Bob Simpson	England	Adelaide	1965-66

10 HIGHEST SCORES IN THIRD INNINGS

Rank	Score	Batsman	Versus	Venue	Series
1.	270	Don Bradman	England	Melbourne	1936–37
2.	212	Don Bradman	England	Adelaide	1936–37
3.	185*	Victor Trumper	England	Sydney	1903–04
4.	184*	David Boon	England	Sydney	1987–88
5.	177	Matthew Hayden	West Indies	St John's	2003
6.	170*	Ross Edwards	England	Nottingham	1972
7.	167	Don Bradman	South Africa	Melbourne	1931–32
8.	166	Victor Trumper	England	Sydney	1907–08
9.	164	Mark Taylor	Sri Lanka	Brisbane	1989–90
10.	163	Allan Border	India	Melbourne	1985–86

10 HIGHEST SCORES IN FOURTH INNINGS

Rank	Score	Batsman	Versus	Venue	Series
1.	189*	Stan McCabe	South Africa	Johannesburg	1935–36
2.	182	Arthur Morris	England	Leeds	1948
3.	173*	Don Bradman	England	Leeds	1948
4.	160	Joe Darling	England	Sydney	1897–98
5.	151*	Neil Harvey	South Africa	Durban	1949–50
6.	149*	Adam Gilchrist	Pakistan	Hobart	1999–00
7.	136	Keith Stackpole	England	Adelaide	1970–71
8.	131	Don Bradman	England	Nottingham	1930
9=.	127*	John Dyson	West Indies	Sydney	1981–82
9=.	127	Justin Langer	Pakistan	Hobart	1999–00

There are 20 other instances of an Australian scoring a century in the fourth innings of a Test match. Five men — Morris, Bradman, Langer, Allan Border and Mark Taylor — have done so twice.

10 AMUSING QUOTES FROM AUSTRALIAN TEST CRICKET HISTORY

3. 'Leave it open, you won't be long.'

– A spectator to Bill Johnston, as the Australian No. 11 tried to shut the boundary-fence gate behind him as he walked on to the Sydney Cricket Ground to face a rampaging Frank Tyson. In fact, Johnston would stay with Neil Harvey while 39 runs were added for the last wicket.

10 BATSMEN WHO SCORED THE HIGHEST PERCENTAGE OF A COMPLETED INNINGS TOTAL

Rank	Player	Versus	Venue	Series	Runs	Total	%Inns
1.	Charles Bannerman	England	Melbourne	1876–77	165*	245	67.35
2.	Michael Slater	England	Sydney	1998–99	123	184	66.85
3.	Graham Yallop	England	Sydney	1978–79	121	198	61.11
4.	Victor Trumper	England	Melbourne	1903–04	74	122	60.66
5.	Don Bradman	England	Leeds	1930	334	566	59.01
6.	Don Bradman	South Africa	Adelaide	1931–32	299*	513	58.28
7.	Clem Hill	England	Melbourne	1897–98	188	323	58.20
8.	Percy McDonnell	England	Sydney	1881–82	147	260	56.54
9.	Bob Cowper	India	Sydney	1967–68	165	292	56.51
10.	Stan McCabe	England	Nottingham	1938	232	411	56.45

There can be few better measures of the quality of a Test-match innings than when one batsman prevails while most or even all of his teammates struggle. Of these 10 fantastic innings, only one was made by the Australian captain — Graham Yallop's defiant innings on the opening day of the final Test of the 1978–79 Ashes series. Only two other batsmen reached double figures; Graeme Wood, who made 15, and Kim Hughes, who scored 16. When Hughes was dismissed to make it 3–67, Yallop was 29. Australia scored another 131 runs, and the skipper made 92 of them.

Percy McDonnell's innings was similarly spectacular. In at 3–16, he scored 147 out of 219 while at the wicket, including one hit clean over the members' pavilion.

10 HIGHEST CAREER AGGREGATES WITHOUT A CENTURY

Rank	Runs	50s	HS	Batsman
1.	2238	8	99	Shane Warne
2.	1507	13	89	Ken Mackay
3.	1427	4	65*	Bert Oldfield
4.	1341	11	92	Bruce Laird
5.	1328	5	80	Alan Davidson
6.	1108	8	94	Alec Bannerman
7.	1032	2	72*	Merv Hughes
8.	1000	6	77	Ian Johnson
9.	978	4	74	Bruce Yardley
10.	955	6	79*	Paul Reiffel

10 BATSMEN WITH MOST CAREER FIFTIES BUT WITHOUT A CENTURY

Rank	50s	Runs	HS	Batsman
1.	13	1507	89	Ken Mackay
2.	11	1341	92	Bruce Laird
3=.	8	2238	99	Shane Warne
3=.	8	1108	94	Alec Bannerman
5.	7	813	88	Tom Veivers
6=.	6	1000	77	Ian Johnson
6=.	6	955	79*	Paul Reiffel
6=.	6	789	66	Graeme Hole
6=.	6	785	91	Michael Bevan
6=.	6	697	91	Rick Darling

10 BATSMEN WHO SCORED THE MOST RUNS FOR A LOSING AUSTRALIAN TEAM

Rank	Runs	Batsman	Scores	Versus	Venue	Series
1.	242	Victor Trumper	214* & 28	South Africa	Adelaide	1910–11
2.	238	Matthew Hayden	203 & 35	India	Chennai	2001
3.	219	Stan McCabe	187* & 32	England	Sydney	1932–33
4.	217	Syd Gregory	201 & 16	England	Sydney	1894–95
5.	216	Ricky Ponting	144 & 72	England	Leeds	2001
6.	212	Neil Harvey	205 & 7	South Africa	Melbourne	1952–53
7.	210	Steve Waugh	199 & 11	West Indies	Bridgetown	1999
8.	207	Percy McDonnell	124 & 83	England	Adelaide	1884–85
9.	204	Allan Border	78 & 126	West Indies	Adelaide	1981–82
10.	202	George Giffen	161 & 41	England	Sydney	1894–95

The only other instance of a batsman scoring 200 or more runs for a losing Australian team was Archie Jackson's effort in his debut Test, when he scored 164 and 36 against England at the Adelaide Oval in 1928–29.

One player very unlikely to appear on this table was Don Bradman. Only two of Bradman's centuries were scored in Tests in which he ended on the losing side, and they were two of the first three hundreds he made in Test cricket. In the third Test against England in 1928–29, Bradman scored 79 and 112, but Australia lost by three wickets. Bradman's second Test century played a part in Australia's victory in the fifth Test, but then in the opening encounter in England in 1930, Bradman scored 131 in Australia's second innings (having made 8 in the first), as the home team won by 93 runs.

10 HIGHEST CAREER AGGREGATES AT ONE VENUE

Rank	Batsman	Venue	Mat	Inns	NO	Runs	HS	Avge	100s
1.	Don Bradman	Melbourne	11	17	4	1671	270	128.54	9
2.	Allan Border	Adelaide	16	29	5	1415	205	58.96	4
3.	Allan Border	Melbourne	20	36	3	1272	163	38.55	4
4.	Steve Waugh	Melbourne	16	29	6	1265	131*	55.00	3
5.	Greg Chappell	Melbourne	17	31	4	1257	121	46.56	4
6.	Allan Border	Sydney	17	29	8	1177	89	56.05	0
7.	Greg Chappell	Sydney	12	22	4	1150	204	63.89	4
8.	David Boon	Sydney	11	21	3	1127	184*	62.61	4
9.	Bill Lawry	Melbourne	8	13	0	1023	205	78.69	4
10.	Greg Chappell	Brisbane	7	11	2	1006	201	111.78	5

10 BATSMEN WHO HIT THE MOST FOURS IN AN INNINGS

Rank	4s	Batsman	Score	Versus	Venue	Series	6s
1.	46	Don Bradman	334	England	Leeds	1930	–
2.	43	Don Bradman	304	England	Leeds	1934	2
3.	34	Stan McCabe	232	England	Nottingham	1938	1
4=	33	Arthur Morris	182	England	Leeds	1948	–
4=	33	Greg Blewett	214	South Africa	Johannesburg	1997	–
6=	32	Don Bradman	244	England	The Oval	1934	1
6=	32	Mark Taylor	334*	Pakistan	Peshawar	1998	1
8=	30	Joe Darling	160	England	Sydney	1897–98	–
8=	30	Greg Chappell	247*	New Zealand	Wellington	1974	1
8=	30	Doug Walters	250	New Zealand	Christchurch	1977	2
8=	30	Justin Langer	223	India	Sydney	1999–2000	–
8=	30	Justin Langer	250	England	Melbourne	2002–03	1

The record for the most sixes in one Test innings by an Australian batsman is eight, by Adam Gilchrist during his 204 not out against South Africa in Johannesburg in 2002. In that innings, Gilchrist also hit 19 fours, giving him 124 runs in boundaries. Gilchrist hit five sixes in an innings of 152 against England at Edgbaston in 2001. Other Australians with five or more sixes in one Test innings are Matthew Hayden (six in his 203 v India at Chennai in 2001), Sam Loxton (five in his 93 v England, Leeds, 1948), Allan Border (five in his 153 v Pakistan, Lahore, 1980) and Michael Slater (five in his 219 v Sri Lanka, Perth, 1995–96).

The most fours from consecutive deliveries hit by an Australian in Tests is five, by David Hookes in the second innings of his debut match, the Centenary Test at the MCG in March 1977.

Until the mid to late 1990s, when — as is clearly occurring in golf — cricket bat manufacturers began providing state-of-the-art equipment that made boundaries shorter and batsmen more adventurous, George Bonnor, Joe Darling and Keith Miller were regarded as our biggest hitters. We see no reason, despite the dazzling exploits of some of Australia's most recent 'sluggers', to argue with this rating.

Our top 10 hitters are:

1. George Bonnor
2. Joe Darling
3. Keith Miller
4. Adam Gilchrist
5. Matthew Hayden
6. Jack Gregory
7. Kim Hughes
8. Mark Waugh
9. Merv Hughes
10. Graham McKenzie

Ralph Barker and Irving Rosenwater, in their 1969 classic *Test Cricket: England v Australia*, record that in a Test in Melbourne in 1882–83, in the days when a ball had to be smashed clean out of the ground before you scored six (hits over the boundary were worth five), George Bonnor hit four deliveries way out of the playing field, one of which would have cleared the members' reserve had it not been snared by the highest branches of one of the trees that bordered the ground. In the following Test, he hit three more fives in an innings of 34. He also, famously, was once caught in a Test as he turned for a *third* run.

In 1894–95, in his first Test series, Joe Darling clubbed a ball from the great English bowler Johnny Briggs onto the lawn tennis courts behind the SCG Members Pavilion, and three years later he attacked Briggs again, pulling a ball over the square-leg fence and out of the ground, the first time this had been done in a first-class match at the Adelaide Oval. With this blow, which took him from 98 to 104, Darling also became the first Australian to reach his hundred with a six, a feat that wouldn't be repeated until 1972–73, when John Benaud hit Pakistan's Intikhab Alam for six at the MCG, to go from 94 to his maiden Test century. (In early 2002, in the second Test against South Africa at Cape Town, Ricky Ponting would take this exploit to a new level, becoming the first man to hit a six that not only took him to his century, but also won the Test for Australia.)

Among Keith Miller's big-hitting feats, at Adelaide in the first Ashes series after World War II, he belted the first ball of a day's play, a no-ball from legspinner Doug Wright, deep into the crowd. Earlier in that series he'd put another Wright delivery onto the roof of the Member's Stand at the Gabba. People lucky enough to have seen Miller bat speak in wonder of drives that were still rising as they rocketed over the boundary fence.

To compare such hitters to modern-day batsmen such as Adam Gilchrist and Matthew Hayden is awkward. Both Gilchrist and Hayden average nearly a six per Test (Gilchrist 40 sixes in 45 Tests; Hayden 39 in 44). The pair will soon pass Mark Waugh as the most prolific six hitters in Australian Test history, though six-hitting records must be treated with some caution, as not all are precise. Waugh hit 41 sixes in 128 Test matches, and of those 41, perhaps the blow he struck against New Zealand at the WACA was his most impressive. The new Lillee–Marsh Stand is five storeys high, but that didn't stop Waugh putting a delivery from left-arm spinner Daniel Vettori up onto its roof.

Jack Gregory still holds the record for the fastest Test century by an Australian — 70 exhilarating minutes in Johannesburg in 1921. 'He hit with tremendous power, knew which game suited him best, and played it,' Johnnie Moyes once wrote of Gregory. 'He often batted with compelling skill, using his long reach to attack, often with low, skimming drives which cleared the infield.' Kim Hughes had a flair for the extravagant, such as the day in 1977–78 when he put the great Indian spinner Bishan Bedi onto the SCG Members Stand roof, or when in 1980 he charged England paceman Chris Old and drove him back over his head, all but clearing the Lord's Pavilion. Merv Hughes might not have been as prolific, consistent or scientific as other big bitters, but in Christchurch in 1993 he hit four sixes in an innings of 45, the only example in Test history of an Australian batsman scoring more than 40 runs in one innings and more than half of them from sixes.

And Graham McKenzie? Well, he's here for just one shot. Barker and Rosenwater tell how at Lord's in 1964, McKenzie swung the medium pacer Len Coldwell way beyond the square-leg boundary and onto the roof of the old Mound Stand. From there, the ball bounced over the top and onto St John's Wood Road, which runs outside the famous ground. Walking on the footpath was Mr Richard Horton, 55, of Camden Town, London, who was struck on the face and had his spectacles smashed.

MERV HUGHES' TOP 10 ATTRIBUTES OF A SUCCESSFUL BIG HITTER

1. A limited desire to run between wickets.

2. Lack of technique, because good batsmen hit the ball along the ground.

3. Improved helmet technology (because if you hit a West Indian fast bowler for six you know what's coming next).

4. Encouragement and support from teammates: ('Gee that boundary at square-leg looks big,' one might say. 'If anyone hits a six out there, I'll give them $50').

5. A heavy bat, because when a six foot four bloke who weighs 100kg swings a three-and-a-half pound bat as hard as he can, he doesn't need much of the bat to hit the five-and-a-half ounce ball to have an impact.

6. A lack of respect for team management. If the captain says to keep your head down and take singles, a big hitter needs to be confident enough to play his own game.

7. A desire to upset specialist batsmen, especially the ones on your own team, because they work so hard to make their ones and twos — hitting sixes with your eyes shut really annoys them.

8. The ability to take physical punishment. When you've got your eyes shut, sometimes you miss.

9. Enormous self-knowledge. It is only when you finally, truly admit to yourself that you will never be a good enough batsman to always keep the ball on the ground that you can justify always trying to hit it in the air.

10. Understanding that the key to being a great batsman is the ability to eliminate modes of dismissal. When you're hitting sixes all the time, you can't get run out.

Who's the best Australian big hitter I've seen? Adam Gilchrist, because he doesn't follow any of these rules.

10 BATSMEN WHO SCORED THE MOST RUNS IN AN INNINGS FROM BOUNDARIES

Rank	Runs	4s	6s	Name	Score	Versus	Venue	Series
1=	184	46	0	Don Bradman	334	England	Leeds	1930
1=	184	43	2	Don Bradman	304	England	Leeds	1934
3.	142	34	1	Stan McCabe	232	England	Nottingham	1938
4=	134	32	1	Don Bradman	244	England	The Oval	1934
4=	134	32	1	Mark Taylor	334*	Pakistan	Peshawar	1998
6=	132	33	0	Arthur Morris	182	England	Leeds	1948
6=	132	30	2	Doug Walters	250	New Zealand	Christchurch	1977
6=	132	33	0	Greg Blewett	214	South Africa	Johannesburg	1997
9=	126	30	1	Greg Chappell	247*	New Zealand	Wellington	1974
9=	126	30	1	Justin Langer	250	England	Melbourne	2002–03

10 BATSMEN WITH THE MOST NINETIES

Rank	90s	Batsman	Not Out
1.	10	Steve Waugh	2
2.	9	Michael Slater	–
3.	6	Clem Hill	1
4.	5	David Boon	1
5=	4	Bob Simpson	–
5=	4	Ian Chappell	–
5=	4	Rod Marsh	1
5=	4	Mark Taylor	–
9=	3	Bill Lawry	–
9=	3	Ian Redpath	–
9=	3	Doug Walters	–
9=	3	Kim Hughes	–
9=	3	Allan Border	2
9=	3	Ricky Ponting	–
9=	3	Greg Blewett	–
9=	3	Matthew Hayden	–

'Not Out' in the above Top 10 indicates the number of times the batsmen have remained not out in the 90s. Thus, Steve Waugh has 10 Test 90s, two of which were undefeated. There have been 138 occasions, involving 69 different men, when an Australian batsman has been dismissed or remained not out in the 90s during a Test match.

The 'leader' of this club, Steve Waugh, has never been dismissed for 99 in a Test, but was left stranded on 99 not out against England at the WACA in

1994–95, after his brother Mark, running for the injured Craig McDermott, was run out at the non-striker's end. Steve was trapped lbw for 199 at Bridgetown in 1999, the second Australian to be dismissed on that score in a Test match, after Matthew Elliott, who missed a double century by a single at Headingley in 1997.

Waugh and Elliott are two of 11 Australians to be dismissed or remain undefeated in the 190s in a Test. Ian Chappell, who made 196 against Pakistan at the Adelaide Oval in 1972–73 and 192 at The Oval in 1975, is the one member of what is an elite group to do so twice (the other Australian near double centuries besides Waugh, Elliott and Chappell are Warren Bardsley, Allan Border, Neil Harvey, Lindsay Hassett, Matthew Hayden, Clem Hill, Arthur Morris and Ricky Ponting). No Australian has been dismissed in the 290s, but Don Bradman did remain 299 not out in Adelaide against South Africa in 1931–32, after No. 11 'Pud' Thurlow was rather infamously run out.

Two of Greg Blewett's three Test 90s ended on 99, and he remains the only Australian to be twice dismissed on this score. In all, 16 Australians have either been out or remained not out on 99, but only one of those — Shane Warne, who scored his 99 against New Zealand at the WACA in 2001–02 — never scored a Test century at some stage of his career. Perhaps Warne's time is still to come? Six players — Roy Minnett, Arthur Richardson, Arthur Chipperfield, Ian Redpath, Bruce Laird and Ricky Ponting — were dismissed in the 90s on their Test debut, with perhaps the most heartbreaking of these being Chipperfield, who went to lunch at Trent Bridge in 1934 on 99, only to be dismissed fourth ball after the break without adding to his score. At least Chipperfield did have the distinction of scoring a Test hundred, 109 in his first Test against South Africa, at Durban in 1935–36, something neither Minnett nor Laird was able to do.

10 AMUSING QUOTES FROM AUSTRALIAN TEST CRICKET HISTORY

4. 'There's Neil Harvey standing at leg slip with his legs wide apart, waiting for a tickle!'

– Legendary English commentator Brian Johnston, saying the first thing that came into his head as the cameras panned to Harvey during the third Ashes Test of 1961.

10 BATSMEN WITH THE MOST CONSECUTIVE INNINGS WITHOUT A DUCK

Rank	Player	Inns w/o Duck	From/to	Career Ducks
1.	Allan Border	89	26.11.82 to 2.12.88 (4435 runs)	11
2.	Doug Walters	68	12.12.69 to 1.1.77 (2508 runs)	4
3.	Mark Waugh	63	23.01.93 to 29.11.96 (2875 runs)	19
4.	Geoff Marsh	62	18.09.86 to 25.01.91 (1999 runs)	3
5.	Justin Langer	60	15.10.98 to 30.11.2001 (2727 runs)	6
6.	Mark Taylor	58	23.03.91 to 25.03.94 (2386 runs)	5
7.	Bob Simpson	54	18.06.64 to 28.01.78 (3086 runs)	8
8.	Rod Marsh	54	16.02.73 to 7.07.77 (1607 runs)	12
9.	Allan Border	52	6.01.79 to 16.07.81 (2198 runs)	11
10=	Bill Lawry	51	30.11.62 to 30.12.65 (2196 runs)	6
10=	Mark Taylor	51	5.10.94 to 3.7.97 (1664 runs)	5
10=	Alan Davidson	51	11.06.53 to 6.7.61 (1076 runs)	1

Four Australian batsmen enjoyed careers of 20 or more innings that never included a duck:

Batsman	Tests	Inns	Runs	Avge	HS
Jim Burke	24	44	1280	34.59	189
Reg Duff	22	40	1317	35.59	146
Herbert Collins	19	31	1352	45.07	203
Tommy Andrews	16	23	592	26.91	94

Each of these four players was dismissed for 1 during their Test career. Collins' is the highest aggregate to not 'include' a duck.

10 BATSMEN WITH MOST DUCKS

Rank	Player	Tests	Inns	NO	Ducks	Pairs
1.	Shane Warne	107	146	13	27	2
2.	Glenn McGrath	95	104	36	26	3
3.	Steve Waugh	162	251	43	21	0
4.	Mark Waugh	128	209	17	19	2
5.	Ian Healy	119	182	23	18	1
6.	David Boon	107	190	20	16	0
7.	Graham McKenzie	60	89	12	15	2
8.	Rodney Hogg	38	58	13	14	2
8=	Jeff Thomson	51	73	20	14	1
10=	Terry Alderman	41	53	22	13	0
10=	Craig McDermott	71	90	13	13	1

Other players with susceptibility for being dismissed for 0 include:

Player	Inns	NO	Ducks	Pairs
John Gleeson	46	8	11	2
Alan Connolly	45	20	10	–
Alan Hurst	20	3	10	3
Wayne Clark	19	2	8	2
Jack Saunders	23	6	8	1
Bob Holland	15	4	7	2

The longest run of ducks suffered in Tests is five, by Bob Holland. In the fifth Test in England in 1985, Holland was out for 0 and 0; he did not play in the sixth Test of that series, but then made ducks in each of his first three innings of the subsequent series against New Zealand, including a pair in the first Test. The record for most ducks in a series is six, set by Alan Hurst in 12 innings during the 1978–79 Ashes series in Australia. Wayne Clark managed five ducks in seven innings in the series in the West Indies in 1978, a feat matched by Glenn McGrath in the 1998–99 Ashes series.

10 LOWEST CAREER BATTING AVERAGES
(Qualification: 20 innings)

Rank	Batsman	Tests	Inns	NO	Runs	HS	100s	50s	Avge
1.	Jack Saunders	14	23	6	39	11*	0	0	2.29
2.	Bert Ironmonger	14	21	5	42	12	0	0	2.63
3.	Bruce Reid	27	34	14	93	13	0	0	4.65
4.	Ernie Jones	19	26	1	126	20	0	0	5.04
5.	Jim Higgs	22	36	16	111	16	0	0	5.55
6.	Alan Hurst	12	20	3	102	26	0	0	6.00
7.	Tim Wall	18	24	5	121	20	0	0	6.37
8.	Terry Alderman	41	53	22	203	26*	0	0	6.55
9.	Glenn McGrath	93	104	36	450	39	0	0	6.62
10.	Bill Howell	18	27	6	158	35	0	0	7.52

Just outside this top 10, in 11th and 12th places respectively, are two tailenders of recent times: Colin Miller (24 innings, 174 runs, 8.29 average) and Stuart MacGill (29, 236, 9.08). Missing out on qualifying because they didn't play sufficient innings are two prominent tailenders of the 1980s: Bob Holland (15, 35, 3.18) and Mike Whitney (19, 68, 6.18).

If you increase the qualification to 30 innings, the following players make the top 10:

Batsman	Tests	Inns	NO	Runs	HS	100s	50s	Avge
Geoff Dymock	21	32	7	236	31*	0	0	9.44
Rodney Hogg	38	58	13	439	52	0	1	9.76
John Gleeson	29	46	8	395	45	0	0	10.39
Bill Johnston	40	49	25	273	29	0	0	11.38
Charlie Turner	17	32	4	323	29	0	0	11.54
Ashley Mallett	38	50	13	430	43*	0	0	11.62

THE 10 AUSTRALIANS WHO PLAYED TEST CRICKET BUT NEVER SCORED A RUN

Rank	Player	Career	Tests	Inns	NO	Bowling	Cght
1.	Hugh Thurlow	1931–32	1	1	0	0–53 & 0–33	0
2.	Roy Park	1920–21	1	1	0	0–9	0
3.	Simon Davis	1986	1	1	0	0–70	0
4.	Paul Wilson	1998	1	2	1	0–50	0
5.	Rex Sellers	1964	1	1	0	0–17	1
6.	Bill Hunt	1931–32	1	1	0	0–25 & 0–14	1
7.	Ken Meuleman	1946	1	1	0	–	1
8.	Jack Wilson	1956	1	0	0	0–39 & 1–25	0
9.	Peter Allan	1965–66	1	0	0	2–58 & 0–25	0
10.	Jack McLaren	1911–12	1	2	2	0–47 & 1–23	0

'Pud' Thurlow gets top billing here, because in his one innings (as a No. 11 in the fourth Test against South Africa at the Adelaide Oval) he managed to get himself run out, leaving Don Bradman not out on 299.

At No. 2, Dr Roy Park's first-ball duck in the second Ashes Test of 1920–21 has entered folklore, because of the unlikely but often told story of his proud wife missing his entire Test batting career because she bent down to pick up a knitting needle just as he was being bowled by Harry Howell. Not as well known is the genuine fact that the good doctor had been up all night caring for a patient.

Paceman Jack McLaren was the first native-born Queenslander to play for Australia, but only after he was the centre of a storm that threatened to tarnish the fourth Ashes Test of 1911–12. Queensland unionists tried to convince their Melbourne comrades to black ban the game if McLaren played, because he had allegedly been involved in some strikebreaking activities on the Brisbane docks. Perhaps fortunately, McLaren was made 12th man, and the matter was resolved before the fifth Test, in Sydney.

10 BATSMEN DISMISSED BY AN OPPOSING BOWLER MOST OFTEN

Rank	Batsman	Bowler	Times Dismissed
1.	Arthur Morris	Alec Bedser (England)	18
2=.	Mark Waugh	Curtly Ambrose (West Indies)	15
2=.	Ian Healy	Courtney Walsh (West Indies)	15
4=.	Victor Trumper	Sydney Barnes (England)	13
4=.	Greg Chappell	Derek Underwood (England)	13
6=.	Neil Harvey	Alec Bedser (England)	12
6=.	Kim Hughes	Ian Botham (England)	12
6=.	Allan Border	Ian Botham (England)	12
6=.	Doug Walters	Derek Underwood (England)	12
6=.	Lindsay Hassett	Doug Wright (England)	12

Curtly Ambrose dismissed Steve Waugh 11 times in Test matches, giving him a total of 26 Waugh dismissals in 27 Tests against Australia.

10 BATSMEN WHO WERE BETTER AT HOME

(Qualification: 10 innings home and away; must average at least 40 at home)

Rank	Batsman	Home Avge	Away Avge	Difference
1.	Bob Cowper	75.79	33.33	42.46
2.	Brett Lee	40.00	9.18	30.82
3.	Rick Darling	41.33	14.36	26.97
4.	Johnny Taylor	45.35	20.55	24.80
5.	Brian Booth	53.80	31.68	22.12
6.	Joe Darling	41.26	20.23	21.03
7.	Bruce Laird	43.71	24.88	18.83
8.	Doug Walters	57.83	39.52	18.31
9.	Michael Slater	52.63	35.29	17.34
10.	Greg Matthews	48.76	31.50	17.26

Victor Trumper was another whose batting average was better at home (45.80) than away (30.61). Trumper scored his first two Test centuries in England, one each in 1899 and 1902, but after he left England the second time he never scored another Test hundred outside Australia. Going even further back in cricket history, the famous hitter George Bonnor was often effective in Tests in Australia, averaging 34.58. But in England he was a rank failure, averaging only 5.39 in 10 Tests spread over five tours.

10 BATSMEN WHO WERE BETTER AWAY FROM HOME

(Qualification: 10 innings home and away; must average at least 40 away from home)

Rank	Batsman	Home Avge	Away Avge	Difference
1.	Rick McCosker	30.20	54.19	23.99
2.	Billy Murdoch	23.47	45.18	21.71
3.	Bill Ponsford	40.90	62.40	19.50
4.	Jim Burke	26.44	40.81	14.37
5.	Jack Fingleton	36.75	50.08	13.33
6.	Arthur Morris	41.18	53.78	12.60
7.	Stan McCabe	42.43	54.63	12.20
8.	Allan Border	45.84	56.57	10.73
9.	Steve Waugh	45.07	55.50	10.43
10.	Warren Bardsley	35.52	45.60	10.08

One tailender with a fair record batting in overseas Tests was Bill Johnston, who averaged just 8.81 in Tests at home, but 29.33 in Tests outside Australia.

❖   ❖   ❖

OPINION
THE TOP 10 SHOTS BY AUSTRALIAN BATSMEN

Rank	Batsman	Shot	Versus	Venue	Series
1.	Doug Walters	Pulls Bob Willis for six	England	Perth	1974–75
2.	Steve Waugh	Cover drives Richard Dawson for four	England	Sydney	2002–03
3.	Ken Mackay	Takes Wes Hall on the chest	West Indies	Adelaide	1960–61
4.	Kim Hughes	Straight drives Chris Old into the pavilion	England	Lord's	1980
5.	Victor Trumper	Jumping out to drive	England	Manchester	1902
6.	George Bonnor	Caught while turning for third run	England	The Oval	1880
7.	Ian Healy	Swings Hansie Cronje away for six	South Africa	Port Elizabeth	1997
8.	Adam Gilchrist	'Scoops' Andy Caddick over the keeper's head	England	Birmingham	2001
9.	Archie Jackson	Square drives Harold Larwood	England	Adelaide	1928–29
10.	David Hookes	Hits Tony Greig for fifth straight four	England	Melbourne	1976–77

For a generation of cricket fans who supported Dougie Walters through many good times and some not quite so good, this was the crowning moment. On the Saturday afternoon of the second Ashes Test, Walters had moved from 3 not out at tea to 93 with seven balls to go. Bob Willis had been bowling two or three bouncers an over, so Walters decided to wait, and when one came he got lucky, miscuing a hook over keeper Alan

Knott's head. For the rest of the over he defended, until the last ball, another short one, which he cracked flat-batted over square-leg, to reach his hundred and also complete a century in a session.

The shot of Steve Waugh (to reach a magic century) and non-shot of Ken Mackay at numbers two and three respectively also came from the final balls of the day, Mackay's from the final ball of a Test. Facing Wes Hall with Australia nine down, after he and Kline had defended for 100 minutes, Mackey took a fast riser on the body rather than risk giving a catch. Ian Healy's shot was also the last of a Test, his six an exciting and emphatic end to a thrilling contest.

George Bonnor's hit went out towards the old gasometer that was situated outside The Oval at the Vauxhall end, and was measured at around 100 metres in length. Its height was such that he was turning for his third when Fred Grace took a clean catch on the boundary's edge. Surely there has never been a more powerful mishit (one presumes that if he'd hit it clean it would have rocketed out of the ground), but it was hardly as glorious as Victor Trumper's lofted drive, captured so superbly by the acclaimed photographer George Beldam during the 1902 Ashes tour (and featured on the cover of this book). That photo of Beldam's is staged; there is no square-leg umpire, no fieldsman, and Beldam admitted that at this time in the early history of cricket photography, he was having trouble taking clear shots of genuine onfield action. But look at the photo and imagine Trumper at Old Trafford, when he became the first batsman to score a century before lunch on the first day of a Test. This is how England captain Archie MacLaren responded to criticism of his tactics on that day …

I knew my man — Victor had half a dozen strokes for the same kind of ball. I exploited the inner and outer ring — a man there, and another man covering him. I told my bowlers to pitch on the short side to the off: I set my heart and brain on every detail of our policy. Well, in the third over of the morning, Victor hit two balls straight into the practice ground, high over the screen behind the bowler. I couldn't very well have had a man fielding in the bloody practice ground, now could I?

At No. 8, Adam Gilchrist's improvisation came from the last ball of an over, when he was 99 not out, with Australia 9–519 and all the fieldsmen patrolling the boundary. The biggest gap was between fine leg and third man, so that's where he aimed. Archie Jackson's blistering square drive from the first ball after lunch also took him to his century; like Jackson, David Hookes was playing in his maiden Test match.

10 LONGEST INNINGS

Rank	Minutes	Batsman	Versus	Venue	Series	Score	Balls Faced#
1.	762	Bob Simpson	England	Manchester	1964	311	740
2.	727	Bob Cowper	England	Melbourne	1965–66	307	589
3.	720	Mark Taylor	Pakistan	Peshawar	1998	334*	564
4.	716	Graham Yallop	Pakistan	Melbourne	1983–84	268	517
5.	642	Sid Barnes	England	Sydney	1946–47	234	661
6.	601	Graeme Wood	England	Nottingham	1985	172	449
7.	599	Allan Border	New Zealand	Adelaide	1987–88	205	485
8=.	578	Jim Burke	South Africa	Cape Town	1957–58	189	N/A
8=.	578	Justin Langer	England	Melbourne	2002–03	250	407
10.	565	Allan Border	England	Leeds	1993	200*	399

where recorded

10 FAST INNINGS

Runs	Minutes	Batsman	Final Score	Versus	Venue	Series
300*	336	Don Bradman	334	England	Leeds	1930
203*	290	Adam Gilchrist	204*	South Africa	Johannesburg	2002
189*	165	Stan McCabe	189*	South Africa	Johannesburg	1935–36
128	115	George Bonnor	128	England	Sydney	1884–85
121	96	Richie Benaud	121	West Indies	Kingston	1955
103*	113	Victor Trumper	104	England	Sydney	1903–04
100*	70	Jack Gregory	119	South Africa	Johannesburg	1921
56	40	Charlie Macartney	56	South Africa	Sydney	1910–11
50*	58	Justin Langer	122*	New Zealand	Hamilton	2000
35	14	Bill Howell	35	England	Sydney	1901–02

We have confined ourselves here to runs scored from the beginning of an innings. Thus an instance of fast scoring such as Stan McCabe's effort in scoring 72 runs in 28 minutes at Trent Bridge in 1938 is not included, because those were the final 72 runs (in a last-wicket stand of 77 with Chuck Fleetwood-Smith) of his famous innings of 232. McCabe took 223 minutes to reach his double century that day; in all, his masterpiece occupied 235 minutes.

Don Bradman's extraordinary innings at Headingley in 1930 remains the fastest triple century by an Australian in Test cricket. He went on to score 309 on the day and 334 in the innings, the final score made off 448 balls in 383 minutes. Bradman took 214 minutes to reach 200, still the fastest double century (in terms of time) by an Australian in Tests. In terms of balls faced, Adam Gilchrist's effort at Johannesburg in 2002, which came from 212 deliveries, is the quickest of all Australian double centuries where the balls faced by individual batsmen were recorded.

George Bonnor was the first man to score a Test century at a run a minute, his first 100 runs at Sydney in 1884–85 taking precisely 100 minutes. He hit four fives in that innings — a hit out over the fence being then worth five not six, meaning that when such a blow was struck, the batsman lost the strike, which most likely slowed him down just a fraction. Victor Trumper, at Leeds in 1902, was the first man to score a 100 before lunch on the opening day of a Test, a feat later matched by Charlie Macartney (Leeds, 1926) and Bradman (Leeds, 1930), and by Pakistan's Majid Khan at Karachi in 1976.

Jack Gregory's century in Johannesburg remains the quickest by an Australian in terms of time and balls faced (67 deliveries). His entire innings of 119 occupied 97 minutes. Next fastest in terms of time taken to reach a century is Richie Benaud's 78-minute hundred in Kingston in 1955. The second fastest, in terms of balls faced, is Adam Gilchrist's 84-ball century at Mumbai in 2001.

Justin Langer's performance in Hamilton came in the fourth innings, after Australia was set what at first glance seemed to be a tricky 210 to win. Langer proceeded to his half century from 42 balls and his century from 102 balls as Australia won comfortably by six wickets. Bill Howell's 35 came from 15 balls, his first 23 runs from just eight balls.

10 SLOW INNINGS

Runs	Minutes	Batsman	Versus	Venue	Series
311	762	Bob Simpson	England	Manchester	1964
205	599	Allan Border	New Zealand	Adelaide	1987–88
91	421	Alec Bannerman	England	Sydney	1891–92
84	330	Bill Lawry	England	Brisbane	1970–71
75	386	Allan Border	West Indies	Sydney	1988–89
40	289	Herbert Collins	England	Manchester	1921
31	264	Ken Mackay	England	Lord's	1956
28*	250	Jim Burke	England	Brisbane	1958–59
9	107	Carl Rackemann	England	Sydney	1990–91
6	106	Damien Martyn	South Africa	Sydney	1993–94

Bob Simpson took 608 minutes to reach 200 and 753 minutes to reach 300 in 1964, the slowest double century and triple century by an Australian in Tests. Allan Border took 596 minutes to reach his double century at

Adelaide in 1987–88, the slowest Test double century by an Australian at home, and 310 minutes to reach 50 at the SCG in 1988–89, the slowest half-century by an Australian in Test matches. At least Border was able to hit fours in both these innings, something Bill Lawry did not do at the Gabba in 1970–71.

In the first Test of 1891–92, in Melbourne, Alec Bannerman scored 45 in 195 minutes in the first innings and 41 in 230 minutes in the second; all up 86 runs in seven hours and five minutes. Thus, his marathon in Sydney soon after (included above) was somewhat rapid by comparison.

The longest time taken by an Australian to reach a century in a Test match is 385 minutes, by Dean Jones at Madras in 1986. Jones went on to make 210 in 503 minutes. The longest time taken to reach a century in a Test match in Australia is 384 minutes, by Mark Taylor against India in Adelaide in 1991–92. Taylor was dismissed 11 minutes after he reached his century that day, without adding to his score. Similarly, Graeme Wood reached 100 against England at the MCG in 1978–79 in 363 minutes, and then batted a further 29 minutes before he was dismissed, without scoring a run.

At the SCG in 1990–91, Carl Rackemann batted for 72 minutes before he scored his first run. Damien Martyn's innings at the same ground three summers later occupied 59 balls, for six singles. Martyn's stubborn innings ended with Australia seven runs short of victory; one run later Glenn McGrath was caught and bowled by Fanie de Villiers and South Africa had won a stunning comeback victory. Of the 10 innings in this Top 10, Martyn's is the only one that came in an Australian defeat. Four (Bannerman, Border in Sydney, Mackay and Burke) were involved in wins; the other five in draws.

10 AMUSING QUOTES FROM AUSTRALIAN TEST CRICKET HISTORY

5. 'If I get hit out there, make sure you stop Mum from jumping the fence.'
   – *Stan McCabe to his father, before he went out to bat in the first innings of the opening Test of the bodyline series, at the Sydney Cricket Ground. McCabe scored 187 not out, and the only jumping Mrs McCabe did was to get to her feet every time her son hooked another four.*

BEST BATTING AVERAGES AT EACH BATTING POSITION

(Qualification: 10 innings played from the specific position in the batting order. In each instance, statistics refer solely to performances made from that position in the batting order)

OPENER

Rank	Batsman	Inns	NO	HS	Runs	Avge	50s	100s
1.	Sid Barnes	14	1	234	928	71.38	4	3
2.	Bob Simpson	70	4	311	3664	55.52	19	8
3.	Justin Langer	40	3	250	2048	55.35	7	8
4.	Bill Ponsford	31	3	266	1517	54.18	4	5
5.	Matthew Hayden	74	6	203	3536	52.00	11	14
6.	Bill Woodfull	44	4	161	2036	50.90	11	7
7.	Bill Brown	29	1	206*	1404	50.14	8	4
8.	Bill Lawry	123	12	210	5234	47.15	27	13
9.	Herbert Collins	27	1	203	1199	46.12	4	4
10.	Arthur Morris	76	2	206	3381	45.69	12	11

NO. 3

Rank	Batsman	Inns	NO	HS	Runs	Avge	50s	100s
1.	Don Bradman	56	7	334	5078	103.63	10	20
2.	Stan McCabe	12	3	189*	625	69.44	–	3
3.	Charlie Macartney	28	2	170	1543	59.35	6	6
4.	Ricky Ponting	47	5	206	2490	59.29	7	10
5.	Lindsay Hassett	19	1	163	1009	56.06	3	4
6.	Rick McCosker	12	2	109*	560	56.00	3	2
7.	Graham Yallop	22	1	268	1101	52.43	3	3
8.	Ian Chappell	91	7	196	4279	50.94	22	13
9.	Kepler Wessels	13	–	173	662	50.92	5	1
10.	Dean Jones	28	4	210	1167	48.63	5	3

---

10 AMUSING QUOTES FROM AUSTRALIAN TEST CRICKET HISTORY

6. 'Burke, I wish you were a statue and I was a pigeon.'

– A line from a barracker from the 1950s, in protest at the slow batting of Test opener Jim Burke.

JUSTIN LANGER'S TOP 10 ATTRIBUTES OF A SUCCESSFUL OPENING BATSMAN

1. Courage. An opener gets to face the fastest bowlers with the new ball — and that's probably the hardest thing any batsman has to do.

2. Preparation. This is crucial, in terms of getting your game in order and being aware of your opponents' strengths and weaknesses. Know yourself and know your opposition.

3. A good game plan. Always look for process over outcome.

4. Aggression. Against fast bowlers with a new ball you need to be decisive in your footwork, your decision making, your strokeplay. You're a sitting duck otherwise.

5. Focus. You've got to be really focused on what you want to achieve.

6. A good partner. Many of the best opening partnerships have been two good mates — think of Slater and Taylor, Boon and Marsh — which must help, because openers have to work as a team. I'm not trying to knock anyone else I've opened the batting with when I say that, for me, batting with Matty Hayden is what opening up is all about. With another partner, it's not quite the same.

7. A good routine, both before and during the game.

8. A sense of humour. Sometimes you've got to go out to bat when there's absolutely nothing to be gained. At Bridgetown in 2003, I had to bat after we'd fielded for three days and we needed eight runs to win. I got a golden duck. What else can you do but laugh in such situations?

9. Luck. But you know the old saying, 'The harder you work, the luckier you get.' And if you think and bat positively, the opposition will be more tense, things will go your way. If you're negative, it feels like the opposition is all over you. That's when you nick one, you get out to an unbelievable catch or an umpire's decision goes against you.

10. An appetite for runs. One thing Steve Waugh always talks about is that you never mess with good form. And Brian Lara once said to me, 'When you have a good day, make it a great day.'

NO. 4

Rank	Batsman	Inns	NO	HS	Runs	Avge	50s	100s
1.	Dean Jones	18	5	216	931	71.62	2	4
2.	Greg Chappell	86	13	247*	4316	59.12	19	15
3.	Norm O'Neill	41	6	181	2010	57.43	10	5
4.	Bob Cowper	13	–	307	745	57.31	2	2
5.	Don Bradman	10	1	112	485	53.89	1	3
6.	Warren Bardsley	11	–	164	590	53.64	3	2
7.	Stan McCabe	16	–	232	830	51.88	4	2
8.	Lindsay Hassett	25	2	198*	1182	51.39	4	3
9.	Doug Walters	29	3	112	1313	50.50	10	4
10.	Allan Border	89	13	205	3792	49.89	21	8

NO. 5

Rank	Batsman	Inns	NO	HS	Runs	Avge	50s	100s
1.	Victor Trumper	10	2	214*	555	69.38	–	3
2.	Greg Chappell	13	4	182*	610	67.78	5	1
3.	Steve Waugh	135	22	200	6434	56.94	26	24
4.	Allan Border	69	11	200*	3062	52.79	15	9
5.	Doug Walters	49	4	242	2134	47.42	14	5
6.	Ross Edwards	20	2	115	839	46.61	8	1
7.	Greg Ritchie	19	3	128	743	46.44	2	2
8.	Ian Redpath	18	3	171	684	45.60	5	1
9.	Stan McCabe	27	2	187*	1114	44.56	8	1
10.	Keith Miller	52	5	145*	1973	41.98	9	5

NO. 6

Rank	Batsman	Inns	NO	HS	Runs	Avge	50s	100s
1.	Brian Booth	10	1	112	578	64.22	3	2
2.	Mark Waugh	13	2	139*	589	53.55	2	2
3.	Allan Border	63	14	153	2556	52.16	17	6
4.	Steve Waugh	77	16	177*	3079	50.48	15	6
5.	Ricky Ponting	44	5	197	1962	50.31	8	7
6.	Damien Martyn	28	5	133	1113	48.39	6	4
7.	Victor Trumper	11	1	135*	482	48.20	2	1
8.	Sam Loxton	10	–	101	481	48.10	3	1
9.	Doug Walters	45	6	250	1869	47.92	9	6
10.	Greg Chappell	11	2	150*	355	39.44	–	2

DEAN JONES' TOP 10 ATTRIBUTES OF A SUCCESSFUL MIDDLE-ORDER BATSMAN

1. At all times a middle-order batsman must want to bat NOW. Many players want to come in at 2–100. I want batsmen to come in and make a difference at 2–0!

2. A middle-order batsman needs to be able to relax before going in. Opening batsmen know when they are going in; middle-order batters don't. So the guys batting four, five and six have to be able to relax, but also be prepared in case there is top-order collapse.

3. Middle-order batsmen must have a presence about them. They must show good body language.

4. It is not the style in which the batsmen in the middle order play that is important, it is the numbers they produce. Allan Border was not the most grandiose of players, but he was the most EFFECTIVE!

5. The best middle-order batsmen read the game better than others. They can recognise which bowlers and fielders are 'on' their games, and which are off.

6. All good batsmen have the ability to leave their egos at the gate. If your batting partner is playing well, give him the strike, watch and learn, and wait for your turn.

7. The best middle-order batsmen can play in all conditions. They have the ability to be openers, and to be attacking, explosive batsmen. They know when to dominate and when to back off.

8. Fitness is a vital ingredient in the making of large scores. Great middle-order players have the ability and are fit enough to make double hundreds.

9. Top class middle-order batsmen must have other strings to their bow. They must be great catchers and perhaps be able to bowl a bit.

10. Middle-order batsmen these days must know how to play the one-day game. All the best middle-order batters can play all forms of the game.

NO. 7

Rank	Batsman	Inns	NO	HS	Runs	Avge	50s	100s
1.	Adam Gilchrist ·	45	10	204*	2253	64.37	10	7
2.	Warwick Armstrong	17	–	158	724	51.71	3	2
3.	Greg Matthews	33	4	128	1317	45.41	10	3
4.	Ken Mackay	10	3	83*	313	44.71	3	–
5.	Colin McCool	11	4	104*	287	41.00	–	1
6.	Wayne B. Phillips	14	1	91	484	37.23	3	–
7.	Steve Waugh	19	3	134*	543	33.94	3	1
8.	Tom Veivers	15	1	88	470	33.57	5	–
9.	Ian Healy	121	11	161*	3041	27.65	17	4
10.	Ray Lindwall	15	1	61	382	27.29	–	–

NO. 8

Rank	Batsman	Inns	NO	HS	Runs	Avge	50s	100s
1.	Paul Reiffel	24	8	79*	560	35.00	5	–
2.	Richie Benaud	16	–	121	537	33.56	3	1
3.	Gary Gilmour	12	1	101	351	31.91	2	1
4.	Ray Lindwall	18	3	118	466	31.07	2	1
5.	Ian Johnson	15	3	77	371	30.92	4	–
6.	Hugh Trumble	18	3	70	449	29.93	2	–
7.	Kerry O'Keeffe	23	6	85	491	28.88	1	–
8.	Alan Davidson	22	3	77*	504	26.53	2	–
9.	Geoff Lawson	18	3	53	388	25.87	2	–
10.	Ian Healy	43	9	71	872	25.65	3	–

NO. 9

Rank	Batsman	Inns	NO	HS	Runs	Avge	50s	100s
1.	Bert Oldfield	15	7	65*	388	48.50	2	–
2.	Jim Kelly	22	10	46*	332	27.67	–	–
3.	Max Walker	11	3	78*	199	24.88	1	–
4.	Hanson Carter	17	4	66	282	21.69	1	–
5.	Paul Reiffel	23	5	54*	374	20.78	1	–
6.	Brett Lee	27	4	62*	468	20.35	2	–
7.	Richie Benaud	13	1	51	242	20.17	1	–
8.	Doug Ring	10	2	65	156	19.50	1	–
9.	Charlie McLeod	10	3	50*	132	18.86	1	–
10.	Ian Johnson	12	1	73	207	18.82	1	–

PAUL REIFFEL'S TOP 10 ATTRIBUTES OF A SUCCESSFUL LOWER-ORDER BATSMAN

1. Keep it simple.

2. Block the straight ones.

3. Hit the not-so-straight ones.

4. Don't run the captain out.

5. Think like a batsman.

6. Practise like a batsman. You are in the team as a bowler, but you must practise your batting with the same degree of application and planning as a top-order batsman.

7. Understand the game and the context of your innings. If there is a top-order batsman at the other end, stay away from the strike.

8. Once you are the senior batsman, remember you are a bowler. Make runs as quickly as you can, because blocking to stay in doesn't help anyone and will eventually lead to you getting yourself out.

9. Be ready for short balls. Bowlers use them aggressively against lower-order batsmen these days; if you can handle them well, you take away one of your opponent's weapons.

10. Enjoy yourself.

The best top-order batsman I shared a partnership with was Steve Waugh, who had the same approach to batting with me as he had when batting with most lower-order guys. He always made me feel that I had ability as a batsman, and that I deserved to be in the middle with him. He was always encouraging and gave me responsibility for the partnership. By making me feel an equal, he gave me confidence, and that meant I performed better with the bat.

The best lower-order batsman I have seen would probably be Merv Hughes — he always enjoyed himself and he was one of the most technically able batsmen I played with. He only had one shot, but he could play it to any part of the ground!

NO. 10

Rank	Batsman	Inns	NO	HS	Runs	Avge	50s	100s
1.	Bert Oldfield	12	2	47	263	26.30	–	–
2.	Ian Johnson	13	6	41	181	25.86	–	–
3.	Tim May	13	7	42*	127	21.17	–	–
4.	Dennis Lillee	30	10	73*	381	19.05	1	–
5.	Shane Warne	21	5	37	303	18.94	–	–
6.	Bill O'Reilly	14	4	56*	181	18.10	1	–
7.	Hanson Carter	14	2	31*	194	16.17	–	–
8.	Jim Kelly	12	4	39	125	15.63	–	–
9.	Gil Langley	22	8	53	204	14.57	1	–
10.	Jason Gillespie	31	13	46	262	14.56	–	–

NO. 11

Rank	Batsman	Inns	NO	HS	Runs	Avge	50s	100s
1.	Max Walker	10	7	34*	93	31.00	–	–
2.	Bill Whitty	15	7	39*	145	18.13	–	–
3.	Ernie Toshack	10	5	20	73	14.60	–	–
4.	Bill Johnston	33	22	28	159	14.45	–	–
5.	Jeff Thomson	24	10	24*	201	14.36	–	–
6.	Fred Spofforth	13	6	50	100	14.29	1	–
7.	Dennis Lillee	12	9	19*	42	14.00	–	–
8.	Arthur Mailey	23	8	46*	184	12.27	–	–
9.	Lindsay Kline	11	8	15*	35	11.67	–	–
10.	Ashley Mallett	12	5	18*	81	11.57	–	–

Can somebody please explain why Don Bradman averaged 103 as a No. 3 in Test cricket, 142 as a No. 5 (from three innings), 97 as a No. 6 (from eight innings) and 162 as a No. 7 (from three innings), but only 53.89 as a No. 4? Bradman did score three Test centuries going in with two wickets down, but the highest of them was only 112, hardly colossal by his standards. Purely on averages at No. 4, Dean Jones, Greg Chappell, Norm O'Neill and Bob Cowper were all more productive batsmen.

An interesting possibility thrown up by these averages is the suggestion that the unique talents of Victor Trumper may have been to a degree wasted by his preference for opening the innings. Going in first 52 times in Test matches, Trumper averaged 33; at numbers five and six he was significantly more productive. Herbert Collins once said of Trumper: 'Believe me when I tell you that it was odds on Trumper hitting the first ball bowled to him for four. That was always his objective.' The great English bowler SF Barnes suggested much the same thing: 'Victor, well, he always gave you a chance, almost daring you to bag his wicket.' This is a laudable policy, but it doesn't lend itself to heavy run-scoring, especially for an opening bat. At the same time, it became the essence of Trumper's magic — that despite going for shots from the jump he was still able to be the most acclaimed batsman of his day. In 1954, the acclaimed cricketer writer AG 'Johnnie' Moyes wrote, when comparing Trumper and Bradman:

> I believe that Trumper could have made more runs than he did, for I know what his attitude to run-getting was, and, indeed, what was the attitude of the times. But the fact is inescapable: Bradman did score the runs; he did it consistently; he so often did it brilliantly. Trumper was the most fascinating of them all. He was a genius. Bradman never lacked the fascinating touch, as is proved by the crowds he drew and held. He also was a genius.

Using only these averages, it is possible to select a 'greatest ever' Australian batting line-up, with the bowlers selected solely for their ability to make runs down the order. One problem in nominating such an XI from these stats is that we have wicketkeepers topping the averages at No. 7 (Adam Gilchrist) and Nos 9 and 10 (both times Bert Oldfield). Another keeper, Jim Kelly, is second among No. 9s. Because Oldfield is ranked highest in two positions, he gets the nod, with Warwick Armstrong (second at No. 7) becoming the team's bowling allrounder and Ian Johnson (second at No. 10) the team's spinner. The line-up in batting order is:

Sid Barnes, Bob Simpson, Don Bradman, Dean Jones, Victor Trumper, Brian Booth, Warwick Armstrong, Paul Reiffel, Bert Oldfield, Ian Johnson and Max Walker.

---

10 AMUSING QUOTES FROM AUSTRALIAN TEST CRICKET HISTORY

7. 'Who can forget Malcolm Devon?'
    – England chairman of selectors Ted Dexter, being serious (we think!) when asked if any positives had come out of the fifth Ashes Test of 1989. Australia had just won the Test by an innings and 181 runs, to take a 4–0 lead in the series, after Mark Taylor and Geoff Marsh had batted throughout the opening day. Derbyshire quick Devon Malcolm made his Test debut in this match.

10 LOWEST BATTING AVERAGES AT NO. 11

(Qualification: 10 innings at No. 11)

Rank	Batsman	Inns	NO	HS	Runs	Avge
1.	Jack Saunders	21	6	11*	36	2.40
2.	Bert Ironmonger	16	4	12	38	3.17
3.	Dave Renneberg	13	7	9	22	3.67
4.	Ernie Jones	11	1	14	45	4.50
5.	Tim Wall	10	3	18	33	4.71
6.	Bruce Reid	28	13	8*	73	4.87
7.	Jim Higgs	27	14	11	64	4.92
8.	Glenn McGrath	98	34	39	423	6.61
9.	Alan Hurst	15	3	26	86	7.17
10.	Mike Whitney	17	8	13	68	7.56

With the qualification being set at 10 innings, Bob Holland is ineligible. His batting record as last man in for Australia in Tests was nine innings, three not out, 10 runs, average: 1.67.

10 HIGHEST PARTNERSHIPS

Rank	Runs	Wkt	Batsmen	Versus	Venue	Series
1.	451	2nd	Bill Ponsford/Don Bradman	England	The Oval	1934
2.	405	5th	Sid Barnes/Don Bradman	England	Sydney	1946–47
3.	388	4th	Bill Ponsford/Don Bradman	England	Leeds	1934
4.	385	5th	Steve Waugh/Greg Blewett	South Africa	Johannesburg	1997
5.	382	1st	Bob Simpson/Bill Lawry	West Indies	Bridgetown	1965
6.	346	6th	Jack Fingleton/Don Bradman	England	Melbourne	1936–37
7.	336	4th	Bill Lawry/Doug Walters	West Indies	Sydney	1968–69
8.	332*	5th	Allan Border/Steve Waugh	England	Leeds	1993
9.	329	1st	Mark Taylor/Geoff Marsh	England	Nottingham	1989
10.	327	5th	Justin Langer/Ricky Ponting	Pakistan	Perth	1999–00

The first century partnership by Australian batsmen was made in cricket's fifth Test match, the first of 1881–82, when Tom Horan and George Giffen added 107 for the fifth wicket. In the third Test of that series, Alec Bannerman and Percy McDonnell put on 199 for the fourth wicket, which remained the Australian record until the third Test of 1884, when Billy Murdoch and Henry Scott added 207 for the third wicket. That wasn't broken until the opening Test of 1896, when Harry Trott and Syd Gregory put on 221 for the fourth wicket, a mark that was not improved until 1907–08, when Clem Hill and Roger Hartigan (who was making his Test debut) combined to add a world record 243 for the eighth wicket during the third Test against England.

In 1930, at The Oval, Don Bradman and Archie Jackson put on 243 for the fourth wicket, to equal Hill and Hartigan. Eighteen months later, against South Africa in Melbourne, Bradman and Bill Woodfull went further, adding 274 for the second wicket. That was the Australian record Bradman and Bill Ponsford broke at Leeds in 1934, with their 388 stand, a figure surpassed a Test later by the same pair's 451 at The Oval.

The three other 300-plus stands made by Australian in Tests are:

Runs	Wkt	Batsmen	Versus	Venue	Series
317	6th	Damien Martyn/Adam Gilchrist	South Africa	Johannesburg	2002
315	3rd	Ricky Ponting/Darren Lehmann	West Indies	Port-of-Spain	2003
301	2nd	Arthur Morris/Don Bradman	England	Leeds	1948

HIGHEST PARTNERSHIPS FOR EACH WICKET

Wkt	Runs	Batsmen	Versus	Venue	Series
1st	382	Bob Simpson/Bill Lawry	West Indies	Bridgetown	1965
2nd	451	Bill Ponsford/Don Bradman	England	The Oval	1934
3rd	315	Ricky Ponting/Darren Lehmann	West Indies	Port-of-Spain	2003
4th	388	Bill Ponsford/Don Bradman	England	Leeds	1934
5th	405	Sid Barnes/Don Bradman	England	Sydney	1946–47
6th	346	Jack Fingleton/Don Bradman	England	Melbourne	1936–37
7th	217	Doug Walters/Gary Gilmour	New Zealand	Christchurch	1977
8th	243	Roger Hartigan/Clem Hill	England	Adelaide	1907–08
9th	154	Syd Gregory/Jack Blackham	England	Sydney	1894–95
10th	127	Johnny Taylor/Arthur Mailey	England	Sydney	1924–25

HIGHEST PARTNERSHIPS FOR EACH WICKET IN AUSTRALIA

Wkt	Runs	Batsmen	Versus	Venue	Series
1st	269	Michael Slater/Greg Blewett	Pakistan	Brisbane	1999–00
2nd	298	Bill Lawry/Ian Chappell	West Indies	Melbourne	1968–69
3rd	276	Don Bradman/Lindsay Hassett	England	Brisbane	1946–47
4th	336	Bill Lawry/Doug Walters	West Indies	Sydney	1968–69
5th	405	Sid Barnes/Don Bradman	England	Sydney	1946–47
6th	346	Jack Fingleton/Don Bradman	England	Melbourne	1936–37
7th	185	Graham Yallop/Greg Matthews	Pakistan	Melbourne	1983–84
8th	243	Roger Hartigan/Clem Hill	England	Adelaide	1907–08
9th	154	Syd Gregory/Jack Blackham	England	Sydney	1894–95
10th	127	Johnny Taylor/Arthur Mailey	England	Sydney	1924–25

HIGHEST PARTNERSHIPS FOR EACH WICKET OUTSIDE AUSTRALIA

Wkt	Runs	Batsmen	Versus	Venue	Series
1st	382	Bob Simpson/Bill Lawry	West Indies	Bridgetown	1965
2nd	451	Bill Ponsford/Don Bradman	England	The Oval	1934
3rd	315	Ricky Ponting/Darren Lehmann	West Indies	Port-of-Spain	2003
4th	388	Bill Ponsford/Don Bradman	England	Leeds	1934
5th	385	Steve Waugh/Greg Blewett	South Africa	Johannesburg	1997
6th	317	Damien Martyn/Adam Gilchrist	South Africa	Johannesburg	2002
7th	217	Doug Walters/Gary Gilmour	New Zealand	Christchurch	1977
8th	137	Richie Benaud/Ian Johnson	West Indies	Kingston	1955
9th	133	Steve Waugh/Jason Gillespie	India	Kolkata	2001
10th	98	Alan Davidson/Graham McKenzie	England	Manchester	1961

10 PAIRS WITH MOST CENTURY PARTNERSHIPS

Rank	Batsmen	Number	Highest
1.	David Boon/Mark Waugh	11	175 v England, Lord's, 1993
2.	Mark Taylor/Michael Slater	10	260 v England, Lord's, 1993
3=	Bill Lawry/Bob Simpson	9	382 v West Indies, Bridgetown, 1965
3=	Dean Jones/Allan Border	9	214 v West Indies, Adelaide, 1988–89
3=	Mark Waugh/Steve Waugh	9	231 v West Indies, Kingston, 1995
3=	Matthew Hayden/Justin Langer	9	242 v West Indies, St John's, 2003
7=	David Boon/Allan Border	8	170 v West Indies, Sydney, 1988–89
7=	Mark Taylor/David Boon	8	221 v India, Adelaide, 1991–92
9=	Bill Woodfull/Don Bradman	7	274 v South Africa, Melbourne, 1931–32
9=	Greg Chappell/Kim Hughes	7	179 v Pakistan, Faisalabad, 1980
9=	Steve Waugh/Ricky Ponting	7	239 v India, Adelaide, 1999–00

Australian batsmen have been involved in a total of 664 century stands in Test matches. Allan Border has shared in the most — 63 hundred partnerships with 23 different batsmen — two clear of Steve Waugh (27 different partners). Others to be involved in 30 or more hundred stands are Mark Waugh (47, 14 partners), Greg Chappell (44, 13), David Boon (42, 12), Mark Taylor (41, 10), Don Bradman (35, 14), Neil Harvey (32, 14), Ricky Ponting (31, 13) and Ian Chappell (30, 12).

The Australian record for most double-century partnerships is held by Matthew Hayden and Justin Langer, who as at the completion of the winter 2003 series against Bangladesh had put together five 200-plus stands, including four in a run of six Tests in Australia in 2001–02. Bill Ponsford/Don Bradman, Bill Lawry/Bob Simpson, and Michael

Slater/Mark Taylor all compiled a next-best three double century partnerships.

Bradman was involved in 14 double century partnerships during his Test career — three with Ponsford, two each with Bill Woodfull, Sid Barnes and Arthur Morris, and one each with Alan Kippax, Archie Jackson, Jack Fingleton, Stan McCabe and Lindsay Hassett. Three batsmen — Steve Waugh, Justin Langer and Ricky Ponting — have been involved in nine 200-plus stands.

10 OPENING BATTING PARTNERSHIPS WITH MOST APPEARANCES *(By innings)*

Rank	Batsmen	Inns	NO	Runs	Highest	100s	Avge
1.	Mark Taylor/Michael Slater	78	2	3837	260	10	50.49
2.	Bob Simpson/Bill Lawry	62	2	3596	382	9	59.93
3.	Geoff Marsh/Mark Taylor	47	3	1980	329	4	45.00
4.	David Boon/Geoff Marsh	41	1	1871	217	5	46.78
5.	Justin Langer/Matthew Hayden	38	1	2521	242	9	68.14
6.	Colin McDonald/Jim Burke	32	3	1132	190	3	39.03
7.	Bill Lawry/Keith Stackpole	31	2	1302	95*	0	44.90
8.	Victor Trumper/Reg Duff	29	1	966	135	3	34.50
9.	Michael Slater/Matthew Hayden	25	1	1046	156	3	43.58
10.	Graeme Wood/John Dyson	24	1	583	80	0	25.35

'NO' indicates undefeated partnerships. '100s' indicates century partnerships.

10 OPENING BATTING PARTNERSHIPS WITH THE HIGHEST AVERAGE *(Qualification: 10 innings)*

Rank	Batsmen	Inns	NO	Runs	Highest	100s	Avge
1.	Justin Langer/Matthew Hayden	38	1	2521	242	9	68.14
2.	Bill Brown/Jack Fingleton	16	0	1020	233	3	63.75
3.	Arthur Morris/Colin McDonald	15	0	949	191	3	63.27
4.	Bob Simpson/Bill Lawry	62	2	3596	382	9	59.93
5.	Sid Barnes/Arthur Morris	13	0	706	122	3	54.31
6.	Mark Taylor/Michael Slater	78	2	3837	260	10	50.49
7.	Herbert Collins/Warren Bardsley	20	1	915	123	3	48.16
8.	Michael Slater/Greg Blewett	22	2	922	269	3	46.10
9.	David Boon/Geoff Marsh	41	1	1871	217	5	46.78
10.	Geoff Marsh/Mark Taylor	47	3	1980	329	4	45.00

'NO' indicates undefeated partnerships. '100s' indicates century partnerships.

One thing that has almost been forgotten when watching the remarkable exploits of the Justin Langer-Matthew Hayden opening partnership is that it came together almost by accident. At the start of 2001 Ashes tour, Justin Langer was not really considered an opening batsman — in fact, there was no clear alternative in the touring party for the established opening pair of Hayden and Michael Slater — and he only got the job for the final Test of that tour because Slater had lost form and there was no other obvious replacement. Langer's first-class batting average for the tour going in to that Test was 20.33, but he scored a century at The Oval, and then through the 2001–02 Australian summer he and Hayden produced a string of mighty partnerships that by season's end had them being compared with any of the great opening pairs of the past.

What was also remarkable was that both Langer and Hayden are left-handed. We say remarkable quite deliberately, because in Australia's Test history only 11 totally left-handed partnerships have opened either the batting or the bowling, and only three have done so in more than 10 innings, as follows:

Partnership	Inns	Role
Justin Langer/Matthew Hayden	38	Batting
Alan Davidson/Ian Meckiff	29	Bowling
Mark Taylor/Matthew Elliott	23	Batting
Mark Taylor/Matthew Hayden	10	Batting
Kepler Wessels/Wayne B Phillips	9	Batting
Jack Saunders/Charlie Macartney	2	Bowling
Bill Lawry/Bob Cowper	2	Batting
Gary Gilmour/Tony Dell	2	Bowling
Bill Whitty/Charlie Macartney	2	Bowling
Kepler Wessels/Graeme Wood	1	Batting
Wayne B Phillips/Greg Matthews	1	Batting

10 AMUSING QUOTES FROM AUSTRALIAN TEST CRICKET HISTORY

8. 'I doubt whether we would recognise him with his clothes on.'
– a Lord's official, when asked if Michael Angelow (that really was his name!) would be allowed into the ground for the last day of the Ashes Test there in 1975. Angelow had become Test cricket's first streaker the previous afternoon, winning a £20 bet (which he lost the following morning when he was fined that same amount at a hearing in the Marylebone Magistrates' Court).

THE TOP 10 PARTNERSHIPS
(Qualification: 100 runs)

Rank	Batsmen	Runs	Wkt	Versus	Venue	Series
1.	Justin Langer/Adam Gilchrist	238	6th	Pakistan	Hobart	1999–00
2.	Richie Benaud/Alan Davidson	134	7th	West Indies	Brisbane	1960–61
3.	Mark Waugh/Steve Waugh	231	4th	West Indies	Kingston	1995
4.	Clem Hill/Hugh Trumble	165	7th	England	Melbourne	1897–98
5.	Bill Ponsford/Don Bradman	451	2nd	England	The Oval	1934
6.	Geoff Marsh/David Boon	187*	3rd	England	Melbourne	1990–91
7.	Ian Chappell/Greg Chappell	159*	3rd	West Indies	Brisbane	1975–76
8.	Arthur Morris/Don Bradman	301	2nd	England	Leeds	1948
9.	Alec Bannerman/Jack Lyons	174	2nd	England	Sydney	1891–92
10.	Jack Fingleton/Don Bradman	346	6th	England	Melbourne	1936–37

We are not so much concerned here with the size of the stands as their significance, and have set the qualification at 100 runs so we don't have to compare these 'dominating' stands with backs-to-the-wall efforts such as Ken Mackay and Lindsay Kline at Adelaide in 1960–61. These are partnerships that changed a game, or a series, that set up an important victory, or brought Australia back when all had seemed lost.

Justin Langer and Adam Gilchrist made their stand against a world-class attack featuring Wasim Akram, Shoaib Akhtar and Saqlain Mushtaq on a Bellerive pitch on which Australia had collapsed to 5–126 chasing 369 to win. We put it ahead of the effort of Richie Benaud and Alan Davidson in the Brisbane Tied Test only because the enormity of the task Langer and Gilchrist faced. At tea at the Gabba, Australia needed 123 in 120 minutes, with only Wally Grout, Ian Meckiff and Kline in hand, but Benaud still went for the win — and would almost certainly have got it had he not gravely underestimated Joe Solomon's throwing ability. Australia needed 7 to win with 13 balls left when Davidson was run out; later Solomon did the same to Kline to seal the tie.

The effort of Mark Waugh and Steve Waugh was an epic that won a series-deciding Test and confirmed that the balance between the two teams had shifted Australia's way. Clem Hill and Hugh Trumble's effort came after Australia had crashed to 6–58 in what proved to be a low-scoring Test. Geoff Marsh and David Boon and Ian Chappell and Greg Chappell were similar stands in that in each case when they came together the Test was evenly poised, perhaps even fractionally tilted the opposition's way. Yet the batsmen were superb enough to win the matches without the loss of another wicket.

On paper, Arthur Morris and Don Bradman's performance looks remarkable, maybe the greatest ever, but fantastic as it was — taking Australia from 1–57 to 2–358 chasing a world record 404 in 344 minutes on the final day — the quality of England's bowling and fielding against them was so poor (Fingleton in *Brightly Fades the Don* described it as 'ignoble' and 'wretched stuff') that the partnership must be marked down, if only slightly. Most likely, many of the home team's mistakes were forced on them by the aggression of the two great batsmen. Jack Lyons and Alec Bannerman, in contrast, rescued Australia and set the stage for a Test win that gave Australia its first series victory in a decade. Australia were trailing by 162 on the first innings, and 1–1 in the second with regular No. 4 Harry Moses injured and unable to bat, when the pair came together. Lyons smashed 134 in three hours, Bannerman crawled to 91 in seven and a half, and by the time the innings ended England needed 230 to win, which proved too many for them.

Bill Ponsford and Bradman and Fingleton and Bradman are Australian records for the second and sixth wickets respectively. The former put the Ashes-deciding fifth Test of 1934 out of England's reach almost before it had started; the latter came after Bradman had out-manoeuvred England captain Gubby Allen on a sticky Melbourne pitch, and set up a crucial Australian win. Both were incredible stands, but as great as they were, in neither case were they batting on fifth-day pitches, or facing bowlers as good as the ones who confronted Langer and Gilchrist many years later at Bellerive Oval. ∎

CHAPTER TWO

THE BOWLERS

Once more, we'll begin by using our 'era by era' method to nominate a 'Top 10 Australian Bowlers' list. While we were more than happy with our Top 10 All Time list, and quite comfortable with our Top 10 Batsmen, we concede that this time our method goes slightly awry in a couple of cases. Still, on the grounds that the opinion-based Top 10s throughout this book are included to generate some healthy debate, we'll stick with the strategy …

Rank	Bowler	Era
1.	Dennis Lillee	1970–1979
2.	Shane Warne	1990–1999
3.	Fred Spofforth	1877–1895
4.	Alan Davidson	1957–1969
5.	Glenn McGrath	2000–2003
6.	Bill O'Reilly	1930–1939
7.	Ray Lindwall	1946–1956
8.	Hugh Trumble	1896–1912
9.	Jack Gregory	1920–1929
10.	Geoff Lawson	1980–1989

It is our view — and we imagine many others, and the Top 10s that follow back us all up — that there are bowlers who should be ranked ahead of Jack Gregory and Geoff Lawson in any Top 10 Aussie bowlers list. Not too many, mind you, but a number. Some will argue that Clarrie Grimmett should be representing the 1920s ahead of Gregory, but as you will soon see, we are of the view that Grimmett is a bowler whose talents might not have been as great as is his reputation today. In the 1920s, for example, between 1925 and 1929, Grimmett played in his first nine Tests, all against England, and took 47 wickets at 32.34. He bowled 3805 deliveries to get those wickets: that's one wicket every 80.96 balls, which isn't a great bowler's 'strike rate'. Compare these returns to Gregory, who took 85 wickets in the decade, at 31.15, with a strike rate of a wicket every 65.67 balls. Arthur Mailey, with 99 Test wickets in the 1920s, at 33.91, with a strike rate of 61.80, is actually a bigger rival than Grimmett to Gregory's claims as Australia's No. 1 bowler of that decade. Both Gregory and Mailey played all their Test cricket in the '20s.

Two bowlers who we believe should definitely be ranked ahead of Gregory, Grimmett and Mailey are Charlie Turner, the 'Terror', the man with the lowest bowling average of all Australians to have taken 50 Test wickets, and Richie Benaud, taker of 248 Test wickets, Australia's finest spin bowler between O'Reilly and Warne. Move forward to the 1980s, and for all Geoff Lawson's sustained excellence between 1982 and 1985, and outstanding form in England after returning from injury in 1989, Graham McKenzie, Jeff Thomson and Jason Gillespie are three superb bowlers from different eras (1960s, 1970s and 2000s respectively) who are probably entitled to be ranked ahead of him. A case can also be argued that four other opening bowlers — Jack Ferris (1887 to 1890), Bill Johnston (late 1940s to early 1950s), Merv Hughes (early 1990s) and Craig McDermott (early to mid 1990s) — were also superior, if only by a small margin. If this was just about bowling in England, Terry Alderman (1981-84, 1988-1991) would have to be a chance, too. If we could, we'd put Turner at No. 8 in our Top 10, and Benaud at No. 10.

Should Dennis Lillee be No. 1? If one Top 10 wins it for him, it is the last one featured in this chapter. Through the tables that follow, the same famous names keep reappearing — Spofforth, Turner, Davidson, Warne and McGrath especially. Lillee's name is a regular, too, in Top 10s for most wickets, best strike rates, most wickets in a calendar year, most five-fors, most 10-fors, and others. Then at the end, we list the Australian bowler who got to 100 wickets fastest, and to 200 wickets, and beyond. This is a measure not just of class, but also of toughness, persistence and greatness over an *entire* career. Lillee was fast to 100 wickets, very fast to 200, and fastest, of three, to 300; he took nine innings less than Shane Warne to get his 300th, and 16 innings less than Glenn McGrath. All three have been truly great bowlers; DK Lillee was just that little bit better.

10 LEADING CAREER WICKET-TAKERS

Rank	Bowler	Tests	Balls	Mdns	Runs	Wkts	Avge	Best	5w	10w
1.	Shane Warne	107	29877	1417	12624	491	25.71	8-71	23	6
2.	Glenn McGrath	95	22374	1115	9338	430	21.72	8-38	23	3
3.	Dennis Lillee	70	18467	652	8493	355	23.92	7-83	23	7
4.	Craig McDermott	71	16586	583	8332	291	28.63	8-97	14	2
5.	Richie Benaud	63	19108	805	6704	248	27.03	7-72	16	1
6.	Graham McKenzie	60	17681	547	7328	246	29.79	8-71	16	3
7.	Ray Lindwall	61	13650	419	5251	228	23.03	7-38	12	0
8.	Clarrie Grimmett	37	14513	736	5231	216	24.22	7-40	21	7
9.	Merv Hughes	53	12285	499	6017	212	28.38	8-87	7	1
10.	Jeff Thomson	51	10535	300	5601	200	28.01	6-46	8	–

Of course, a bowler has to be exceptional, in terms of both talent and fitness, to play a mountain of Tests, so no one can deny Shane Warne or Glenn McGrath their places at the top of this table. Indeed, McGrath's bowling average, 1.31 runs better than anyone else in the top 10, suggests that, if anything, we underrate a truly great bowler.

At first glance, Clarrie Grimmett's effort in making this top 10 while only playing in 37 Tests is outstanding. But a closer examination suggests that Grimmett might well owe his reputation as a truly great legspinner to the fact that in those Tests he did play in he bowled a lot of deliveries, sometimes to very ordinary batsmen. He took 11 wickets in his debut Test, the final Test of the 1924–25 Ashes series, and an astounding 44 in his final series, against a poor South African team. In between, at Test level, he had his good days and his not so good.

If you ignore that debut Test, Grimmett bowled in five Ashes series. He was dropped from the side during two of them — in 1926 and during the bodyline series. In the latter, he took five wickets in the first three Tests, at 65.20. In 21 Ashes Tests between 1926 and 1934, Grimmett took 95 wickets from 1496.1 overs, a wicket every 94.49 deliveries. In two Ashes series in Australia (1928–29 and 1932–33) he took 28 wickets from 545.2 overs, a wicket every 116.85 balls (that's one every 19 and a half overs). His best Ashes series was in England in 1930, when Don Bradman made so many runs so quickly that Grimmett could take his time spinning people out. Grimmett's best performance in that series was at Lord's, when he took 6–167 from 53 overs in England's second innings. In the deciding fifth Test at The Oval, a match with no time limit, he took 5–225 for the match from 109.2 six-ball overs. This is good bowling, especially on what were clearly batsman-friendly wickets, but in our view, it is hardly the stuff of greatness. Grimmett was a good leggie, canny and accurate, who made his reputation mainly on his Test debut, in the Sheffield Shield and against the minor Test-playing nations of his time.

Outside this top 10, Jason Gillespie has moved into 13th place, with 174 wickets from 45 Tests. Brett Lee (125 wickets from 33 Tests) is 23rd, Stuart MacGill (131, 23) is 21st.

10 BEST STRIKE RATES *(Qualification: 50 wickets)*

Rank	Player	Tests	Balls	Mdns	Runs	Wkts	Avge	Best	SR
1.	Fred Spofforth	18	4185	416	1731	94	18.41	7–44	44.52
2.	Jack Saunders	14	3565	116	1796	79	22.73	7–34	45.13
3.	Gary Gilmour	15	2661	51	1406	54	26.04	6–85	49.28
4.	Brett Lee	33	6337	218	3703	125	29.62	5–47	50.70
5.	Charlie Turner	17	5179	457	1670	101	16.53	7–43	51.44
6=.	Bill Whitty	14	3357	163	1373	65	21.12	6–17	51.65
6=.	Jason Gillespie	45	8987	415	4337	174	24.93	7–37	51.65
8.	Stuart MacGill	25	6799	251	3435	131	26.22	7–50	51.90
9.	Dennis Lillee	70	18467	652	8493	355	23.92	7–83	52.02
10.	Glenn McGrath	95	22374	1115	9338	430	21.72	8–38	52.03

'SR' indicates strike rate, calculated simply by dividing wickets taken by balls bowled, the lower the strike rate the better.

A study of Australia's Test bowling scorecards from before 1900 — and a reading of contemporary reports and reminiscences — suggests most strongly that our finest two bowlers of that era were Fred 'The Demon' Spofforth and Charlie 'The Terror' Turner. That the pitches of their day were more bowler-friendly is reflected in the lower overall batting averages, compared especially with the decades after World War I, but still these were two genuinely great bowlers. Who was better?

George Giffen, who played with both, thought Turner to be something of a 'genius', but also wrote that while Turner might have been deadly on a sticky wicket, he did not have 'quite the same command of the ball that Spofforth had'. Giffen quickly added that to have been *more* venomous than the Demon on a sticky was impossible.

'He was unique as a fast bowler and practically established a school of bowlers,' wrote WG Grace of Spofforth in 1899, four years after Turner's final Test. When Spofforth was at his peak, from 1877 to 1885, Australia matched it with England, winning six Tests and losing five. Through Turner's career, Australia won five but lost 11. Yet perhaps Australia leant more heavily on Turner (and his partner in bowling crime, Jack Ferris) than it had on Spofforth, who was usually supported by Harry Boyle or the outstanding George Palmer, or sometimes both. While Spofforth's strike rate is better, Turner had a nearly two-run better Test bowling average. Still, the opinion of the day leaned to Spofforth. As magnificent as the Terror quite obviously was, almost certainly the Demon was even better.

One striking fact about this top 10 is the total absence of bowlers from the 1920s through to the 1960s. No O'Reilly, no Lindwall, no Davidson. These were times of flatter wickets, most notably between the wars, and mostly defensive mindsets, especially post-Bradman. Lillee and Jeff Thomson (ranked 12th on the list, with Tibby Cotter at No. 11) broke a trend with their aggression, a philosophy support players such as Gary Gilmour and Len Pascoe (ranked 13th) were happy to continue.

Into the 1990s, and especially under Steve Waugh's captaincy, the Australians have focused on getting their opponents out. The fact that Lee, Gillespie and McGrath (not to mention MacGill) all feature in this Top 10 underlines the fact that the current-day Australian bowling line-up represents at least one of Australia's most lethal attacks of all time.

10 LEADING CAREER BOWLING AVERAGES
(Qualification: 50 wickets)

Rank	Player	Tests	Balls	Mdns	Runs	Wkts	Avge	Best	5w	10w
1.	Charlie Turner	17	5179	457	1670	101	16.53	7–43	11	2
2.	Bert Ironmonger	14	4695	328	1330	74	17.97	7–23	4	2
3.	Fred Spofforth	18	4185	416	1731	94	18.41	7–44	7	4
4.	Alan Davidson	44	11587	431	3819	186	20.53	7–93	14	2
5.	Bill Whitty	14	3357	163	1373	65	21.12	6–17	3	0
6.	George Palmer	17	4517	452	1678	78	21.51	7–65	6	2
7.	Glenn McGrath	95	22374	1115	9338	430	21.72	8–38	23	3
8.	Hugh Trumble	32	8099	452	3072	141	21.79	8–65	9	3
9.	Bill O'Reilly	27	10024	585	3254	144	22.60	7–54	11	3
10.	Jack Saunders	14	3565	116	1796	79	22.73	7–34	6	0

Besides once more highlighting the fantastic wicket-taking exploits of Turner and Spofforth, here is a table that highlights the extraordinary Test-match achievements of Glenn McGrath. No one else on the table has played even half as many Tests as McGrath has. By way of comparison, Keith Miller's career bowling average is 22.98 (placing him at No. 11 on this list), Ray Lindwall's is 23.03 (12th), Dennis Lillee's 23.92 (14th). McGrath's contemporaries are even further behind: Jason Gillespie (24.93 average), Shane Warne (25.71), Merv Hughes (28.38), Craig McDermott (28.63), and Brett Lee (29.62).

Bert Ironmonger's appearance on this table is something of an aberration, the product of two Tests on sticky pitches at the MCG. Ironmonger took 11–79 in Melbourne against the West Indies in 1930–31 and 11–24 there versus South Africa a year later. Take those two Tests out and his Test bowling average is a still very respectable 23.60, but it's no longer Demonesque.

One thing this top 10 does quite clearly is highlight Alan Davidson's superb bowling career. Davidson didn't become the spearhead of the Australian bowling attack until the tour to South Africa in 1957–58, after Keith Miller retired and Ray Lindwall was left out. Before then, he had played in 12 Tests, taking 16 wickets at 34.06. From the first Test in South Africa until he retired at the end of the 1962–63 Ashes series, 'Davo' took 170 wickets in 32 Tests, at 19.26, without ever having a regular opening partner in the way Gregory had McDonald, Lindwall had Miller, Lillee had Thomson and McGrath has Gillespie and Lee. Davidson's most regular accomplices were Ian Meckiff early on and Graham McKenzie late.

In recent times, experts from Sir Donald Bradman down have been keen to tag Pakistan's wonderfully gifted Wasim Akram as the greatest left-hand quick of all time. In our view, Alan Davidson was at least not far behind.

10 BEST BOWLING FIGURES IN AN INNINGS

Rank	Bowling	Bowler	Versus	Venue	Series
1.	9–121	Arthur Mailey	England	Melbourne	1920–21
2.	8–31	Frank Laver	England	Manchester	1909
3.	8–38	Glenn McGrath	England	Lord's	1997
4.	8–43	Albert Trott	England	Adelaide	1894–95
5.	8–53	Bob Massie	England	Lord's	1972
6.	8–59	Ashley Mallett	Pakistan	Adelaide	1972–73
7.	8–65	Hugh Trumble	England	The Oval	1902
8=.	8–71	Graham McKenzie	West Indies	Melbourne	1968–69
8=.	8–71	Shane Warne	England	Brisbane	1994–95
10.	8–84	Bob Massie	England	Lord's	1972

It is curious indeed how many of these performances came from debutants of one kind or another. Arthur Mailey was bowling in his first Test series, Albert Trott and Bob Massie in their first Tests. Glenn McGrath was playing in his first Test at Lord's, Ashley Mallett in his first Test against Pakistan, and Shane Warne in his first Ashes Test in Australia.

There are five other instances of Australians taking eight wickets in a Test innings, as follows:

8–87	Merv Hughes	West Indies	Perth	1988–89
8–97	Craig McDermott	England	Perth	1990–91
8–112	Geoff Lawson	West Indies	Adelaide	1984–85
8–141	Craig McDermott	England	Manchester	1985
8–143	Max Walker	England	Melbourne	1974–75

THE TOP 10 BOWLING PERFORMANCES
(Bowling in a match)

Rank	Bowler	Figures	Versus	Venue	Series
1.	Fred Spofforth	7–46 & 7–44	England	The Oval	1882
2.	Dennis Lillee	6–26 & 5–139	England	Melbourne	1976–77
3.	Bruce Reid	6–97 & 7–51	England	Melbourne	1990–91
4.	Bob Massie	8–84 & 8–53	England	Lord's	1972
5.	Glenn McGrath	6–17 & 4–10	West Indies	Brisbane	2000–01
6.	Monty Noble	7–17 & 6–60	England	Melbourne	1901–02
7.	Shane Warne	5–75 & 6–34	South Africa	Sydney	1997–98
8.	Bill O'Reilly	4–75 & 7–54	England	Nottingham	1934
9.	Dennis Lillee	7–83 & 3–44	West Indies	Melbourne	1981–82
10.	Herbert Hordern	5–85 & 7–90	England	Sydney	1911–12

When we finalised this Top 10, we were surprised by the number of Ashes Tests included. So we rechecked, looking again for notable Australian performances against teams other than England, and quickly came up with Shane Warne's 11–77 against Pakistan at the Gabba in 1995–96 and Dennis Lillee's 11–123 at Auckland in 1976–77. Three performances for losing Australian sides also stand out: Merv Hughes was something of a relentless one-man battering ram in taking 13–217 against the mighty West Indies in Perth in 1988–89; Warne captured 12–128 versus South Africa in Sydney in 1993–94; and Alan Davidson took 12–124 from 77.4 overs at Kanpur in 1959–60.

But, still, despite the Ashes bias, we left our Top 10 as it was. Almost certainly, Fred Spofforth's effort at The Oval in 1882, bowling England out for 77 when they needed 85 to win, should be No. 1. Fired up by WG Grace's discredited run out of Sammy Jones, Spofforth told his teammates that 'this can be done', and strode out to send down 28 (four-ball) overs, 15 of them maidens, to get Australia home. His last 11 overs yielded four wickets for two runs. The next day, the *Sporting Times* published their mock obituary and the legend of the Ashes was born; the Demon, it can be easily argued, was even more responsible than the newspaper's editor for the birth of the legend.

Lillee's efforts in Melbourne were triumphs not just for his great skill, but also his courage, staying power and rare ability to adapt to the conditions. In England's first innings of the Centenary Test in 1977 he was as sharp as he'd been in three years, three years later he slowed his pace and went through England with a combination of leg and off cutters; in 1981–82, the Test in which he broke Lance Gibbs' Test wicket-taking record, he smashed through the Windies top order, Viv Richards and all, late on the first day, reducing them to 4–10.

Bruce Reid's analysis is the best ever achieved by an Australian left-arm bowler; had he stayed fit, who knows how many Test wickets he might have taken. Bob Massie's 16 wickets came in his maiden Test; the only thing stranger than his remarkable debut figures was that within a year he had lost the ability to swing the ball, and was lost to international cricket. Glenn McGrath bowled 33 overs to take his 10–27, Monty Noble 33.4 to take his 13–77. Warne's 11 wickets in Sydney in January 1998 included his 300th in Tests, Jacques Kallis bowled as the great legspinner led Australia to a decisive win.

Two more legspinners round out the Top 10. O'Reilly's performance at Trent Bridge was notable for the way he bailed out his captain, Bill Woodfull, who was so conservative with his last-day declaration that he almost cost Australia victory. Woodfull delayed until England, who held the Ashes, needed all of 380 runs in 285 minutes on a wearing pitch, and when Ames and Leyland batted well into the final session a draw seemed likely. Then O'Reilly took over, the last five wickets fell for seven runs and Australia won with 10 minutes to spare. Hordern's achievement came in his first Ashes Test, having made his debut against South Africa the previous summer. Immediately, his googlies seemed so special that he was heralded as Test cricket's new superstar, but as the series wore on the tourists seemed to work him out, and though he took another 10 wickets in the final Test, he was happy enough at summer's end to retire so he could concentrate on his career as a dentist. ∎

10 BEST BOWLING FIGURES IN A MATCH

Rank	Bowling	Bowler	Versus	Venue	Series
1.	16-137	Bob Massie	England	Lord's	1972
2.	14-90	Fred Spofforth	England	The Oval	1882
3.	14-199	Clarrie Grimmett	South Africa	Adelaide	1931-32
4.	13-77	Monty Noble	England	Melbourne	1901-02
5.	13-110	Fred Spofforth	England	Melbourne	1878-79
6.	13-148	Bruce Reid	England	Melbourne	1990-91
7.	13-173	Clarrie Grimmett	South Africa	Durban	1935-36
8.	13-217	Merv Hughes	West Indies	Perth	1988-89
9.	13-236	Arthur Mailey	England	Melbourne	1920-21
10.	12-87	Charlie Turner	England	Sydney	1887-88

There are eight other instances of Australians taking 12 wickets in a Test:

12-89	Hugh Trumble	England	The Oval	1896
12-107	Stuart MacGill	England	Sydney	1998-99
12-124	Alan Davidson	India	Kanpur	1959-60
12-126	Bruce Reid	India	Melbourne	1991-92
12-128	Shane Warne	South Africa	Sydney	1993-94
12-166	Geoff Dymock	India	Kanpur	1979
12-173	Hugh Trumble	England	The Oval	1902
12-175	Herbert Hordern	England	Sydney	1911-12

10 BEST BOWLING FIGURES IN AN INNINGS ON DEBUT

Rank	Bowling	Inns	Bowler	Versus	Venue	Series
1.	8-43	2nd	Albert Trott	England	Adelaide	1894-95
2.	8-53	2nd	Bob Massie	England	Lord's	1972
3.	8-84	1st	Bob Massie	England	Lord's	1972
4.	7-55	2nd	Tom Kendall	England	Melbourne	1876-77
5.	6-15	1st	Charlie Turner	England	Sydney	1886-87
6.	6-37	2nd	Clarrie Grimmett	England	Sydney	1924-25
7.	6-49	2nd	Monty Noble	England	Melbourne	1897-98
8.	6-58	2nd	Tony Dodemaide	New Zealand	Melbourne	1987-88
9.	6-74	1st	Rodney Hogg	England	Brisbane	1978-79
10.	6-78	1st	Peter Taylor	England	Sydney	1986-87

Bob Massie at Lord's and Clarrie Grimmett at Sydney (5–45 in the first innings) provide the only examples of Australian bowlers taking 10 wickets in their debut Test. For Massie, this was the ultimate 'one-off';

he would take a further five Test wickets in the third Ashes Test of 1972 (his second of the series, having missed the opener though injury), none in the fourth, two in the fifth, and eight more in his career, which ended as suddenly — but not nearly as spectacularly — as it began, in 1973.

Ian Johnson took 6–42 in England's first innings of the second Ashes Test of 1946–47. It was Johnson's third Test, but his first Test spell, as he had not been required to bowl in Australia's substantial victories on wet wickets at Wellington in March 1946 and at Brisbane in the opening Test of 1946–47.

The best innings bowling figures achieved by an Australian in his second Test are 7–60 by Keith Miller at the Gabba in 1946–47. The best match figures by an Australian bowler in his second Test are 13–110 (6–48 and 7–62) by Fred Spofforth at the MCG in 1879–80.

Rodney Hogg took at least five wickets in each of his first five complete innings as a bowler in Test cricket.

10 HIGHEST AGGREGATES IN A CALENDAR YEAR

Rank	Player	Year	Balls	Mdns	Runs	Wkts	Avge
1.	Dennis Lillee	1981	3710	147	1781	85	20.95
2.	Shane Warne	1993	5054	316	1697	72	23.57
3.	Graham McKenzie	1964	3746	119	1737	71	24.46
4.	Shane Warne	1994	3774	217	1274	70	18.20
5=	Glenn McGrath	2001	3508	196	1473	68	21.66
5=	Shane Warne	1997	4091	194	1661	68	24.43
7=	Glenn McGrath	1999	3364	167	1425	67	21.27
7=	Shane Warne	2002	2874	109	1310	67	19.55
9.	Glenn McGrath	1997	3113	151	1347	63	21.38
10.	Shane Warne	2001	3501	113	1809	58	31.19

Of course, this is going to be a table that reflects the heavy schedules of the current era; hence the multi-appearances of Warne and McGrath. Besides these top 10, there have been another 10 instances of Australian bowlers taking 50 wickets in one year and four of them are from the 1990s: Merv Hughes (57 wickets) in 1993, Craig McDermott (56) in 1991, and McGrath and Warne (both 52) in 1995.

McGrath's effort in 1995 came from 386.3 overs; the only other instance of an Australian bowler taking 50 wickets in a year in which he bowled fewer than 400 overs occurred back in 1902, when Monty Noble took 51 wickets from 368 overs. In the first seven Tests of 2003, Stuart MacGill took 42 wickets in 359.2 overs.

10 INSTANCES OF BOWLERS WHO DISMISSED AN OPPOSING BATSMAN MOST OFTEN

Rank	Bowler	Batsman	Times Dismissed
1.	Glenn McGrath	Mike Atherton (England)	19
2.	Hugh Trumble	Tom Hayward (England)	15
3=	Geoff Lawson	David Gower (England)	14
3=	Monty Noble	Arthur Lilley (England)	14
3=	Shane Warne	Alec Stewart (England)	14
6=	Glenn McGrath	Brian Lara (West Indies)	13
6=	Hugh Trumble	Archie MacLaren (England)	13
8=	Dennis Lillee	Alan Knott (England)	12
8=	Glenn McGrath	Jimmy Adams (West Indies)	12
8=	Hugh Trumble	Arthur Lilley (England)	12

Glenn McGrath has dismissed the West Indian opening batsman Sherwin Campbell 11 times. Clarrie Grimmett dismissed Maurice Tate of England 11 times, and Shane Warne did the same to another Englishman, Nasser Hussain.

10 BOWLERS WITH THE MOST FIVE-FORS

Rank	Bowler	Tests	5w	Best
1=	Dennis Lillee	70	23	7–83
1=	Shane Warne	107	23	8–71
1=	Glenn McGrath	93	23	8–38
4.	Clarrie Grimmett	37	21	7–40
5=	Richie Benaud	63	16	7–72
5=	Graham McKenzie	60	16	8–71
7=	Alan Davidson	44	14	7–93
7=	Terry Alderman	41	14	6–47
7=	Craig McDermott	71	14	8–97
10.	Ray Lindwall	61	12	7–38

Shane Warne has taken five wickets in a Test innings on 15 different grounds, an Australian record. Glenn McGrath has done so on 14 grounds, Graham McKenzie did so on 13, Richie Benaud on 12, Clarrie Grimmett on 11, Ray Lindwall and Terry Alderman on 10. Alderman is unique among Australian bowlers in that he took a Test five-for on each of the six current major Test grounds in England. Craig McDermott and Warne are the only men with Test five-fors on five different Australian grounds.

McGrath is the only Australian to take a five-for against seven different Test-playing teams. He needs only to do so against Zimbabwe and Bangladesh to complete his 'set'. Warne has not taken a five-for in Tests against India or Zimbabwe, and has not played against Bangladesh. Benaud, McKenzie and McDermott are the only three Australians besides McGrath and Warne to take five-fors against five different Test opponents.

McKenzie and Warne are the only Australians to take five wickets in a Test innings in six different countries (counting the West Indies as one country). Ray Lindwall, Benaud and McGrath are the three others to do so in five different countries.

Charlie Turner, Grimmett, Dennis Lillee and Alderman jointly hold the record for most five-fors against one country, all with 11 against England. Lillee, with 15 five-fors against various opponents on Australian grounds, has taken the most five-fors in Australia. Alderman, with 10 in England, holds the mark for the most taken by an Australian in any one country outside Australia.

10 BOWLERS WITH THE MOST 10-FORS

Rank	Bowler	Tests	10w	Best
1=	Clarrie Grimmett	37	7	14–199
1=	Dennis Lillee	70	7	11–123
3.	Shane Warne	107	6	12–128
4.	Fred Spofforth	18	4	14–90
5=	Hugh Trumble	32	3	12–89
5=	Bill O'Reilly	27	3	11–129
5=	Graham McKenzie	60	3	10–91
5=	Glenn McGrath	93	3	10–27
9=	George Palmer	17	2	11–165
9=	Charlie Turner	17	2	12–87
9=	Monty Noble	42	2	13–77
9=	Herbert Hordern	7	2	12–175
9=	Arthur Mailey	21	2	13–236
9=	Bert Ironmonger	14	2	11–24
9=	Alan Davidson	44	2	12–124
9=	Rodney Hogg	38	2	10–66
9=	Geoff Lawson	46	2	11–134
9=	Bob Holland	11	2	10–144
9=	Craig McDermott	71	2	11–157
9=	Bruce Reid	27	2	13–148
9=	Stuart MacGill	25	2	12–107

10 BOWLERS WHO WERE BETTER AT HOME

(Qualification: 750 deliveries home and away; must average less than 30 at home)

Rank	Bowler	Home Avge	Away Avge	Difference
1.	Mike Whitney	22.00	88.71	66.71
2.	Tim Wall	25.54	56.05	30.51
3.	Leslie Fleetwood-Smith	24.37	48.13	23.76
4.	Rodney Hogg	24.31	44.84	20.53
5.	Bob Cowper	21.00	39.24	18.24
6.	Bruce Reid	20.06	37.90	17.84
7.	Monty Noble	20.77	32.67	11.90
8.	Jim Higgs	26.24	37.45	11.21
9.	Colin Miller	20.79	30.05	9.26
10.	Eric Freeman	29.40	38.57	9.17

Mike Whitney played in three series outside Australia. In England in 1981, with a grand total of six first-class matches behind him, Whitney suddenly came into the Australian side for the final two Tests after a succession of quick or medium-pace bowlers — Geoff Lawson, Rodney Hogg, Graeme Beard, Jeff Thomson and Carl Rackemann among them — dropped out because of injury, illness or loss of form. And he did reasonably well, having David Gower dropped off his fourth ball in Test cricket, dismissing Gower in his second over and finishing the series with five wickets and a much enhanced reputation. However, as far as overseas Tests were concerned for M. Whitney, that was it for almost a decade. The reasons for this were varied, and included injuries and a mysterious decision by the selectors in 1989 not to pick him for that year's Ashes adventure despite the fact he'd taken 7–89 and 2–60 in the Test against the West Indies that immediately preceded the tour (not to mention his 58 first-class wickets for the 1988–89 season, the most by any bowler). When the popular NSW left-hander finally played another Test offshore it was in the West Indies in early 1991, where he failed to take a wicket in either of the first two Tests of the series. Finally, in Sri Lanka in 1992, 'Whit' played in the first two Tests, contributing with both bat and ball in Australia's stirring comeback victory at the Sinhalese Sports Club in Colombo, then getting few opportunities in the rain-interrupted second Test before missing the third with a shoulder problem.

One bowler unlucky to be in this Top 10 is 'Chuck' Fleetwood-Smith, whose record is skewed disastrously by the fact that he played at The Oval in 1938, when Len Hutton scored 364, England declared at 7–903, and he took 1–298. Things might have been different if keeper Ben Barnett hadn't missed a routine stumping chance off Fleetwood-Smith when Hutton was just 40.

TERRY JENNER'S TOP 10 ATTRIBUTES OF A SUCCESSFUL SPIN BOWLER

1. A Stock Ball. It is vital to have a reliable stock ball, such as a leg break or off break, and to be prepared to bowl it for the majority of a spell.

2. A Capable Wicketkeeper. Like a pair of opening batsmen who work well together, a good relationship between spinner and keeper is very important and rewarding. They need each other. Spinners rely on their keeper for wickets and advice.

3. Patience. There is often a long wait before the spinner is given his chance in a match. When the moment arrives, he must not be too anxious. Anxiety leads to a short spell.

4. Planning. With his captain, a spinner needs to plan each batsman's dismissal and patiently work to that plan.

5. Tactical Awareness. A spinner has to be able to adapt to different pitch conditions and match situations. Knowing when to attack and when to defend is a sign of class.

6. Variations. Knowing the right time to introduce the wrong 'un, for example, is one thing; having the confidence to bowl it is another. Regardless, a spinner needs to show the batsman he has more than a stock ball in his repertoire.

7. Courage. After being hit for fours and/or sixes, being able to come back to the bowling crease and continue to risk runs to take a wicket is a special gift.

8. Resilience. Certain pitch conditions or one average performance are often enough for the selectors to omit the spin bowler. He has to accept the situation, and wait patiently for another opportunity to show his worth.

9. A Sense of Humour. Given the way batsmen can sometimes make the spinner look a bit ordinary, you need to be able to have a laugh and come back tomorrow.

10. Selflessness. A spinner needs to know that on occasions he will need to do things for the team that may not benefit his own statistics.

10 BOWLERS WHO WERE BETTER AWAY FROM HOME

(Qualification: 750 deliveries home and away; must average less than 40 away from home)

Rank	Bowler	Home Avge	Away Avge	Difference
1.	Frank Laver	65.00	22.62	42.38
2.	Ray Bright	68.63	36.24	32.39
3.	Greg Matthews	60.11	38.15	21.96
4.	Tom Veivers	57.50	36.60	20.90
5.	Charlie Macartney	40.92	22.70	18.22
6.	Ken Mackay	45.62	30.49	15.13
7.	Andy Bichel	37.74	23.79	13.95
8.	Alan Connolly	37.58	24.67	12.91
9.	Terry Jenner	36.55	26.69	9.86
10.	Richie Benaud	30.74	24.35	6.39

The left-handed wrist spinner Lindsay Kline, who played 13 Tests between 1957 and 1961, doesn't qualify for this table because he bowled only 480 deliveries at home, taking three wickets in four Tests at an average of exactly 100. His greatest claim to fame as far as Tests in Australia are concerned is being involved right at the death of the highly dramatic first and fourth Tests of the 1960–61 series against the West Indies. On both those occasions, he had the bat in his hand; with the ball, unfortunately, he was unsuccessful, taking 3–52 and 0–14 in Brisbane and 0–109 and 0–48 in Adelaide. Away from Australia, Kline played in nine Tests — in South Africa, Pakistan and India — and took 31 wickets, including a hat-trick at Cape Town in January 1958, at 15.35.

10 HIGHEST AGGREGATES IN A SERIES

Rank	Wickets	Bowler	Versus	Series	Tests
1.	44	Clarrie Grimmett	South Africa	1935–36	5
2.	42	Terry Alderman	England	1981	6
3=.	41	Rodney Hogg	England	1978–79	6
3=.	41	Terry Alderman	England	1989	6
5.	39	Dennis Lillee	England	1981	6
6.	37	Bill Whitty	South Africa	1910–11	5
7=.	36	Arthur Mailey	England	1920–21	5
7=.	36	Glenn McGrath	England	1997	6
9=.	34	George Giffen	England	1894–95	5
9=.	34	Geoff Lawson	England	1982–83	5
9=.	34	Shane Warne	England	1993	6

Arthur Mailey played in all five Tests of the 1920–21 Ashes series, but only bowled in four of them. In the second Test, seven Australians bowled, but for some reason the Australian captain, Warwick Armstrong, decided Mailey, who batted No. 11 and was a specialist legspinner, wouldn't be one of them. In the other four Tests, the captain was in a better mood and Mailey sent down 243.5 overs. In 1931–32, Clarrie Grimmett played in all five Tests against South Africa, and finished with 33 wickets, but he didn't get a bowl in the final Test, when Laurie Nash, Bert Ironmonger and Bill O'Reilly so demoralised the South Africans on a sticky MCG pitch that Grimmett wasn't needed.

The most wickets taken by an Australian in a four-Test series is 30, by Glenn McGrath in the West Indies in 1999. Alan Davidson took 33 wickets in four Tests against the West Indies in 1960–61, when he missed the fourth Test through injury. The most wickets taken in a three-Test series is 27, by Shane Warne against Pakistan in Sri Lanka and Sharjah in 2002. Hugh Trumble took one less in the 1902 Ashes series in England, despite missing the opening two matches of that five-Test series.

❖   ❖   ❖

OPINION
THE TOP 10 DELIVERIES

Rank	Bowler	Delivery	Versus	Venue	Series
1.	Shane Warne	A leg break that bowled Mike Gatting	England	Manchester	1993
2.	Ernie Jones	A bouncer that went through WG Grace's beard	England	Lord's	1896
3.	Dennis Lillee	A full-pitched ball that Viv Richards played on	West Indies	Melbourne	1981–82
4.	Ray Lindwall	A yorker that bowled Len Hutton second ball for 0	England	Leeds	1953
5.	Jeff Thomson	A 'sandshoe crusher' that bowled Tony Greig	England	Brisbane	1974–75
6.	Richie Benaud	A leg break that bowled Peter May round his legs	England	Manchester	1961
7.	Leslie Fleetwood-Smith	An off-break that bowled Wally Hammond	England	Adelaide	1936–37
8.	Shane Warne	A flipper that bowled Richie Richardson	West Indies	Melbourne	1992–93
9.	Arthur Mailey	A full toss that bowled Jack Hobbs	England	Melbourne	1924–25
10.	Ken Eastwood	A full toss that Keith Fletcher spooned to mid-on	England	Sydney	1970–71

Shane Warne's famous first-up delivery to Mike Gatting was much more than just a 'leg break'. It was a wonder of physics that started on an off-stump line, drifted cruelly so it pitched around 15 centimetres outside the leg-stump, then fizzed back to take the off bail. This was Warne's debut delivery in Ashes cricket, Gatting (a masterful player of spin bowling) reacted as if he'd seen a ghost, and a mystique about Warne was immediately established, an aura that for English batsmen at least continues to this day. Six months earlier, Warne had knocked over Richie Richardson, the West Indies captain, with a stunning flipper that demonstrated he was Test-class. After one ball in England he was a magician.

While there is no doubt that Ernie Jones did get a very quick short one through Dr Grace's beard, there is some conjecture as to when it took place. In his superb biography, *W.G. Grace*, the cricket historian Simon Rae explains that some thought it occurred at Lord's, others in the opening game of the Australians' tour, at Sheffield Park. The weight of opinion might be slightly in favour of the Test, so we're happy to include it here. There is also disagreement as to Grace's reaction, though most agree that he was at least ruffled, and that he most likely did say something to the bowler. It certainly would have been in his nature. Jones is reputed to have replied, 'Sorry, doc, she slipped.'

Jones was the fastest Australian bowler of his time. One senses he would have enjoyed the efforts of those who followed in his footsteps, men such as Dennis Lillee, Ray Lindwall and Jeff Thomson. Lillee's last-ball-of-the-day dismissal of Viv Richards so delighted the MCG faithful that they were still cheering and chanting his name for half an hour after the players had left the field. Lindwall's act in knocking over Hutton, the local Yorkshire hero, second ball of the Test, sent a hush over Headingley more likely not to be heard at a funeral. Thomson's express yorker was the last thing Tony Greig expected, and for all the bouncers and bumpers fired down during the series, it became something of a Thommo trademark.

Vastly different in style from Thomson, but just as crafty, Richie Benaud's dismissal of Peter May, the England captain, at Old Trafford in 1961 turned not just a Test finish but the fate of the Ashes. The series was tied at one-all after three matches, and on the final afternoon of the fourth Test England were 2–150, chasing 256, with May newly arrived at the crease after the dismissal of Ted Dexter, who had batted brilliantly for 76 in 84 minutes. The Australian skipper had settled on a plan of landing his leg breaks in bowlers' footmarks left outside the batsmen's leg stump, and second ball to May he got it exactly right, spinning a delivery sharply around his pads and hitting the leg stump.

The delivery 'Chuck' Fleetwood-Smith bowled to dismiss Wally Hammond in February 1937 was in terms of spin and drift the left-hander's version of the Gatting ball. Hammond was in stirring form, and so clearly the key man if England (3–148 at the start of the last day) were to reach their target of 392. But he didn't survive the first over, bowled by a wickedly turning off-break that started on the line of the off-stump, but began, like a tease, to drift away. Then, when it pitched, it spun back viciously through the gap between bat and pad that the drift had created, to knock back the English master batsman's off-stump. Fleetwood-Smith fell to his knees, looked over at his captain, Bradman, and grinned, 'Was that what you wanted?'

In the 1924–25 series, the Australians stayed up half the night trying to find a way to dismiss Jack Hobbs and Herbert Sutcliffe, who had batted throughout the previous day for 283 runs. All sorts of plans were considered, and then Hobbs was bowled second ball by Mailey's full-pitcher. History sort of repeated itself in 1970–71, when Ian Chappell gave Ken Eastwood an over in what proved to be his only Test. Eastwood had hardly bowled in Shield cricket, but the new Australian captain had been troubled by his wrong 'un in the nets and thought the Englishmen mightn't be able to pick the 'rookie' left-hander either. The googly didn't do the trick, but Keith Fletcher was still confused enough to hit a full toss to Keith Stackpole. Eastwood finished his international career with figures of 1–21 from five overs. ∎

10 BOWLERS WHO HAVE BOWLED THE MOST DELIVERIES IN A CAREER

Rank	Balls	Bowler	Tests
1.	29877	Shane Warne	107
2.	22374	Glenn McGrath	95
3.	19108	Richie Benaud	63
4.	18467	Dennis Lillee	70
5.	17681	Graham McKenzie	60
6.	16586	Craig McDermott	71
7.	14513	Clarrie Grimmett	37
8.	13650	Ray Lindwall	61
9.	12285	Merv Hughes	53
10.	11587	Alan Davidson	44

Other Australians to have bowled more than 10,000 deliveries in Test cricket are Terry Alderman (10,181 balls), Bill Johnston (11,048), Geoff Lawson (11,118), Keith Miller (10,461), Bill O'Reilly (10,024), Jeff Thomson (10,535) and Max Walker (10,094).

10 BOWLERS TO TAKE 100 TEST WICKETS IN THE LEAST NUMBER OF INNINGS

Rank	Bowler	Tests	Inns	Best	Avge	5w	10w
1.	Charlie Turner	17	30	7–83	16.53	11	2
2.	Clarrie Grimmett	17	31	7–87	28.06	11	3
3.	Bill O'Reilly	20	36	7–54	23.78	7	2
4=	Bruce Reid	25	38	7–51	25.63	3	1
4=	Stuart MacGill	21	38	7–50	27.96	5	1
6.	Jeff Thomson	22	39	6–46	25.34	5	–
7=	George Giffen	30	41	7–117	26.96	7	1
7=	Shane Warne	23	41	7–52	24.19	5	1
9=	Bill Johnston	22	42	6–44	18.81	4	–
9=	Graham McKenzie	23	42	7–153	26.96	6	1
9=	Dennis Lillee	22	42	6–66	23.72	5	1
9=	Geoff Lawson	25	42	7–81	28.16	8	1

The youngest to reach 100 Test wickets was McKenzie, at 23 years, 163 days, from Warne, 24 years, 141 days, then Craig McDermott (27 Tests, 45 innings, aged 25 years, 326 days). The quickest to get there, from date of first wicket to date of 100th, was Warne (two years and 30 days), then Max Walker (24 Tests, 43 innings, three years and six days) and Brett Lee (27 Tests, 53 innings, three years and nine days).

Charlie Turner, the Terror, took 6–15 in his first Test innings, giving him a Test bowling average after one innings of 2.50. Inevitably, from there, his average gradually got worse, but it took a while. After five Tests, his bowling average was 9.40 (45 wickets for 423 runs), after 10 it was 12.97 (78 for 1073), after 15 it was as high as it ever got: 17.30 (86 for 1488).

A study of the fluctuations in Bill Johnston's career average suggests that he might well be one of the most underrated of all Australian bowlers. Perhaps he had the advantage of bowling with Ray Lindwall and Keith Miller, and because he could bowl fast medium or spinners he was adaptable, but it is a fact that it wasn't until he'd played in 26 Tests that his career bowling average climbed above 20. By the end of the series at home against the West Indies in 1951–52, by which time Johnston had played 24 Tests and been a Test cricketer for four years, his Test bowling average was 19.22, one and a half runs better than Miller's career average at that time and more than a run better than Lindwall's. Johnston's international career continued on to 1955, and he retired with 160 wickets at a still impressive 23.91, but for the final three years he was hindered by a knee injury suffered at the beginning of the 1953 Ashes tour.

10 BOWLERS TO TAKE 200 WICKETS IN THE LEAST NUMBER OF INNINGS

Rank	Bowler	Tests	Inns	Best	Avge	5w	10w
1.	Clarrie Grimmett	36	65	7–40	24.91	19	6
2.	Dennis Lillee	38	73	6–26	23.34	14	4
3.	Shane Warne	42	76	8–71	22.92	10	3
4.	Craig McDermott	50	83	8–97	29.17	9	2
5=.	Glenn McGrath	45	86	8–38	23.36	11	–
5=.	Graham McKenzie	46	86	8–71	28.42	14	3
7.	Richie Benaud	49	88	7–72	24.73	13	1
8.	Merv Hughes	49	89	8–87	27.08	7	1
9.	Jeff Thomson	51	91	6–46	28.00	8	–
10.	Ray Lindwall	52	94	7–38	22.38	11	–

The youngest to reach 200 Test wickets was Warne, at 26 years 89 days. The quickest to get there, from date of 101st wicket to date of 200th, was also Warne (three years and 343 days).

Three Australian bowlers have taken more than 300 Test wickets. The speed they took to get there is as follows:

Rank	Bowler	Tests	Inns	Best	Avge	5w	10w
1.	Dennis Lillee	56	107	7–89	22.96	21	6
2.	Shane Warne	63	116	8–71	23.56	14	4
3.	Glenn McGrath	64	123	8–38	21.70	18	3

McGrath took 168 innings to reach 400 Test wickets, Warne 169.

10 BOWLERS WHO HAVE BOWLED THE MOST DELIVERIES IN AN INNINGS

Rank	Balls	Bowler	Analysis	Versus	Venue	Series
1.	571	Tom Veivers	3–155	England	Manchester	1964
2.	522	Leslie Fleetwood-Smith	1–298	England	The Oval	1938
3.	510	Bill O'Reilly	3–178	England	The Oval	1938
4.	478	Jim Higgs	5–148	England	Sydney	1978–79
5.	470	George Giffen	6–155	England	Melbourne	1894–95
6.	450	George Giffen	4–164	England	Sydney	1894–95
7.	432	Mervyn Waite	1–150	England	The Oval	1938
8.	424	Kerry O'Keeffe	3–166	Pakistan	Adelaide	1976–77
9.	408	Bert Ironmonger	2–142	England	Sydney	1928–29
10.	408	Ken Mackay	5–121	England	The Oval	1961

Jim Higgs in 1978–79 and Kerry O'Keeffe two years earlier were bowling eight-ball overs. The number of deliveries does not include wides and no balls.

In his autobiography *Captain's Story*, Bob Simpson told the story of how, near the end of the high-scoring fourth Test of 1964, at Manchester, it was discovered Tom Veivers was closing in on West Indian Sonny Ramadhin's world record for most deliveries bowled in an innings. So a plan was hatched with England No. 11 John Price, that Veivers would bowl wide of the stumps and Price would leave such deliveries alone until the record was broken. However, Veivers was in such a groove — after aiming over after over at the stumps — that he couldn't change his line, and Price was bowled 17 deliveries short of Ramadhin's mark. 'Tom had virtually mesmerised himself out of the record,' Simpson recalled.

10 BEST INNINGS FIGURES (BOWLING FIRST OVER)

Rank	Analysis	Bowler	Versus	Venue	Series
1.	8–38	Glenn McGrath	England	Lord's	1997
2.	8–65	Hugh Trumble	England	The Oval	1902
3.	8–71	Graham McKenzie	West Indies	Melbourne	1968–69
4.	8–87	Merv Hughes	West Indies	Perth	1988–89
5.	8–112	Geoff Lawson	West Indies	Adelaide	1984–85
6.	7–38	Ray Lindwall	India	Adelaide	1947–48
7=.	7–43	Charlie Turner	England	Sydney	1887–88
7=.	7–43	Ray Lindwall	India	Madras	1956
9=.	7–44	Fred Spofforth	England	The Oval	1882
9=.	7–44	Fred Spofforth	England	Sydney	1882–83

10 BEST INNINGS FIGURES (BOWLING SECOND OVER)

Rank	Analysis	Bowler	Versus	Venue	Series
1.	8–53	Bob Massie	England	Lord's	1972
2.	8–84	Bob Massie	England	Lord's	1972
3.	8–97	Craig McDermott	England	Perth	1990–91
4.	8–141	Craig McDermott	England	Manchester	1985
5.	8–143	Max Walker	England	Melbourne	1974–75
6.	7–17	Monty Noble	England	Melbourne	1901–02
7.	7–34	Jack Saunders	South Africa	Johannesburg	1902
8.	7–36	Michael Kasprowicz	England	The Oval	1997
9.	7–51	Bruce Reid	England	Melbourne	1990–91
10.	7–58	Charlie Macartney	England	Leeds	1909

GEOFF LAWSON'S TOP 10 ATTRIBUTES OF A SUCCESSFUL FAST BOWLER

1. Aggression.

2. Stamina.

3. Resilience.

4. Intelligence.

5. A dislike, bordering on absolute hatred of batsmen.

6. The ability to adapt to different conditions.

7. A dislike of umpires.

8. In the 1970s it was Zapata moustaches; in the 21st century you need cool sunglasses and blond tips. The more times change, the more they stay the same.

9. Athleticism (Merv Hughes being the exception that proves the rule).

10. High pain tolerance.

No one captured these attributes better than DK Lillee. He was not as much a natural athlete as his fellow 'frightener' Jeff Thomson was, but he had a fierce competitiveness and a will to go on when his body screamed that there was nothing left. That mindset, along with an almost perfect technical bowling action that produced the legcutter at pace, made him consistently lethal — even if his speed declined a little in the latter part of his career. His effectiveness never declined.

In full cry, Dennis Lillee was the archetypal speed man, snarling and ferocious and bristling with disgust and annoyance when the umpire did not concur with one of his bellowing, demanding appeals. He was truly intimidating … and truly great.

10 BEST INNINGS FIGURES (BOWLING FIRST CHANGE)

Rank	Analysis	Bowler	Versus	Venue	Series
1.	9–121	Arthur Mailey	England	Melbourne	1920–21
2.	8–31	Frank Laver	England	Manchester	1909
3.	8–43	Albert Trott	England	Adelaide	1894–95
4.	8–71	Shane Warne	England	Brisbane	1994–95
5=	7–23	Bert Ironmonger	West Indies	Melbourne	1930–31
5=	7–23	Shane Warne	Pakistan	Brisbane	1995–96
7.	7–25	Gerry Hazlitt	England	The Oval	1912
8.	7–28	Hugh Trumble	England	Melbourne	1903–04
9.	7–37	Jason Gillespie	England	Leeds	1997
10.	7–40	Clarrie Grimmett	South Africa	Johannesburg	1935–36

10 BEST INNINGS FIGURES (BOWLING SECOND CHANGE)

Rank	Analysis	Bowler	Versus	Venue	Series
1.	8–59	Ashley Mallett	Pakistan	Adelaide	1972–73
2.	7–27	Mike Whitney	India	Perth	1991–92
3.	7–44	Ian Johnson	West Indies	Georgetown	1955
4.	7–52	Shane Warne	West Indies	Melbourne	1992–93
5.	7–54	Bill O'Reilly	England	Nottingham	1934
6.	7–75	Lindsay Kline	Pakistan	Lahore	1959–60
7.	7–83	Clarrie Grimmett	South Africa	Adelaide	1931–32
8.	7–92	Percy Hornibrook	England	The Oval	1930
9.	7–94	Shane Warne	Pakistan	Colombo	2002
10.	7–116	Clarrie Grimmett	South Africa	Adelaide	1931–32

10 BEST INNINGS FIGURES (BOWLING THIRD CHANGE)

Rank	Analysis	Bowler	Versus	Venue	Series
1.	7–46	Allan Border	West Indies	Sydney	1988–89
2.	6–31	Shane Warne	New Zealand	Hobart	1993–94
3=	6–42	Ian Johnson	England	Sydney	1946–47
3=	6–42	Ken Mackay	Pakistan	Dacca	1959–60
5.	6–49	Monty Noble	England	Melbourne	1897–98
6.	6–80	Doug Ring	West Indies	Brisbane	1951–52
7.	6–94	Don Blackie	England	Melbourne	1928–29
8.	6–106	Bob Holland	New Zealand	Sydney	1985–86
9.	5–27	Warwick Armstrong	England	Birmingham	1909
10.	5–28	Steve Waugh	South Africa	Cape Town	1994

10 BEST INNINGS FIGURES (BOWLING FOURTH CHANGE OR LATER)

Rank	Analysis	Bowler	Change	Opponent	Venue	Series
1.	5–68	Allan Border	Fourth	West Indies	Georgetown	1991
2.	5–109	Colin McCool	Fourth	England	Sydney	1946–47
3.	4–25	Jim Higgs	Fourth	New Zealand	Perth	1980–81
4.	4–26	Steve Waugh	Fourth	South Africa	Adelaide	1993–94
5.	4–34	Doug Walters	Fourth	England	The Oval	1975
6.	4–41	Norm O'Neill	Sixth	West Indies	Port-of-Spain	1965
7.	4–47	Sammy Jones	Fifth	England	Melbourne	1884–85
8.	4–50	Allan Border	Fourth	West Indies	Sydney	1988–89
9.	4–54	Bob Simpson	Fifth	India	Calcutta	1964
10.	4–63	Ashley Mallett	Fourth	New Zealand	Melbourne	1973–74

❖ ❖ ❖

OPINION
THE TOP 10 HAT-TRICKS

Rank	Bowler	Versus	Venue	Series	Batsmen dismissed (batting position)
1.	Damien Fleming	Pakistan	Rawalpindi	1994	Aamer Malik (5), Inzamam-ul-Haq (6), Salim Malik (4)
2.	Glenn McGrath	West Indies	Perth	2000–01	Campbell (1), Lara (4), Adams (5)
3.	Merv Hughes	West Indies	Perth	1988–89	Ambrose (9), Patterson (11), Greenidge (1)
4.	Jimmy Matthews	South Africa	Manchester	1912	Taylor (5), Schwarz (8), Ward (9)
5.	Hugh Trumble	England	Melbourne	1903–04	Bosanquet (7), Warner (5), Lilley (9)
6.	Shane Warne	England	Melbourne	1994–95	de Freitas (8), Gough (9), Malcolm (10)
7.	Hugh Trumble	England	Melbourne	1901–02	Jones (8), J Gunn (9), Barnes (10)
8.	Fred Spofforth	England	Melbourne	1878–79	Royle (6), Mackinnon (7), Emmett (8)
9.	Lindsay Kline	South Africa	Cape Town	1957–58	Fuller (9), Tayfield (10), Adcock (11)
10.	Tom Matthews	South Africa	Manchester	1912	Beaumont (9), Pegler (10), Ward (11)

There have been 10 Test-match hat-tricks taken by Australians, most of them achieved by Victorians. Spofforth, from Sydney, completed Australia's first Test-match hat-trick — at the Melbourne Cricket Ground — but the next eight men to do so were all Victorians. We've ranked the 10 here according to the bowler's personal situation, the game situation when the hat-trick occurred and the quality of the batsmen dismissed.

It is doubtful that any Test bowler on a hat-trick has been less likely to complete the trifecta than was Damien Fleming in Rawalpindi in October 1994. He was bowling to the Pakistan captain, Salim Malik, who was 237 not out. Even though Fleming had taken wickets with the last two balls of his previous over, the home team was 5–478 in its second innings as the game plodded to a high-scoring draw. Salim would finish the series with 557 runs, the most ever by a batsman in a three-Test series. Yet when Fleming reached the end of his run he looked at Craig McDermott at mid-on, and David Boon at mid-off and, as Boon recalls in his autobiography, announced …

Salim Malik, you are about to become a part of history …

Which he surely did, edging the perfect outswinger to Ian Healy. Fleming became the third man from any country to take a hat-trick on his Test debut. At Adelaide in December 1999, against India, Shane Warne dropped a slip catch that would have made Fleming the second man, after Pakistan's Wasim Akram, to achieve a Test hat-trick at home and away.

McGrath is ranked at No. 2, if only because the great Lara was part of the hat-trick, and the Australian quick's 300th Test wicket as well. At No. 3, Hughes' hat-trick is unique among these 10, as it was spread across two innings, and included Greenidge straight after Hughes' fast-bowling teammate Geoff Lawson had had his jaw broken by a Curtly Ambrose bouncer.

Remarkably, Jimmy Matthews' twin hat-tricks were taken on the same day; the second is ranked higher because of this feat. Adding to the wonder of this achievement, the South African wicketkeeper Tommy Ward was the third leg of both hat-tricks, out for a 'king' pair on his Test debut. Ward, who batted at No. 11 in the first innings and at No. 9 in the second, was lbw and then out caught and bowled. But though his performances against Matthews on this day might not have suggested it, he was actually a very tough and handy cricketer, who would go on to play 23 Tests, many of them after World War I, and even open the batting for his country.

The remainder of our top 10 feature almost exclusively tailenders, but Hugh Trumble's two hat-tricks and Shane Warne's receive greater marks because they occurred dramatically on these two great bowlers' home ground, the Melbourne Cricket Ground. Trumble's higher-ranked hat-trick occurred in the fourth innings of his final Test — the fourth, fifth and sixth wickets in a spell that brought him 7–28 from 6.5 overs. ■

10 BOWLERS WHO WERE FASTEST TO TAKE THEIR FIRST TEST WICKET

Rank	Ball	Bowler	Versus	Venue	Series	Batsman	How Out
1.	1	Arthur Coningham	England	Melbourne	1894–95	AC MacLaren	caught
2=.	2	Colin McCool	New Zealand	Wellington	1946	DA McRae	caught
2=.	2	Frank Misson	West Indies	Melbourne	1960–61	CC Hunte	caught
2=.	2	Peter Philpott	West Indies	Kingston	1965	CC Hunte	cght (wk)
2=.	2	Geoff Dymock	New Zealand	Adelaide	1973–74	JM Parker	cght (wk)
6=.	3	Ian Johnson	England	Sydney	1946–47	L Hutton	cght (wk)
6=.	3	Eric Freeman	India	Brisbane	1967–68	S Abid Ali	caught
8=.	4	Fred Freer	England	Sydney	1946–47	C Washbrook	bowled
8=.	4	Brett Lee	India	Melbourne	1999–00	S Ramesh	bowled
10.	5	Ashley Mallett	England	The Oval	1968	MC Cowdrey	lbw

The three other Australian bowlers to take a wicket in their first over in Test cricket are 'Chuck' Fleetwood-Smith, who bowled South Africa's Ken Viljoen with his sixth delivery at Durban in 1935–36; Ron Gaunt, who bowled Dick Westcott with his seventh ball at Durban in 1957–58; and Tony Mann, who had India's Gundappa Viswanath caught with his seventh delivery at the Gabba in 1977–78.

Arthur Coningham's only real claim to fame in cricket history is the fact that he took a ball with his first delivery in Tests (it was one of two he took for 76 in his only match), but elsewhere he developed a reputation as an eccentric that reached its height in 1900 when he sued his wife for divorce on the grounds that she was having an affair with a senior priest of Sydney's St Mary's Cathedral. In court, Alice Coningham tearfully admitted the adultery, but eventually both she and her husband were shown to be cruelly conspiring against the Church. This verdict, though, was not reached until after a moment of high drama, when the Test cricketer suddenly brandished a revolver in court, and threatened to shoot the innocent priest at the centre of the false allegations.

Ian Johnson was a specialist offspinner, but he didn't get a bowl until his third Test, when he immediately dismissed England's best batsman, Len Hutton. Fred Freer's instant success had occurred earlier in the same game, when he bowled the other English opener, Cyril Washbrook.

Eric Freeman took a wicket with his third and 10th balls in Test cricket. Earlier in his debut Test, his first scoring stroke had been a six over midwicket off the Indian offspinner Erapally Prasanna.

THE 10 PLAYERS WHO TOOK MORE WICKETS THAN SCORED RUNS IN A CAREER *(Qualification: three Tests)*

Rank	W/R	Player	Tests	HS	Runs	Avge	Wkts	Avge
1.	7.00	Jack Iverson	5	1*	3	0.75	21	15.24
2.	3.66	Sam Gannon	3	3*	3	3.00	11	32.82
3.	2.40	Grahame Corling	5	3	5	1.66	12	37.25
4.	2.02	Jack Saunders	14	11*	39	2.29	79	22.73
5.	1.76	Bert Ironmonger	14	12	42	2.63	74	17.97
6.	1.30	Greg Campbell	4	6	10	2.50	13	38.69
7.	1.21	Bruce Reid	27	13	93	4.65	113	24.64
8.	1.16	Ron Gaunt	3	3	6	3.00	7	44.29
9.	1.11	Gordon Rorke	4	7	9	4.50	10	20.30
10.	1.04	Dave Renneberg	8	9	22	3.66	23	36.09

W/R indicates career wickets divided by career runs.

10 BOWLERS WHO HAVE OPENED THE BOWLING MOST TIMES *(By innings)*

Rank	Inns	Bowler	Tests
1.	174	Glenn McGrath	95
2.	124	Dennis Lillee	70
3.	115	Craig McDermott	71
4.	113	Graham McKenzie	60
5.	108	Ray Lindwall	61
6.	73	Keith Miller	55
7.	67	Terry Alderman	41
8.	63	Jeff Thomson	51
9.	62	Alan Davidson	44
10.	62	Jason Gillespie	45

During a career that ran from the second Ashes Test at Lord's in 1961 to the fourth Ashes Test at the SCG in 1970–71, Graham McKenzie bowled in 113 Test innings and bowled either the first or second over every time (Jeff Thomson, by way of comparison, opened the bowling in 63 of the 90 Test innings in which he bowled). This is unique among the bowlers in this Top 10. McKenzie's Tests stats are intriguing, in that there is little in them — no low average (he ended with 246 wickets at 29.79) or low strike rate (he took a wicket every 71.87 balls), for example — to suggest he was a truly great bowler, yet for a decade he was far and away Australia's No. 1 bowler in a manner perhaps only Bill O'Reilly in the 1930s can match. One can imagine opponents throughout the '60s adopting a policy of 'let's see off McKenzie and score our runs elsewhere'. When he was perhaps prematurely dropped from the Australian team, McKenzie was only two wickets short of Richie Benaud's Australian Test record, having played three fewer Tests and bowled 1427 fewer deliveries than the great legspinner, and having bowled through a decade where defensive batting mindsets often prevailed, and the pitches were often batsman-friendly. Had he bowled in the 1950s, with Lindwall, or the '70s, with Lillee, Graham McKenzie's career figures might have been sensational.

10 PARTNERSHIPS THAT OPENED THE BOWLING
MOST OFTEN *(By innings)*

Rank	Bowlers	Inns	Wickets	Avge wickets
1.	Ray Lindwall/Keith Miller	62	236	3.81
2.	Glenn McGrath/Jason Gillespie	55	246	4.47
3.	Graham McKenzie/Alan Connolly	33	123	3.73
4.	Graham McKenzie/Neil Hawke	30	142	4.73
5=.	Alan Davidson/Ian Meckiff	29	125	4.31
5=.	Glenn McGrath/Damien Fleming	29	132	4.55
7.	Craig McDermott/Merv Hughes	26	115	4.42
8=.	Ray Lindwall/Bill Johnston	23	103	4.48
8=.	Dennis Lillee/Jeff Thomson	23	116	5.04
8=.	Dennis Lillee/Terry Alderman	23	131	5.70

'Wickets' indicates wickets taken in those innings in which the two men opened the bowling. 'Average wickets' indicates the average number of wickets taken in the innings where the duos opened the attack.

The most successful Australian opening partnership, based on the average wickets per Test as an opening pair measuring stick, is Charlie Turner and Jack Ferris. In 14 innings between 1887 and 1890, this dynamic duo took 104 wickets — 7.43 wickets per innings.

CHAPTER THREE

WICKETKEEPERS AND FIELDSMEN

If there is one thing about changes in cricket standards that is beyond dispute, it is that the quality of fielding has improved dramatically through the decades, especially in the past 25 years as one-day cricket has sharpened catching, ground fielding and throwing skills, and a wide variety of fielding drills have become an integral part of pre-match preparations. The first 100 years of Australian Test cricket did produce a succession of superb fieldsmen — natural athletes such as Clem Hill, Tommy Andrews, 'Nip' Pellew, Vic Richardson, Don Bradman, Ernie Bromley, Neil Harvey, Norm O'Neill, Doug Walters, Paul Sheahan and Ross Edwards — but also some very ordinary ones, none more so than Bert 'Dainty' Ironmonger, who once caught England's Bob Wyatt in a Test at the SCG during the bodyline series. Bill O'Reilly, who had been complaining about his misfortune as Wyatt scraped his way to a streaky half century, walked up to the dismissed batsman and muttered, 'And I thought I was unlucky!'

It wasn't until after World War II that slip fielding became an art in itself. It is hard to think of too many prewar catchers outside Jack Gregory who were renowned for snaring sharp edges. Captains of those times often put their fast bowlers in the slips so they wouldn't have their energy wasted chasing boundaries; only in the past 50 years have champions such as Keith Miller, Bob Simpson, Ian and Greg Chappell, Mark Taylor and Mark Waugh proved the true value of a hungry and classy slip cordon.

In 1926, Monty Noble nominated Vernon Ransford as the best Australian outfielder he had seen, Syd Gregory the best cover, Ernie Jones the best mid-off, and Jack Gregory the finest at first slip. To start this chapter we've come up with a Top 10 from post-1926 that would have to be at least close to the greatest fielding combination that Australia could ever put on the paddock.

First slip:	Bob Simpson	*Mid-on:*	Alan Davidson
Second slip:	Mark Waugh	*Short leg:*	Vic Richardson
Third slip:	Greg Chappell	*Square leg:*	Ricky Ponting
Gully:	Ashley Mallett	*Fine leg:*	Brett Lee
Cover:	Neil Harvey	*Bowler:*	Jeff Thomson

This is a Top 10 that was deliberately chosen as a team: Simpson and Richardson to open the batting; Chappell, Waugh, Harvey and Ponting in the middle order; Mallett as the spinner; Thomson, Davidson and Lee as the three quicks. You can add the wicketkeeper of your choice (we would go for Jack Blackham, a choice we justify on page 97). In most cases, the men we've nominated could field superbly in much more than just their specific fielding position; for example, we'd certainly feel extremely comfortable putting Harvey and Ponting — arguably the two best all-round fieldsmen Australia has had — in the slip cordon or the outfield if a game situation so demanded. Choosing Harvey and Ponting means we can't find a place for Bradman, who many believe to have been Australia's best outfielder between the wars. If we were choosing a 12th man, The Don would be it.

As good as David Boon was at short leg, and as much as we accept that fielding standards have improved in recent times, we cannot ignore the claims of Richardson, who was once chaired from the field by the fans in Sydney after a day's play in an Ashes Test in 1928–29, purely because of his heroics fielding close in and in the covers while a batting line-up led by Wally Hammond slaughtered the Australian bowlers. The next morning, *The Sydney Morning Herald* featured an article that began: 'Is Richardson human?'

Ashley Mallett edges Richie Benaud out of this side on the back of his extraordinary series in 1974–75, when he took a number of brilliant catches in the gully. Elsewhere, Mallett could be awkward; in the gully he was fabulous. Alan Davidson, aka 'The Claw', could field anywhere and always do it superbly, Brett Lee has taken fielding standards for fast bowlers to a new level, and before Jeff Thomson damaged his shoulder he had a throwing arm from the boundary that was the equal of any outfielder. Thomson was also a safe, sometimes spectacular catcher, and off his own bowling he could be magnificent; at Trent Bridge in 1977 he made Geoff Boycott look silly in an incident that led to the run out of the home-town hero. Derek Randall. Boycott, making his return to Test cricket after a three-year exile, pushed a ball back up the onside of the pitch and called for a quick single. Quick suddenly became suicidal when Thommo was able to stop and turn like a rugby league halfback, get at the ball before it was past him, and flick it back to Rod Marsh. Boycott kept running, and Randall, his partner, was run out by half the length of the pitch.

10 AUSTRALIANS WITH MOST CAREER FIELDING DISMISSALS *(Including wicketkeepers)*

Rank	Player	Tests	Caught	Stumped	Dismissals
1.	Ian Healy	119	366	29	395
2.	Rod Marsh	96	343	12	355
3.	Adam Gilchrist	45	176	16	192
4.	Wally Grout	51	163	24	187
5.	Mark Waugh	128	181	–	181
6.	Mark Taylor	104	157	–	157
7.	Allan Border	156	156	–	156
8.	Bert Oldfield	54	78	52	130
9.	Greg Chappell	87	122	–	122
10.	Bob Simpson	62	110	–	110

The only other Australians with 100 such dismissals are Steve Waugh, who has taken 109 catches in 162 Tests, and Ian Chappell, who took 105 catches in 75 Tests. David Boon took 99 catches, Ricky Ponting has taken 85 and Ian Redpath caught 83.

The next five wicketkeepers with most dismissals (after Healy, Marsh, Grout, Gilchrist and Oldfield), to make a top 10 keepers list, are as follows:

Rank	Keeper	Tests	Caught	Stumped	Dismissals
6.	Gil Langley	26	83	15	98
7.	Hanson Carter	28	44	21	65
8.	Jim Kelly	36	43	20	63
9=.	Jack Blackham	34	36	24	60
9=.	Brian Taber	16	56	4	60

Blackham played one more Test (in addition to the 34 above), in which he did not keep at any stage and took one catch. In two other Tests, he kept for only part of the match.

Strangely, only one of Taber's 16 Test matches was played in Australia. He made his Test debut in South Africa in 1966–67, when Barry Jarman was unavailable to tour, substituted for the injured Jarman at Edgbaston in 1968, replaced the dropped Jarman for the final Test against the West

Indies at the SCG in 1968–69, and was first choice in India and South Africa throughout the 1969–70 tour. And that was his Test career. For the Ashes series that followed, the selectors preferred Rod Marsh, who never missed a Test until 1977, joined World Series Cricket, and then after 'peace' was restored continued on unchallenged as Test keeper until January 1984.

Taber's eight dismissals (seven catches and a stumping) in the first Test of the 1966–67 series, at Johannesburg, remains the most completed by an Australian keeper in his debut Test. It was also the first time in his life that Taber had ever attended a Test match.

10 WICKETKEEPERS WITH MOST STUMPINGS

Rank	Stumpings	Keeper	Tests	Dismissals
1.	52	Bert Oldfield	54	130
2.	29	Ian Healy	119	395
3=	24	Jack Blackham	32	60
3=	24	Wally Grout	51	187
5.	21	Hanson Carter	28	65
6.	20	Jim Kelly	36	63
7.	16	Adam Gilchrist	45	192
8.	15	Gil Langley	26	98
9.	12	Rod Marsh	96	355
10.	9	Affie Jarvis	8	16

Rod Marsh's ratio of one stumping every eight Tests is the lowest of any Australian keeper to make a stumping in a Test match, with the exception of Tim Zoehrer, who completed one stumping in 10 Test-match appearances.

Many would be surprised by Don Tallon's absence from this Top 10, but the fact is he did not make a stumping in either of the 1948 or 1950–51 Ashes series. While Tallon made eight stumpings in his first 10 Tests (1946–48), and three in one match against England at the SCG in 1946–47, he didn't make another in his final 11 (the first of which was the fifth Test v India in 1947–48 and the last being the opening Ashes Test of 1953). When Tallon missed the 1949–50 tour of South Africa, his replacement, Ron Saggers, completed eight stumpings in five Tests. And when Tallon was unavailable through the 1951–52 and 1952–53 Australian seasons, Gil Langley managed eight stumpings in 10 Tests, including four on his Test debut against the West Indies at the Gabba in 1951–52.

The most stumpings by an Australian keeper in one Test innings is four, by Bert Oldfield at the MCG against England in 1924–25. Oldfield made his stumpings off three different bowlers, two of whom — Jack Ryder and Charles Kelleway — bowled at a brisk medium pace. There have been nine instances of a keeper making three stumpings in one innings, but none since Langley did so against the West Indies at Georgetown in 1955.

The most stumpings achieved in one Test match is four, by Jack Blackham at Lord's in 1888, Affie Jarvis against England at the SCG in 1894–95, Bert Oldfield three times (in the fourth and fifth Tests of the 1924–25 Ashes series and against the West Indies in 1930–31), Saggers at Port Elizabeth in 1949–50, and Langley. All four of Oldfield's stumpings in the fifth Test of 1924–25 came from the bowling of Test debutant Clarrie Grimmett.

10 BOWLER/KEEPER COMBINATIONS WITH MOST STUMPINGS

Rank	Stumpings	Bowler	Keeper	Tests	Years
1.	28	Clarrie Grimmett	Bert Oldfield	37	1925–1936
2.	15	Shane Warne	Ian Healy	74	1992–1999
3=.	11	Arthur Mailey	Hanson Carter	6	1921
3=.	11	Richie Benaud	Wally Grout	34	1957–1964
5.	9	Shane Warne	Adam Gilchrist	32	1999–2002
6=.	7	Arthur Mailey	Bert Oldfield	15	1920–1926
6=.	7	Ashley Mallett	Rod Marsh	30	1971–1980
6=.	7	Tim May	Ian Healy	22	1988–1995
9=.	6	Jack Saunders	Jim Kelly	9	1902–1905
9=.	6	Colin McCool	Ron Saggers	5	1949–1950
9=.	6	Ian Johnson	Gil Langley	16	1951–1956
9=.	6	Stuart MacGill	Adam Gilchrist	13	2000–2003

10 TOP BOWLER/WICKETKEEPER COMBINATIONS

Rank	CB	St	Total	Bowler	Keeper	Tests	Years
1.	95	0	95	Dennis Lillee	Rod Marsh	69	1971–84
2.	58	0	58	Glenn McGrath	Ian Healy	52	1993–99
3.	55	0	55	Craig McDermott	Ian Healy	48	1988–96
4.	53	0	53	Glenn McGrath	Adam Gilchrist	42	1999–03
5.	34	15	49	Shane Warne	Ian Healy	74	1992–99
6.	46	0	46	Merv Hughes	Ian Healy	46	1988–94
7.	44	1	45	Alan Davidson	Wally Grout	28	1957–63
8.	39	0	39	Jason Gillespie	Adam Gilchrist	31	2000–03
9.	9	28	37	Clarrie Grimmett	Bert Oldfield	37	1925–36
10.	36	0	36	Max Walker	Rod Marsh	34	1972–77

At the conclusion of the 2003 Bangladesh series, the Brett Lee/Adam Gilchrist combination had 35 dismissals, equal 11th here with Jeff Thomson/Rod Marsh.

10 TOP BOWLER/FIELDSMAN COMBINATIONS
(Not including wicketkeepers)

Rank	Catches	Bowler	Fieldsman	Tests	Years
1.	51	Shane Warne	Mark Taylor	66	1992–1999
2.	39	Shane Warne	Mark Waugh	103	1992–2002
3.	34	Glenn McGrath	Mark Waugh	87	1993–2002
4=.	22	Dennis Lillee	Greg Chappell	64	1971–1984
4=.	22	Shane Warne	Ricky Ponting	51	1995–2003
4=.	22	Glenn McGrath	Ricky Ponting	60	1995–2003
7.	21	Richie Benaud	Neil Harvey	57	1952–1963
8.	19	Glenn McGrath	Shane Warne	76	1993–2002
9=.	17	Ashley Mallett	Ian Chappell	37	1968–1980
9=.	17	Craig McDermott	Mark Waugh	45	1991–1996

Also on 17 catches are two caught-and-bowled combinations: caught and bowled Richie Benaud (17 in 63 Tests) and caught and bowled Shane Warne (17 in 107 Tests).

❖ ❖ ❖

OPINION
THE TOP 10 WICKETKEEPERS *(Ignoring batting ability)*

1.	Jack Blackham
2.	Ian Healy
3.	Rod Marsh
4.	Wally Grout
5.	Hanson Carter
6.	Bert Oldfield
7.	Don Tallon
8.	Gil Langley
9.	Adam Gilchrist
10=.	Jim Kelly
10=.	Barry Jarman

Jack McCarthy Blackham, known in his day as the 'Prince of Wicketkeepers', was very clearly Australia's top keeper from 1877 to 1894, and during that time he revolutionised the art of wicketkeeping. He was tough, superb and consistent, to the point that he is recognised in England as well as Australia as the man who made the use of a longstop obsolete. In 1899, WG Grace wrote of Blackham:

> *Clean, quick as lightning, and quiet, he stood as close to the wickets as the laws of cricket permit and took the fastest bowling with consummate ease. To stand up to Spofforth's fastest bowling was in itself an achievement, but to keep wicket against the Demon without permitting a bye to pass was a phenomenal performance. The batsman who stirred out of his ground when Blackham was at the wicket knew he had to hit the ball off his innings was over. There was no element of chance in Blackham's stumping; it was a case of inevitability. His hands might get damaged, or the ball might bump on a rough wicket, but Blackham was upon it. [Lancashire's Richard] Pilling was his only rival behind the wicket, and Pilling was only in the cricket field for a few years, while Blackham stuck to his guns for twenty ...*

One of Blackham's more incredible achievements was his role in Fred Spofforth's first Test wicket, taken at the MCG in 1877. The Melbourne paper, *The Argus*, reported that Spofforth 'hurled the ball forwards with a velocity and recklessness as to the consequences enough to make all timid people tremble for the safety of the batsman'. Even so, Blackham stumped Alfred Shaw in the Demon's fourth over.

Few statistics better reflect the way cricket has changed over the decades than keeping stats. In reality, it is impossible to compare keepers of different eras. Adam Gilchrist today uses vastly superior equipment to keep to faster bowlers on less dangerous wickets than did Jack Blackham, and his dismissals-per-Test average is much better, but Blackham was so clearly the best keeper of his time and so important a figure in the evolution of the keeper's role that we feel he should be ranked No. 1.

In our view, there is little between the keepers we've put immediately behind Blackham, from No. 2 to No. 6. Ian Healy is ranked second mainly because of his immaculate work keeping to Shane Warne, and Rod Marsh is third due to his heroics handling Dennis Lillee and Jeff Thomson. There are some who wanted to denigrate Marsh's efforts keeping to the spinners, but the truth is that when he was required to stand over the stumps he invariably did a good job, sometimes a fantastic job. A stumping of the Indian Viswanath off Jim Higgs at the SCG in 1980–81 was quite magnificent.

The reputation of Don Tallon, on the other hand, has grown to the point that he is generally regarded as having been close to perfect. But was he? 'I have never seen a stumper to equal Tallon in speed,' wrote Jack Fingleton in his book of the 1948 Ashes tour, *Brightly Fades the Don*, '[but] he missed a number of chances ...' Tallon took 12 catches in four Tests during that series, a couple of them fabulous, but he did have his mediocre days, most notably when he spilt three straightforward chances in England's first innings of the third Test. From 1950, his form fell away, a fact documented by AG Moyes in his tour book of the 1950–51 Ashes series. 'He [Tallon] moved more slowly than in other seasons, lacked that amazing ability to cover wide areas, and he made too many mistakes,' he wrote.

Fingleton, a good Test opening bat before World War II and a superb cricket writer, thought Tallon superior to Bert Oldfield, but Arthur Mailey, another Test man turned journalist, wrote in the 1960s that Oldfield was the best Australian keeper he ever saw. However, in 1921 the selectors preferred the 43-year-old Hanson Carter to Oldfield, who was 17 years younger. From the time he took over from Jim Kelly in 1907–08 until he declined to go to England in 1912, 'Sammy' Carter never missed a Test. Warwick Armstrong described him as 'sureness itself'. Now long forgotten in most quarters, he might just have been one of the best keepers there ever was.

Considering all this, we have put Tallon as low as No. 7 on this list, fully aware that the sheer weight of expert opinion is on his side. Sir Donald Bradman was a strong Tallon supporter. As we noted in the introduction to this book, in *The Top 100 and the 1st XI* Philip Derriman asked a number of eminent cricket people to select their all-time Australia XIs. All went for Tallon as their wicketkeeper.

What to do with Gil Langley, who took over very efficiently from Tallon? If byes are an issue then Steve Rixon — an underrated keeper who was terrific up at the stumps — should be included. And what of Barry Jarman, who almost beat Wally Grout for the No. 1 job on the tour to South Africa in 1957–58? If Peter Burge, the third selector on that South Africa trip, had not voted for Grout then Jarman and not Grout would have been making his debut in the first Test, and many times in cricket history it has been proved that it is much harder for a new keeper to get in than get dropped. Another conundrum is where to rank Adam Gilchrist. There is no doubt that he is not as immaculate a gloveman as his immediate predecessor, Healy. However, the current Australian keeper's record behind the stumps is still impressive (see '10 Wicketkeepers with Most Dismissals Per Test'). The sheer weight of his keeping statistics entitle him to a place in a 'best ever' Australian top 10. ∎

10 WICKETKEEPERS WITH MOST DISMISSALS PER TEST

(Qualification 50 dismissals)

Rank	Keeper	Tests	Catches	Stumpings	Total	Dismissals per Test
1.	Adam Gilchrist	45	176	16	192	4.27
2.	Gil Langley	26	83	15	98	3.77
3.	Brian Taber	16	56	4	60	3.75
4.	Rod Marsh	96	343	12	355	3.70
5.	Wally Grout	51	163	24	187	3.67
6.	Ian Healy	119	366	29	395	3.32
7.	Barry Jarman	19	50	4	54	2.84
8.	Don Tallon	21	50	8	58	2.76
9.	Bert Oldfield	54	78	52	130	2.40
10.	Hanson Carter	28	44	21	65	2.32

The stats for Australia's two finest keepers from before World War I are as follows:

Keeper	Tests	Catches	Stumpings	Total	Dismissals per Test
Jack Blackham	32	36	24	60	1.88
Jim Kelly	36	43	20	63	1.75

As we have said, times have changed. The only Australian Test keepers besides Gilchrist to average more than four dismissals per Test are Phil Emery (five catches and a stumping in his only Test appearance, in 1994–95) and John Maclean (18 catches in four Tests in 1978–79).

The most dismissals made by Jack Blackham in one series was 10 (six catches and four stumpings), in the four Tests of 1881–82. Bert Oldfield's highest return in one series was 18 (10 catches and eight stumpings) in five Ashes Tests of 1924–25, while Don Tallon's best was 20 (16 and 4) in his first full Test series, against England in 1946–47.

---

10 AMUSING QUOTES FROM AUSTRALIAN TEST CRICKET HISTORY

10=. 'Leave the flies alone, Jardine. They're the only friends you've got in Australia.'
> *– To Douglas Jardine, during a break in play in the bodyline summer.*

10=. 'Don't give the bastard a drink. Let him die of thirst.'
> *– Another shot at Jardine during the same series. Strangely, the much vilified England captain apparently saw the humour in this barracker's crack, more so than the jibe about the flies.*

GOOD BYES

Rank	Keeper	Tests	Runs	Byes	Byes/Runs*
1.	Steve Rixon	13	7245	50	0.690
2.	Brian Taber	16	8848	84	0.949
3.	Wayne B Phillips	18	9230	90	0.975
4.	Ian Healy	119	56810	736	1.296
5.	Rod Marsh	96	47622	625	1.312
6.	Kevin Wright	10	4962	69	1.390
7.	Barry Jarman	19	10273	143	1.392
8.	Adam Gilchrist	45	22625	323	1.428
9.	Bert Oldfield	54	27205	424	1.559
10.	Hanson Carter	28	13255	213	1.607

'Runs' indicates runs scored by Australia's opponents in Tests in which the wicketkeeper kept for all or most of the match. Thus, in a Test such as the second Test against Pakistan in Faisalabad in 1980, when after tea on the final day, with the home team past 300 and only two wickets down in their first innings, Rod Marsh took off the gloves to bowl and field, he is still credited with all the byes conceded in that innings. 'Byes/Runs' indicates byes conceded per 100 runs scored.

Six other Australian keepers have appeared in 10 or more Tests. Their byes per 100 balls scores are Wally Grout (1.635), Gil Langley (1.647), Tim Zoehrer (1.669), Jim Kelly (1.757), Jack Blackham (3.288) and, surprisingly, in 16th place Don Tallon (3.336).

Byes conceded has often been regarded as a good measuring stick for a keeper, but we wonder. In England's first five innings of the 1928–29 Ashes series, Bert Oldfield allowed all of three byes while the tourists accumulated 1932 runs, a byes-per-100-runs score of 0.155. But on a wet wicket in England's second innings of the third Test, he conceded 15 while 332 runs were scored. Oldfield was most likely excellent in all six innings, but the scorecards don't instantly reveal this.

And consider the experience of Brian Taber, who in South Africa in 1970 conceded just eight byes in the four Tests, while the home team piled on 2704 runs. That's a byes-per-100-balls rate of 0.295. Yet, one of his teammates wrote 18 months later: 'It is fair to say that he [Taber] didn't have a particularly good series with the gloves.' Australia lost all four Tests in South Africa, and when the Australian selectors sat down to pick the Test team for the first match of the following series, against England, Taber was replaced by Rodney Marsh.

10 WICKETKEEPERS WITH MOST DISMISSALS IN A SERIES

Rank	Dis	Cght	St	Keeper	Versus	Tests	Series
1.	28	28	–	Rod Marsh	England	5	1982-83
2.	27	25	2	Ian Healy	England	6	1997
3=.	26	26	–	Rod Marsh	West Indies	6	1975-76
3=.	26	21	5	Ian Healy	England	6	1993
3=.	26	24	2	Adam Gilchrist	England	5	2001
6=.	25	23	2	Ian Healy	England	5	1994-95
6=.	25	23	2	Adam Gilchrist	England	5	2002-03
8.	24	24	–	Ian Healy	England	5	1990-91
9=.	23	20	3	Wally Grout	West Indies	5	1960-61
9=.	23	21	2	Rod Marsh	England	5	1972
9=.	23	23	–	Rod Marsh	England	6	1981
9=.	23	19	4	Ian Healy	West Indies	5	1992-93

The most dismissals by a keeper in a four-Test series is 18 (16 catches and two stumpings), by Brian Taber in South Africa in 1970. The most in a three-Test series is 19 (17 catches, two stumpings), by Ian Healy against Sri Lanka in Australia in 1995–96.

The most dismissals by an Australian keeper in one Test match is 10, by Adam Gilchrist against New Zealand at Hamilton in early 2000. Gilchrist took five catches in each innings. This was one short of the world record of England's Jack Russell, and one more than the nine taken by Australia's Gil Langley (eight catches, one stumping v England, Lord's, 1956), Rod Marsh (nine catches v England, Brisbane, 1982–83) and Ian Healy (nine catches v England, Brisbane, 1994–95). There have been 13 instances of an Australian keeper completing eight dismissals in a Test: four by Marsh, three by Healy, two by Wally Grout, and one each by Jim Kelly, Langley, Taber and Gilchrist.

The most dismissals in one Test innings is six, by Grout (v South Africa, Johannesburg, 1957–58), Marsh (v England, Brisbane, 1982–83) and Healy (v England, Birmingham, 1997). In all three cases, there were no stumpings involved. Marsh made five dismissals in a Test innings a world record 11 times, one more than Healy.

The most dismissals made by Jack Blackham in one series was 10 (six catches and four stumpings), in the four Tests of 1881–82. Bert Oldfield's highest return in one series was 18 (10 catches and eight stumpings) in five Ashes Tests of 1924–25, while Don Tallon's best was 20 (16 and 4) in his first full Test series, against England in 1946–47.

10 NON-WICKETKEEPERS WITH MOST CATCHES IN A SERIES

Rank	Catches	Fieldsman	Versus	Tests	Series
1.	15	Jack Gregory	England	5	1920–21
2.	14	Greg Chappell	England	6	1974–75
3=	13	Bob Simpson	South Africa	5	1957–58
3=	13	Bob Simpson	West Indies	5	1960–61
5=	12	Dav Whatmore	India	5	1979
5=	12	Allan Border	England	6	1981
7=	11	Bob Simpson	West Indies	5	1965
7=	11	Ian Chappell	England	6	1974–75
7=	11	Ian Redpath	England	6	1974–75
7=	11	Allan Border	England	6	1985
7=	11	Mark Taylor	England	6	1993
7=	11	Mark Waugh	West Indies	5	2000–01
7=	11	Ricky Ponting	South Africa	3	2001–02

In India in 1979, Dav Whatmore did not play in the second Test of what was a six-Test series.

The most catches by an Australian in a four-Test series is 10, by Mark Taylor in the West Indies in 1995.

The most catches taken by an Australian in one Test is seven, by Greg Chappell against England at the WACA in 1974–75. There are six instances of Australians taking six catches in a Test — Jack Gregory (v England, Sydney, 1920–21), Vic Richardson (v South Africa, Durban, 1935–36), Neil Harvey (v England, Sydney, 1962–63), Ian Chappell (v New Zealand, Adelaide, 1973–74), Dav Whatmore (v India, Kanpur, 1979) and Mark Waugh (v India, Chennai, 2001).

The most catches taken by an Australian in one Test innings is five, by Vic Richardson in Durban in 1935–36. This was the 41-year-old Richardson's final Test match.

---

10 NOTABLE QUOTES FROM AUSTRALIAN CRICKET HISTORY

1. 'In affectionate remembrance of English cricket, which died at The Oval on 29th August, 1882, deeply lamented by a large circle of sorrowful friends and acquaintances. R.I.P. NB: The body will be cremated and the ashes taken to Australia.'

— The famous 'death notice' published in The Sporting Times *after Australia beat the All England team at The Oval in 1882, an event that led to the birth of 'The Ashes'.*

THE TOP 10 CATCHES

Rank	Fieldsman	Batsman Out	Bowler	Versus	Venue	Series
1.	Clem Hill	'Dick' Lilley	Hugh Trumble	England	Manchester	1902
2.	Geoff Marsh	Ijaz Ahmed	Merv Hughes	Pakistan	Melbourne	1989–90
3.	Bob Simpson	David Allen	Richie Benaud	England	Manchester	1961
4.	Glenn McGrath	Michael Vaughan	Shane Warne	England	Adelaide	2002–03
5.	Richie Benaud	Colin Cowdrey	Ken Mackay	England	Lord's	1956
6.	Mark Waugh	Alec Stewart	Paul Reiffel	England	Leeds	1993
7.	Ross Edwards	Sadiq Mohammad	Bob Massie	Pakistan	Sydney	1972–73
8.	Don Tallon	Len Hutton	Ray Lindwall	England	The Oval	1948
9.	Bert Oldfield	Jack Hobbs	Jack Gregory	England	Sydney	1924–25
10.	John Dyson	Sylvester Clarke	Bruce Yardley	West Indies	Sydney	1981–82

Of all the opinion-based Top 10s in this book, this one was the toughest to finalise. Besides the 10 we settled on, just from the past 30 years there are fabulous alternatives, such as a catch Jeff Thomson took in front of the old Brewongle Stand to dismiss Deryck Murray at the SCG in 1975–76, a full-length dive by Allan Border off New Zealand's John Reid at the Gabba 10 years later, an astonishing reflex grab by Mark Waugh to get Inzamam-ul-Haq in Hobart in late 1999, a couple made to look easy by Ricky Ponting at silly point.

Those catches of Ponting's underline the point that the greatest catches are not always spectacular; sometimes courage and rapid-fire reflexes, rather than flamboyance, make for an extraordinary catch.

Yet having said all this, we have next to no doubt — considering all factors, most notably the game situation — that Clem Hill took the greatest Test-match catch of all time. As Dick Lilley faced Hugh Trumble at Old Trafford in 1902, England needed just 8 to win with two wickets in hand. Time was not a factor but still the batsman chanced his arm and aimed a cross-bat heave over square-leg — no easy task against so great a bowler. Yet Lilley seemed to middle the slog perfectly, and the crowd, which had been sadly and nervously watching England throw away a certain victory, roared the boundary. But then they saw Hill, who had been fielding in front of the pavilion on the midwicket fence, set off, hard as he could, to try to save the four. More than that, after sprinting for 25 metres he dived headlong, and in a blur seemed to grab the ball one-handed. And on the full! Everyone held their breath … Hill somersaulted twice … and came up, sheepish and triumphant, with the catch. Four runs later, Fred Tate was bowled by Jack Saunders, and Australia retained the Ashes.

Geoff Marsh's catch was another matchwinner, coming in the last session of the match just as it seemed Ijaz Ahmed would steer Pakistan to the safety of a draw. The batsman, well past his century, flayed Merv Hughes away through point, for Marsh to dive full-length and take an astounding catch with his left hand. Pakistan lost its last five wickets for 45 runs, and Australia won with less than 10 overs to spare. Bob Simpson's catch at first slip of David Allen came on the final afternoon of what proved to be the Ashes-deciding Test of '61. Richie Benaud was bowling over the wicket but sometimes aiming at the rough patches on and outside leg stump; Allen drove at one that gripped, edged it, and as the ball shot like a bullet just past keeper Wally Grout's gloves, Simpson, momentarily unsighted, lunged to his left and backwards to snare a chance few other slip fieldsman in the world would have even touched.

Glenn McGrath's diving catch in the deep in Adelaide won him many a slow-motion replay and the odd memorabilia contract, Benaud's self-preservation effort in the gully stopped what might have been the hardest hit ball caught in Test history. Mark Waugh thought his full-length dive to take Alec Stewart one-handed was his best Test catch, which is quite an accolade considering the quality of his collection. Ross Edwards' catch, running metres and then diving to snatch another drive that seemed destined for four, was described by Ian Chappell in his book *Passing Tests* as being 'miraculous', 'incredible', 'fantastic' and 'one of the greatest catches ever seen on a cricket field', which almost does it justice. It also set off a batting collapse that led to an unlikely Australian victory. The efforts of keepers Don Tallon and Bert Oldfield were similarly superb — both had to show rare anticipation and move many metres to the legside to catch genuine leg glances from great batsmen.

John Dyson's is the only one of this Top 10 that was not part of an Australian victory. Yet it was such a phenomenal outfield catch, moving backwards and then leaping high and backwards some more, like a full forward snaring a mark, that it has to be here. Because the ball hung in the air for so long, no one at the ground missed seeing this catch, yet it was so unlikely, so spectacular an out, that for a moment no one could comprehend exactly what they'd seen. Dyson himself was as astonished as anyone. Clem Hill would have been proud of him. ■

CHAPTER FOUR

THE ALLROUNDERS

The reason we have ranked Adam Gilchrist so highly in the Top 10 Greatest All-Time Australian cricketers is because of the immense allround value he brings to the Australian side. We believe his status as an allrounder is indisputable, but some people like to argue that cricketers who can bat and bowl well are the only players who should be considered as allrounders.

The wicketkeeping art is as distinct from both batting and bowling as batting is from bowling and bowling from batting. In our view, there is no doubt that a keeper/batsman such as Gilchrist brings an 'allround' value to a side that is at least very similar to the worth of a batting/bowling allrounder such as Keith Miller. Going even further, there is no doubt that great fieldsmen have an allround value that should not be devalued. The examples of the Australian XI in 1999, which undoubtedly took time to adjust to being without Mark Taylor at first slip, and in 2002, when the absence of Mark Waugh in the slip cordon, and at first slip to Shane Warne, became a factor, are proof of this.

Consequently, wicketkeepers are included in many of the Top 10s in this chapter. Going further, in the first Top 10 — 10 Australians with Most Allrounder 'Points' — we have given a value to outfielding as well as wicketkeeping. The objective of this Top 10 is to produce a list for allrounders akin to a 'Most Runs' or 'Most Wickets' table; it should be looked at in this light. The players who head this Top 10 are not necessarily the greatest allrounders Australia has ever had, but they are excellent allround cricketers who have served their country well over a long period.

After this first Top 10, we do produce some tables that might offer some indicators as to who have been Australia's greatest ever allrounders. The results may not be as you expect …

❖   ❖   ❖

10 AUSTRALIANS WITH MOST ALLROUNDER 'POINTS'

(Qualifications: 1000 runs and 50 wickets or 1000 runs and 50 wicketkeeping dismissals)
Scoring method: One point for a run; 20 points for a wicket; 10 points for an outfield catch;
20 points for a wicketkeeping catch or a stumping

Rank	Player	Batting	Bowling	Fielding	Total
1.	Steve Waugh	10521	1820	1090	13431
2.	Shane Warne	2238	9820	860	12918
3.	Ian Healy	4356	–	7900	12256
4.	Mark Waugh	8029	1180	1810	11019
5.	Rod Marsh	3633	–	7100	10733
6.	Richie Benaud	2201	4960	650	7811
7.	Bob Simpson	4869	1420	1100	7389
8.	Adam Gilchrist	2940	–	3840	6780
9.	Keith Miller	2958	3400	380	6738
10.	Ray Lindwall	1502	4560	260	6322

This Top 10 reflects not so much allround excellence as durability and longevity. The points system was devised using the basic (and, we concede, arguable) premise that taking 500 Test wickets is equivalent to scoring 10,000 Tests runs or making 400 wicketkeeping dismissals.

The 'allrounder' qualification clause of 1000 runs/50 wickets or 50 keeping dismissals was necessary to preclude predominantly great run-scorers or wicket-takers from making this table. For example, Allan Border, with 11,174 runs, 39 wickets and 156 catches, would have topped this table with 13,514 points, but a cricketer who takes just 39 wickets in 156 Tests can hardly be considered an allrounder. Can he? Even a non-bowler/non-wicketkeeper such as David Boon scores 8412 points, through his 7422 runs and 99 catches.

Two other high point scorers who didn't meet the qualifications for this Top 10 were Greg Chappell (7110 runs, 47 wickets, 122 catches, 9270 points) and Dennis Lillee (905 runs, 355 wickets, 23 catches, 8235 points). It is intriguing to apply part of the method we have used here to compare Chappell, Lillee and Rod Marsh, whose careers all began in the same Ashes series of 1970–71 and finished on the same day, 6 January 1984. Chappell, the finest Australian batsman of his time, scores 7110 batting points; Lillee, the master fast bowler, scores 7100 bowling points; Marsh, the great wicketkeeper, scores 7100 fielding points.

10 LEADING CAREER ALLROUNDERS

(Excluding wicketkeepers. Qualification: 1000 runs and 50 wickets; ranking based on career batting average divided by career bowling average, the higher the score the better)

Rank	Player	Tests	Runs	Avge	Wkts	Avge	Score
1.	Keith Miller	55	2958	36.98	170	22.98	1.609
2.	Steve Waugh	162	10521	51.07	91	36.48	1.399
3.	Monty Noble	42	1997	30.26	121	25.00	1.210
4.	Alan Davidson	44	1328	24.59	186	20.53	1.198
5.	Jack Gregory	24	1146	36.97	85	31.15	1.187
6.	Charles Kelleway	26	1422	37.42	52	32.37	1.156
7.	Warwick Armstrong	50	2863	38.69	87	33.60	1.151
8.	Bob Simpson	62	4869	46.82	71	42.27	1.108
9.	Mark Waugh	128	8029	41.82	59	41.17	1.016
10.	Ken Mackay	37	1507	33.49	50	34.42	0.973

Keepers have to be barred here, because there is no equivalent stat to a batting or bowling average with which we can measure them. In all, 17 Australians meet the 1000 runs/50 wickets qualification. The other seven, in order 11 to 17, are Ray Lindwall, Richie Benaud, George Giffen, Greg Matthews, Shane Warne, Ian Johnson and Merv Hughes. Of the 17, five also took 50 catches during their Test career: Mark Waugh (181 catches), Simpson (110), Steve Waugh (109), Warne (86) and Benaud (65).

Doug Walters (5357 runs at 48.26 and 49 wickets at 29.08) misses qualifying for this table by just one wicket. Divide his Test career batting average by his bowling average and the result is 1.660, which — if he was eligible — would put him top of the list.

Three other players who aren't eligible, but who would finish high in this Top 10 if the qualifications were broadened, are Charlie Macartney, Bob Cowper and Greg Chappell. Macartney hit 2131 runs in his Test career at 41.78 and took 45 wickets at 27.56, which gives him a score of 1.516. Cowper compiled 2061 runs at 46.84, and took 36 wickets at 31.63, for a score of 1.465. Chappell, with 7110 runs at 53.86 and 47 wickets at 40.70, scores 1.323. Even if the qualifications are broadened to as little as 500 runs and 20 wickets, of Australian cricketers only the first nine players in this Top 10 plus Walters, Macartney, Cowper, Chappell, Allan Border (1.293), Stan McCabe (1.125) and Michael Bevan (1.199) record positive results. Of these 16, only Davidson, Miller and Bevan have a career bowling average of less than 25.

OPINION

TOP 10 ALLROUND MATCH PERFORMANCES

(Performance must include at least two of the following: 70 runs for the Test, eight wickets for the match, five fielding dismissals)

Rank	Player	Batting	Bowling	Fielding	Versus	Venue	Series
1.	Richie Benaud	100	4-70 & 5-84	1c	South Africa	Johannesburg	1957–58
2.	Alan Davidson	44 & 80	5-135 & 6-87	1c	West Indies	Brisbane	1960–61
3.	Allan Border	75 & 16*	7-46 & 4-50	–	West Indies	Sydney	1988–89
4.	Jack Gregory	100	7-69 & 1-32	1c	England	Melbourne	1920–21
5.	Michael Bevan	85*	4-31 & 6-82	1c	West Indies	Adelaide	1996–97
6.	Adam Gilchrist	75 & 0*	–	10c	New Zealand	Hamilton	2000
7.	Greg Matthews	44 & 27*	5-103 & 5-146	1c	India	Madras	1986
8.	George Giffen	161 & 41	4-75 & 4-164	2c	England	Sydney	1894–95
9.	Rod Marsh	28 & 110*	–	5c	England	Melbourne	1976–77
10.	Keith Miller	79	7-60 & 2-17	–	England	Brisbane	1946–47

Of these 10 instances, Richie Benaud's is the only example where, in terms of runs scored and wickets taken, the player was the leading Australian batsman *and* bowler in the Test concerned. Australia went into the fourth Test in Jo'burg in February 1958 leading the series 1–0; Benaud, batting four, scored his century as Australia totalled 401 in their first innings, and then was the leading wicket-taker in both innings as South Africa struggled to 203 and 198. We rank this fractionally ahead of Alan Davidson's performance in the first Tied Test. But only just: we happily concede that Davidson's second innings 80 was superior to many a century, as he became the first man to score 100 runs and take 10 wickets in one Test.

Allan Border had the added responsibility of the captaincy when he dominated the Windies at the SCG in 1988–89. Jack Gregory scored his century from No. 9 in the batting order, while Michael Bevan was more a specialist batsman who had one special day in Test cricket as a left-arm wrist spinner. Adam Gilchrist's effort in scoring 75 while breaking the Australian record for most dismissals in a Test is a rare example of an Australian keeper making multiple dismissals in a Test in which he also scores substantial runs.

Greg Matthews and George Giffen produced their marathon efforts in famous Tests: Matthews in the Tied Test in Madras (in which he took the final wicket off the fifth ball of the last possible over), Giffen in the SCG Test that England won despite being forced to follow on. Rod Marsh chose as his stage the Centenary Test, in the process breaking Wally Grout's then Australian record for most wicketkeeping dismissals and then becoming the first Aussie keeper to score a Test century against England.

Surprisingly, Keith Miller rarely produced outstanding batting and bowling performances in the same Test match. Usually, one brilliant performance did the trick. The only time Miller scored a century and took five wickets in an innings in a Test occurred at Kingston in 1955, when he scored 109 and took 6–107 and 2–58. However, the quality of that effort must be marked down slightly because his hundred was just one of five made by Australians in their only innings of 8–758 (declared). One of the blokes who outscored him was Benaud, who this time scored 121 from No. 8, reaching his century in just 78 minutes. ■

10 HIGHEST INNINGS BY A BOWLING ALLROUNDER
(Qualification: The batsman must also have bowled 15 per cent of Australia's overs in the Test match concerned)

Rank	Score	Batsman	Versus	Venue	Series
1.	165	Bob Cowper	India	Sydney	1967–68
2.	161	George Giffen	England	Sydney	1894–95
3=	153	Bob Simpson	Pakistan	Karachi	1964
3=	153	Bob Simpson	South Africa	Cape Town	1966–67
5.	151	Charlie Macartney	England	Leeds	1926
6.	147	Keith Miller	West Indies	Kingston	1955
7.	137	Keith Miller	West Indies	Bridgetown	1955
8=	133	Monty Noble	England	Sydney	1903–04
8=	133*	Charlie Macartney	England	Lord's	1926
10.	130	Greg Matthews	New Zealand	Wellington	1986

Not only did Simpson score 153 at Karachi in 1964, he also captained Australia, scored 115 in the second innings and bowled 50 overs. Only two of the 17 Australian allrounders to score 1000 career runs and take 50 career wickets have scored a Test double century. Simpson did so three times — 311 at Manchester in 1964, 225 at Adelaide in 1965–66 and 201 at Bridgetown in 1965 — but he hardly bowled in any of these matches. Steve Waugh scored 200 at Kingston in 1999, a Test in which he took 2–23 in the match, from 15 overs.

In the fifth Test of that Ashes series in which Simpson made his 225, Bob Cowper scored 307, still the highest score made in a Test in Australia, but though he tops this table here, and although seven Australians bowled in the match, Cowper was not one of those seven. Perhaps his captain, Simpson, was shrewdly keeping him fresh for batting? Despite that 307, Cowper has strangely become something of a forgotten cricketer, even though he scored more than 2000 Test runs and averaged little more than

30 with the ball. His right-hand off-breaks might not have been quite Test class, but as a left-handed batsman he certainly was. In 27 Tests, Cowper hit five hundreds, including two batting three against Hall, Griffith and Sobers in the Caribbean in 1965.

Monty Noble scored the 133 that puts him eighth in this Top 10 in his first Test as Australia captain. Nine seasons earlier, with regular captain Jack Blackham sidelined with a badly cut thumb, George Giffen skippered Australia on the field late in England's first innings and throughout their second (in between he scored the 161 that puts him second here). Giffen clearly relished the responsibilities of leadership, bowling 75 of Australia's 181.4 overs in the second innings and taking 4–164.

10 BEST INNINGS BOWLING FIGURES BY A TOP-ORDER BATSMAN

(Qualification: Bowler must have batted in the top six in at least one innings of the Test concerned)

Rank	Score	Bowler	Versus	Venue	Series
1.	7–17	Monty Noble	England	Melbourne	1901–02
2.	7–46	Allan Border	West Indies	Sydney	1988–89
3.	7–60	Keith Miller	England	Brisbane	1946–47
4.	7–100	Monty Noble	England	Sydney	1903–04
5.	7–117	George Giffen	England	Sydney	1884–85
6.	7–128	George Giffen	England	The Oval	1893
7.	6–40	Tom Horan	England	Sydney	1884–85
8.	6–52	Monty Noble	England	Sheffield	1902
9.	6–58	Jack Gregory	England	Nottingham	1921
10.	6–60	Monty Noble	England	Melbourne	1901–02

Monty Noble's two bowling figures from Melbourne in 1901–02 above were achieved in the same Test, giving him 13–77 for the Test. In the Test, played on a wet wicket, Noble batted at No. 9 in Australia's second innings, having batted at No. 5 on the first day (Victor Trumper batted at No. 8 in that second innings, Reg Duff, usually an opener, at No. 10 and Warwick Armstrong at 11). Noble also took 6–98 in the fifth Test of 1901–02, in a Test in which he batted at five in both innings. At Sheffield in 1902, he took 5–51 in the first innings, giving him 11–103 for the match.

Besides the instances above, George Giffen twice more took six wickets in an innings in a Test in which he batted in the top six.

10 HIGHEST INNINGS BY A WICKETKEEPER

Rank	Score	Batsman	Versus	Venue	Series
1.	204*	Adam Gilchrist	South Africa	Johannesburg	2002
2.	161*	Ian Healy	West Indies	Brisbane	1996–97
3.	152	Adam Gilchrist	England	Birmingham	2001
4.	149*	Adam Gilchrist	Pakistan	Hobart	1999–00
5.	138*	Adam Gilchrist	South Africa	Cape Town	2001–02
6.	134	Ian Healy	England	Brisbane	1998–99
7.	133	Adam Gilchrist	England	Sydney	2002–03
8.	132	Rod Marsh	New Zealand	Adelaide	1973–74
9.	122	Adam Gilchrist	India	Mumbai	2001
10.	120	Wayne B Phillips	West Indies	Bridgetown	1984

The four players featured in this top 10 are the only Australian wicketkeepers to score Test centuries. Gilchrist has scored seven Test hundreds, Healy four, Marsh three and Phillips one. The highest score by an Australian wicketkeeper against Sri Lanka is 71, by Healy in Moratuwa in 1992. Healy was the keeper in Australia's only Test against Zimbabwe, scoring 5. Gilchrist kept in the two Tests against Bangladesh in 2003, scoring 43 in his only innings.

The highest match aggregate by an Aussie keeper-batsman is 206 (161 not out and 45 not out), by Ian Healy against the West Indies in Brisbane in 1996–97.

10 LEADING CAREER BATTING AVERAGES BY A WICKETKEEPER *(Qualification: 400 Test runs)*

Rank	Keeper	Tests	Inns	NO	Runs	HS	100s	50s	Avge	DPT	Score
1.	Adam Gilchrist	45	62	12	2940	204*	8	16	58.80	4.26	250.49
2.	Wayne B Phillips	18	34	1	961	120	1	5	29.12	2.39	69.60
3.	Ian Healy	119	182	23	4356	161*	4	22	27.40	3.32	90.97
4.	Rod Marsh	96	150	13	3633	132	4	15	26.52	3.70	98.12
5.	Hanson Carter	28	47	9	873	72	–	4	22.97	2.32	53.29
6.	Bert Oldfield	54	80	17	1427	65*	–	4	22.65	2.40	54.36
7.	Jim Kelly	36	56	17	664	46*	–	–	17.03	1.75	29.80
8.	Jack Blackham	34	60	11	772	74	–	4	15.75	1.88	29.61
9.	Wally Grout	51	67	8	890	74	–	3	15.08	3.67	55.34
10.	Barry Jarman	19	30	3	400	78	–	2	14.81	2.84	42.06

This Top 10 demonstrates just how far ahead Adam Gilchrist the batsman is from all the other Australian keeper/batsmen. And to make this table something of a companion to the '10 Leading Career Allrounders' on page 107, we have added a column in which a score is derived by multiplying the keeper's career batting average by his dismissals-per-Test (DPT) ratio. Gilchrist, who possesses the best DPT of any Australian Test keeper with more than 20 dismissals, shoots even further ahead.

When, at the start of the 1970–71 Ashes series, Rod Marsh was preferred to Brian Taber as Australia's wicketkeeper, much was made of the fact that Marsh was a superior batsman to Taber. In the previous season, while Taber was scoring 187 runs in 15 Test innings (three not outs, average 15.58), Marsh was averaging more than 35 with the bat in the Sheffield Shield. The new man was seen as representing something of a new philosophy, one opposed to the old maxim that you always picked the best gloveman regardless of his ability with the bat. Within two seasons, Marsh was recognised as the best keeper in the country anyway; still the highest point his Test batting average would ever reach was 38.34, after his 22nd Test (v New Zealand in Adelaide, when he made 132, his highest Test score), which is a long way behind what Gilchrist has achieved. Marsh's batting average after his 45th Test (the number Gilchrist has played after the 2003 winter matches against Bangladesh) was 33.14.

No Australian Test wicketkeeper bar Gilchrist has a career Test batting average of more than 30. In an encounter with England in 1881–82, Billy Murdoch donned the gloves for most of the game and also scored 10 and 49. This was the only Test in which Murdoch kept. Ben Barnett kept throughout the 1938 Ashes series, his only four Tests, and averaged 27.86. The highest career averages otherwise are those of Wayne Phillips, Ian Healy and Marsh.

The statistics in this table do not include runs scored in Tests in which the keepers did not keep at any stage. Phillips scored 524 runs, including one century (on debut), in nine Tests in which he was selected as a batsman. Blackham scored 28 runs in the one Test in which he played but never wore the gloves.

CHAPTER FIVE

THE CAPTAINS

In his book *Benaud on Reflection*, Richie Benaud wrote that the 'very best' captain he ever played under was Keith Miller. In his autobiography, *Anything But ... An Autobiography*, Benaud revealed that the best advice he ever received about bowling came from Bill O'Reilly. Clearly, Miller and O'Reilly both possessed outstanding cricket brains, yet neither captained Australia. Nor did a number of other famous cricketers, who might have done outstanding jobs had they been given the chance — great names such as Victor Trumper, Stan McCabe, Arthur Morris, Rod Marsh, Ian Healy and Shane Warne.

Of the men who did captain Australia, some came to the job at the 'right' time — when the Australian team was on the rise or already in outstanding form. Mark Taylor (1994–1999) and Steve Waugh (1999–2003) were both in this position, though no one could complain about the job they did leading the Australian team to even higher levels. Others took over when the team was in the initial stages of a sharp decline, and were perhaps unfairly blamed for a run of outs. Jack Ryder in 1928–29 might be the best example of this, being forced to take on a powerful England batting line-up with what was perhaps Australia's weakest ever bowling 'attack'. Some took over just as great players were emerging — how shrewd an operator would Bill Woodfull have been in 1930 if 21-year-old Don Bradman was not suddenly scoring double century after double century? Others won the job at exactly the wrong time, and thus hardly had the chance to show whether they were good captains or not. Kim Hughes in 1984 had to cope with a team shattered by the retirements of

Dennis Lillee, Greg Chappell and Rod Marsh. Two decades earlier, Bob Simpson had to make do without Alan Davidson, Neil Harvey and Richie Benaud. Under these circumstances, Simpson's effort in leading Australian teams that retained the Ashes in 1964 and 1965–66 was not too bad at all.

The long captaincy career of Allan Border offers the best evidence that most captains are only as good as their players. Early on, Border was hardly impressive as a leader, and probably only kept the job in 1986 because there was no one to replace him. But as outstanding cricketers such as David Boon, Steve Waugh, Dean Jones, Ian Healy, Mark Taylor, Craig McDermott, Merv Hughes and Mark Waugh flourished under his tutelage, and 'old hands' such as Terry Alderman and Geoff Lawson came back to make significant contributions, Border's leadership fortunes turned just about full circle. When Shane Warne arrived in 1993, the last piece in the jigsaw, Border's third Ashes tour as captain became a triumphant finale.

Similarly, Don Bradman had reasonable success as Test captain before World War II, when — O'Reilly apart — the Australian bowling was mediocre, but was unbeatable afterwards, when England were struggling and Australia's batting order included Morris, Barnes, Hassett, Harvey, Miller, Lindwall, Tallon and Johnston. And, of course, The Don always captained sides that included himself; a colossal advantage. No wonder he usually won.

The only people who can really measure whether skippers truly make a difference are the cricketers who play under them. Consequently, we have not attempted to compile a 'Top 10 Australian Captains'. However, we will recognise three occasions where skippers came to power at what seemed, at least on the day they were first appointed, to be a 'wrong' time for them. However, in each instance — and the captains can take much credit for this — Australia quickly turned the corner and began a golden run ...

HARRY TROTT

When Harry Trott reluctantly took up the captaincy for the 1896 Ashes tour, he became leader of a side that included nine men making their first tour of England. Champions such as Charlie Turner and Jack Blackham had retired, George Giffen was well past his best, but still Trott inspired his men, and but for a wet pitch and a lost toss in the third and deciding Test they might have brought home the Ashes. By 1897–98, the Australians were superb — winning the rubber by four Tests to one, at that time easily Australia's most decisive series victory. Joe Darling then took over, and led Australia to three straight series wins over England, before Monty Noble captained Australia to success in 1903–04. Clem Hill, who played through all these series, later commented: 'As a captain Harry Trott was in a class by himself, the best I ever played under.'

IAN CRAIG AND RICHIE BENAUD

When the Australian selectors sat down to pick the team for the 1957–58 tour of South Africa, they not only had to choose a new captain, they also needed to find a way to replace Keith Miller and Gil Langley, who had retired, and Ron Archer, who was injured. Australia had been humbled in the third and fourth Tests in England in 1956, enough to lose the series, and the selectors opted for not so much a generational change as a revolution — making 22-year-old Ian Craig captain and dropping 36-year-old Ray Lindwall. It seemed dire times were ahead, but instead Craig's team showed terrific spirit to win 3–0 in South Africa, with Benaud and Alan Davidson in dazzling form. Then, after Craig unluckily had to withdraw due to a bout of hepatitis, Benaud took over and Australia thrashed England 4–0 at home in 1958–59, as the momentum first generated in South Africa was more than maintained.

IAN CHAPPELL

By the end of the 1970–71 Ashes series, there didn't seem to be too much to be optimistic about when it came to the Australian Test team. Nine players had made their debuts during that series, but only two — Greg Chappell and Dennis Lillee — looked genuine Test class. The captain, Bill Lawry, had been sacked (replaced by Ian Chappell for the final Test, which England won to take the series 2–0), the team's strike bowler, Graham McKenzie, was also discarded, and some batting stalwarts, most notably Ian Redpath and Doug Walters, had struggled for much of the series. Chappell was lucky in that his brother, Lillee, and also Rod Marsh quickly showed themselves to be champions, but still his aggressive nature, tactical nous and rare motivational powers were key factors as Australia quickly fought back to earn a 2–2 draw in the 1972 Ashes series in England and then went on to dominate international cricket from 1973 to 1976.

---

10 NOTABLE QUOTES FROM AUSTRALIAN CRICKET HISTORY

2. 'Mr Warner, there are two teams out there on that field, and one is playing cricket and the other is not. That is all I have to say. Good afternoon.'

– Bill Woodfull to the manager of the English touring team, Pelham Warner, during the third Test of the bodyline series, 1932–33. Warner had come to the Australian dressing room to make sure Woodfull was all right, after the Australian captain had been struck by a Harold Larwood riser during the home team's first innings.

---

10 AUSTRALIANS WITH MOST TESTS AS CAPTAIN

Rank	Player	Tests	Won	Tied	Lost	Drawn	Toss	Win %
1.	Allan Border	93	32	1	22	38	47	34.41
2.	Steve Waugh	51	38	–	8	5	30	74.51
3.	Mark Taylor	50	26	–	13	11	26	52.00
4.	Greg Chappell	48	21	–	13	14	29	43.75
5.	Bob Simpson	39	12	–	12	15	19	30.77
6.	Ian Chappell	30	15	–	5	10	17	50.00
7=.	Richie Benaud	28	12	1	4	11	11	42.86
7=.	Kim Hughes	28	4	–	13	11	13	14.29
9=.	Bill Lawry	25	9	–	8	8	8	36.00
9=.	Bill Woodfull	25	14	–	7	4	12	56.00

'Toss' indicates the number of times the captain won the toss. Just outside this top 10 are three of Australia's most notable leaders: Don Bradman (24 Tests as captain, 15 victories), Lindsay Hassett (24, 14) and Joe Darling (21, 7).

The captaincy reigns of Allan Border, Mark Taylor, Ian Chappell and Bill Woodfull were uninterrupted.

10 MOST SUCCESSFUL CAPTAINS *(Qualification: 10 Tests as captain)*

Rank	Player	Tests	Won	Lost	Drawn	Toss	Win %
1.	Warwick Armstrong	10	8	–	2	4	80.00
2.	Steve Waugh	51	38	8	5	30	74.51
3.	Don Bradman	24	15	3	6	10	62.50
4.	Lindsay Hassett	24	14	4	6	18	58.33
5.	Bill Woodfull	25	14	7	4	12	56.00
6.	Monty Noble	15	8	5	2	11	53.33
7.	Mark Taylor	50	26	13	11	26	52.00
8=.	Ian Chappell	30	15	5	10	17	50.00
8=.	Clem Hill	10	5	5	0	5	50.00
10.	Herbert Collins	11	5	2	4	7	45.45

Outside this top 10 are some notable figures: Greg Chappell is No. 11 and Richie Benaud is 12th. Benaud lost only four times as captain, but was involved in 11 draws and, of course, that fabulous tie against Frank Worrell's West Indians at the Gabba in 1960–61.

Allan Border (32 wins from 93 starts as captain) is 15th, behind two much-maligned skippers in Ian Johnson (17 Tests for seven wins) and Bill Lawry (25 Tests, nine wins). Dividing Border's captaincy career into two parts offers an interesting reflection on his leadership capabilities. In his first 37 Tests in charge, from the third Test against the West Indies in 1984–85 to the third Windies Test of 1988–89, Border led Australia in six victories (plus one tie, 17 draws and 13 losses). However, from there to the end of Australia's tour of South Africa in 1994, he captained Australia in a further 56 Tests, for 26 wins (plus 21 draws and nine losses), a success rate of 46.43 per cent.

Four Australian cricket captains — Hugh Massie, Hugh Trumble, Bill Brown and Neil Harvey — have a 100-per-cent winning record. Trumble (two Tests for two wins) is the only one of this quartet to lead Australia more than once. Vic Richardson led Australia only in the 1935–36 series in South Africa, after Woodfull had retired and while Bradman was recovering from serious illness, for four wins out of five, despite winning just one toss. Other Australian skippers with success rates greater than 60 per cent are Dave Gregory, who was in charge as Australia won two of its first three Test matches, and Harry Trott, who was captain during the 1896 and 1897–98 Ashes series, winning five Tests out of eight.

Across all Test teams, of those with at least 20 Tests as captain, Steve Waugh, Don Bradman and Lindsay Hassett rank one, two and three in the table of most success-prone leaders. England's Mike Brearley (18 wins from 31 Tests as captain) ranks fourth, with Bill Woodfull fifth, Viv Richards sixth, then Sean Pollock, Mark Taylor, Hansie Cronje and Ian Chappell.

Waugh's 38 victories is the most achieved by any Test leader, two better than Clive Lloyd's 36 wins from 74 starts as West Indies captain between 1974 and 1985.

10 HIGHEST INNINGS BY A CAPTAIN

Rank	Score	Captain	Versus	Venue	Series
1.	334*	Mark Taylor	Pakistan	Peshawar	1998
2.	311	Bob Simpson	England	Manchester	1964
3.	270	Don Bradman	England	Melbourne	1936–37
4.	235	Greg Chappell	Pakistan	Faisalabad	1980
5.	234	Don Bradman	England	Sydney	1946–47
6.	225	Bob Simpson	England	Adelaide	1965–66
7.	212	Don Bradman	England	Adelaide	1936–37
8.	211	Billy Murdoch	England	The Oval	1884
9=.	205	Bill Lawry	West Indies	Melbourne	1968–69
9=.	205	Allan Border	New Zealand	Adelaide	1987–88

There have been six other instances of captains making double centuries: Greg Chappell 204 v India in Sydney, 1980–81, and 201 v Pakistan in Brisbane, 1981–82, Herbert Collins 203 v South Africa in Johannesburg 1921, Don Bradman 201 v India in Adelaide 1947–48, Bob Simpson 201 v West Indies in Bridgetown 1965 and Allan Border 200 not out v England 1993.

Don Bradman made eight scores of 150 or better as Australian captain. Next best are Bob Simpson and Steve Waugh (highest: 199 v West Indies Bridgetown 1999) with six, then Greg Chappell and Allan Border with five. Waugh, with 15, has the most 100s as captain.

10 BEST INNINGS BOWLING FIGURES BY A CAPTAIN

Rank	Figures	Captain	Versus	Venue	Series
1.	7–44	Ian Johnson	West Indies	Georgetown	1955
2.	7–46	Allan Border	West Indies	Sydney	1988–89
3.	7–100	Monty Noble	England	Sydney	1903–04
4.	6–70	Richie Benaud	England	Manchester	1961
5.	6–115	Richie Benaud	England	Brisbane	1962–63
6.	6–155	George Giffen	England	Melbourne	1894–95
7.	5–26	George Giffen	England	Sydney	1894–95
8.	5–43	Richie Benaud	India	Madras	1959–60
9.	5–62	Hugh Trumble	England	Melbourne	1901–02
10=.	5–68	Allan Border	West Indies	Georgetown	1991
10=.	5–68	Richie Benaud	South Africa	Brisbane	1963–64

Richie Benaud took five wickets in a Test innings nine times as captain, easily an Australian record. Next best, with three, is George Giffen. The only other captain to do so more than once is Allan Border, as above. Border, who took 4–50 in the second innings in Sydney in 1988–89, is also the only Australian leader to take 10 or more wickets in a Test in which he was captain.

Ian Johnson's standing at the top of this table is at first glance surprising, if only for the fact that in 17 Tests as captain he took a total of 39 wickets. Take out Georgetown in 1955 and he averaged a fraction worse than two wickets per Test, so to collect seven in one innings was unexpected. Still, this rare burst of wicket-taking was nothing compared with the strike rate of the man who finishes second here. In 93 Tests as captain, Allan Border took 24 wickets. Eleven of them came in one remarkable Test against the West Indies in Sydney, another five were captured at Georgetown in 1991, and the remainder were taken over eight innings during his other 91 matches in charge. In 45 of his Tests as captain, Border didn't bowl a solitary delivery.

STEVE WAUGH'S 10 THINGS A CAPTAIN SHOULD LOOK FOR IN HIS PLAYERS

1. The ability to be yourself, not someone else. Be natural and use your talent. (Have heroes but don't automatically copy everything they do.)

2. A strong desire to be involved, especially in tough conditions. Glenn McGrath offers an outstanding example of a bowler with this habit. The opposition can sense when a player is reluctant to have a go.

3. Good body language, which is extremely important. Positive words and gestures are always a good thing at practice and on the field.

4. A keenness to share your knowledge with teammates. The best batsmen and bowlers work in partnerships — McGrath and Shane Warne are excellent examples of two great bowlers who do this; Matthew Hayden and Justin Langer are similarly excellent as a batting pair. The best teams work to a plan. There is nothing wrong with suggesting thoughts and ideas to your captain.

5. Alertness in the field. Don't switch off, and always watch the captain. Fielding is the truest indicator of whether or not you are a team player, because you don't get rewarded statistically in the way you do when batting or bowling.

6. Bowlers who work hard on their batting technique, starting with the basics, such as defence, and then on one or two shots. Batsmen should work on developing a bowling style that may help the team achieve a better balance through these extra skills.

7. Good fitness, stamina, strength and diet, which are all important in preparing for the games ahead.

8. Enjoyment. It is possible to intimidate the opposition simply by enjoying your cricket. It's always a sport; never look on it as a job, as something you have to do.

9. A realisation that money or other 'off-field' rewards can't be the reason you play.

10. A good attitude. Be prepared to bat on tough wickets, against the best bowlers, to bowl into the wind, to contribute when you're suffering from a 'niggling' injury or feeling slightly off-colour. A maxim we have in the Australian team is this: Attitudes are contagious; is yours worth catching?

THE TOP 10 BIZARRE DECISIONS MADE BY AUSTRALIAN SELECTORS

Rank	Selectors' Decision	Reason for Controversy
1.	Ken Burn picked as a keeper for 1890 Ashes tour	Burn had never kept wicket in his life
2.	Peter Taylor picked for fifth Ashes Test, 1986–87	'Peter Who', aged 30, had played just six first-class matches
3.	Keith Miller left out of 1949–50 tour to South Africa	Miller was the allround star of Australian cricket
4.	Bill Lawry sacked as Australian captain, 1971	Lawry, still an excellent bat, was also dropped from the team
5.	Jack Ryder sacked as Australian captain, 1930	Ryder was ambushed by his fellow selectors
6.	Don Bradman 12th man, second Test, 1928–29	Bradman, 20, was the best young cricketer in the country
7.	Doug Walters dropped from 1981 Ashes tour	Walters had topped the Test averages for the previous season
8.	Allan Border 12th man, sixth Test, SCG, 1978–79	Border had made 60* & 45* two Tests earlier at the SCG
9.	Albert Trott omitted from 1896 tour of England	Trott had starred in the most recent Ashes series in Australia
10.	Jack Blackham preferred as Australian keeper, 1877	Fred Spofforth wanted Billy Murdoch to keep wicket

Tasmania's Kenny Burn wasn't a bad cricketer (he'd been considered seriously for the 1888 tour of England), and actually played in both Tests on the 1890 tour, though with little success. His selection in 1890 came about after 12 of the 13 players for the tour had been announced, with the 13th to be the reserve keeper behind Jack Blackham. Most thought either NSW's Sid Deane or Victoria's Jack Harry would get the nod, but apparently Blackham pushed hard for Burn, who he knew was quite a good batsman. He had seen in print that 'Burn' had made some stumpings in Tasmania, and assumed that keeper to be Kenny, when in truth it was Kenny's brother, a fact the selectors weren't made aware of until the touring team assembled in Adelaide.

With hindsight, Peter Taylor's elevation to Test cricket was something of a masterstroke; he took eight wickets on debut and over the following six years showed himself to be a good and very sensible cricketer. But at the time his selection was such a shock that one TV crew rang *Mark* Taylor, Peter's teammate in club and state cricket, to offer congratulations on his 'Test selection' and to arrange an interview.

With the retirement of Don Bradman after the 1948 Ashes tour, Keith Miller was the biggest star in the Australian game. Consequently, his omission from the 1949–50 tour to South Africa was a colossal shock, an almost absurdly conservative move considering that players such as Sam Loxton, Geff Noblett and Alan Walker were picked instead. In contrast, many thought that the captaincy change in 1970–71, from Bill Lawry to Ian Chappell, was a bold move worth taking, but surely Chappell could have used Lawry's runs. Lawry's replacement, Ken Eastwood, scored 5 and 0 and never played Test cricket again. Four decades earlier, Jack Ryder was sacked because his fellow selectors had decided on a youth policy. It was a pity they never had the courage to let him know before the final selection meeting. Eighteen months before this, the young Bradman had been left out after just one Test appearance (making 18 and 1) when it was decided that while Bill Ponsford's technique was not up to opening the batting he was still worth a place in the middle order. Vic Richardson came in to bat first and Bradman carried the drinks, despite the fact that even after the double failure in Brisbane he was averaging 85.29 for the 1928–29 first-class season. Ironically, Ponsford broke his hand facing Harold Larwood, and the young substitute had to field right through England's marathon first innings of 636. Two weeks later, he scored his first Test century, and was never dropped again.

Doug Walters had toured England four times, without once scoring a Test century, so the selectors decided he'd had his chances and went for Trevor Chappell, Dirk Wellham and Martin Kent for the '81 tour instead. However, in the previous Test in Melbourne, when Australia had collapsed to 83 all out chasing 143, Walters had been the one batsman to stand firm. How valuable might he have been in those dramatic third and fourth Ashes Tests in 1981, when Australia collapsed twice more chasing small totals? Perhaps the Members of Parliament who made speeches protesting against his omission were right. In a similar example of shortsightedness, it's hard to understand how the selectors could have omitted Allan Border in early 1979, so soon after he'd demonstrated how adept he was against the English bowlers on the spinning SCG square. It wasn't as if that Australian team, down 4–1 in the series, was swimming in runs.

Albert Trott and Billy Murdoch, two great cricketers, reacted quite differently to their omissions. Soon after being left out of the 1896 touring squad, Trott set sail for Middlesex and a very successful life as a full-time professional. He never played for Australia again, thus famously keeping his Test batting average for Australia at 102.50 (205 runs for twice out, highest score 85 not out). Two decades earlier, Spofforth's refusal to play in cricket's first Test after Blackham was preferred to Murdoch seemed imprudent at the time and, as the Victorian's reputation continued to grow, it looked ever more foolish. Murdoch, meanwhile, set about making his name as a Test run-getter and did so to the point that by as early as 1880 he was Australian captain and regarded as Australia's greatest ever batsman, better even than Charlie Bannerman. In 1890, after five years out of Test cricket, he made a comeback to captain the Australians in England once more, and irony of ironies, also became the team's reserve wicketkeeper when it was discovered that Kenny Burn was not all he might have been. ■

10 LUCKIEST COIN TOSSERS *(Qualification: five Tests as captain)*

Rank	Captain	Tests	Tosses won	% Tosses won	Win %
1.	Graham Yallop	7	6	85.71	14.29
2.	Lindsay Hassett	24	18	75.00	58.33
3.	Monty Noble	15	11	73.33	53.33
4.	Percy McDonnell	6	4	66.67	16.67
5.	Herbert Collins	11	7	63.64	45.45
6.	Harry Trott	8	5	62.50	62.50
7.	Greg Chappell	48	29	60.42	43.75
8.	Steve Waugh	51	30	58.82	74.51
9.	Ian Chappell	30	17	56.67	50.00
10.	Mark Taylor	50	26	52.00	52.00

Inevitably, the man who has won and lost the most tosses is the man with the most captaincy appearances. Allan Border won 46 of his 93 tosses, a success rate with the coin of 49.46 per cent. Graham Yallop (one victory in seven Tests as skipper) has the unfortunate distinction of having the best coin-tossing record and the equal worst winning percentage of any of the 26 men to captain Australia in five or more Tests. Kim Hughes (four wins in 28 Tests) also has a winning percentage of 14.29%.

10 NOTABLE QUOTES FROM AUSTRALIAN CRICKET HISTORY

3. 'We're going for a win, of course ...'
– Richie Benaud's response to Sir Donald Bradman's question as to what Australia's tactics might be in the final session of the first Test against the West Indies at the Gabba in 1960–61. Australia needed 123 to win in two hours, with just four wickets in hand. 'I'm very pleased to hear it,' The Don replied.

10 UNLUCKIEST COIN TOSSERS *(Qualification: five Tests as captain)*

Rank	Captain	Tests	Tosses won	% Tosses won	Win %
1.	Syd Gregory	6	1	16.67	33.33
2.	Vic Richardson	5	1	20.00	80.00
3.	Bill Lawry	25	8	32.00	36.00
4.	Joe Darling	21	7	33.33	33.33
5.	Ian Johnson	17	6	35.29	41.18
6.	Richie Benaud	28	11	39.29	42.86
7=.	Warwick Armstrong	10	4	40.00	80.00
7=.	Jack Ryder	5	2	40.00	20.00
9.	Don Bradman	24	10	41.67	62.50
10.	Billy Murdoch	16	7	43.75	31.25

10 CAPTAINS WHO MOST OFTEN SENT THE OPPOSITION IN TO BAT

Rank	Captain	Times	Wins	Losses	Draws
1.	Greg Chappell	14	8	3	3
2.	Allan Border	13	5	4	4
3.	Steve Waugh	11	11	–	–
4.	Bob Simpson	5	1	2	2
5.	Kim Hughes	5	3	1	1
6.	Mark Taylor	5	3	1	1
7.	Ian Chappell	4	1	1	2
8.	Richie Benaud	3	3	–	–
9.	Bill Lawry	3	2	–	1
10.	Graham Yallop	3	–	3	–

Clearly, pundits predicting the outcome of Australian Test matches should pay attention when Steve Waugh decides to bowl first. Besides Waugh and Richie Benaud, the only other Australian skipper with a perfect win record when he sent the opposition in is Monty Noble, who did so for the only time in his Test captaincy career at Lord's in 1909 and was rewarded with a nine-wicket victory.

In Australia's first 340 Test matches, the captain won the toss and decided to bowl just four times, and never between that Lord's Test of 1909 and the second Test against the West Indies in Sydney in 1951–52, when Lindsay Hassett asked the West Indies to bat first and Australia went on to win comfortably by seven wickets. Some of Australia's greatest captains before World War II, including Billy Murdoch, Joe Darling, Warwick Armstrong, Bill Woodfull and Don Bradman, always took first innings when they won the toss. Today's captains seem much happier to bowl first, but against this modern trend, it wasn't until Mark's Taylor's 26th Test as captain, the second Test in South Africa in 1997, that he did so. Before Glenn McGrath established himself as a great fast bowler, it seemed Taylor was always keen to have Shane Warne bowling in the fourth innings (which meant, of course, that Taylor would be opening the batting on the first morning).

Also interesting is the fact that of Kim Hughes' four victories as Australian captain (in 28 attempts), three of them came after he decided to bowl first. Hughes' record apart from when he sent the opposition in was 23 Tests, one win, 12 losses, 10 draws.

CHAPTER SIX

THE TEAMS

Australia has been involved in 642 Test matches, from the first against England in mid-March 1877 (actually a game between a combined Victoria and New South Wales XI and James Lillywhite's professional touring team) to the second Test against Bangladesh in Cairns in late-July 2003. This does not include three Tests — one each in 1890, 1938 and 1970–71 — that were abandoned without a ball being bowled. Australia's record in these Tests is as follows:

Opponent	Tests	Won	Tied	Drawn	Lost	Win %
Bangladesh	2	2	–	–	–	100.00
England	306	125	–	86	95	40.85
India	60	29	1	17	13	48.33
New Zealand	41	18	–	16	7	43.90
Pakistan	49	21	–	17	11	42.86
South Africa	71	39	–	17	15	54.93
Sri Lanka	13	7	–	5	1	53.85
West Indies	99	45	1	21	32	45.45
Zimbabwe	1	1	–	–	–	100.00
Total	642	287	2	179	174	44.70

'Win %' is calculated by dividing wins by total Tests played.

One interesting exercise is to compare these win rates with those of the current Australian team. From the time Steve Waugh became captain, after the 1998–99 Ashes series, to the end of the winter 2003 series against

Bangladesh, Australia played 53 Tests, 51 times under Waugh's leadership and twice with Adam Gilchrist filling in as skipper. Australia won 39 of those Tests, a win rate of 73.58 per cent, lost nine (16.98 per cent) and drew only five (9.43 per cent). That remarkably low percentage of draws (since 1877 Australia has drawn 27.88 per cent of its Tests), is made even more amazing by the fact that two of them came in one series in Sri Lanka in 1999 and the other three in a three-Test series against New Zealand in late 2001.

At the end of July 2003, Waugh's team had a perfect record against Bangladesh (two wins from two), Pakistan (six from six) and Zimbabwe (one from one). It had also dominated England (eight from 10), South Africa (five from six) and the West Indies (10 from 13), while the winning percentages against India (four from six) and New Zealand (three from six) are also superior to Australia's all-time marks. Only Sri Lanka, who in the only series the two teams have played since 1999 drew two and won one, has a positive win–loss record against a Steve Waugh-led Australian team.

❖   ❖   ❖

10 HIGHEST INNINGS TOTALS BY AUSTRALIA

Rank	Total	Inns	Versus	Venue	Series
1.	8–758d	Second	West Indies	Kingston	1955
2.	6–729d	Second	England	Lord's	1930
3.	701	First	England	The Oval	1934
4.	695	Second	England	The Oval	1930
5.	674	First	India	Adelaide	1947–48
6.	668	First	West Indies	Bridgetown	1955
7.	8–659d	Second	England	Sydney	1946–47
8.	8–656d	First	England	Manchester	1964
9.	4–653d	First	England	Leeds	1993
10.	7–652d	First	South Africa	Johannesburg	2002

10 NOTABLE QUOTES FROM AUSTRALIAN CRICKET HISTORY

4. 'It's beach cricket only for me from now on.'
   – *Ian Meckiff, after being no-balled for throwing during the first Test against South Africa, the Gabba, 1963–64.*

Australia has made more than 550 in the third innings of a match five times, as follows:

Total	First Inns	Versus	Venue	Series
582	354	England	Adelaide	1920–21
581	267	England	Sydney	1920–21
578	328	South Africa	Melbourne	1910–11
564	9–200d	England	Melbourne	1936–37
554	198	South Africa	Melbourne	1931–32

Australia has made more than 350 in the fourth innings of a match five times, as follows:

Total	Chasing	Versus	Venue	Series
3–404	404	England	Leeds	1948
402	505	England	Manchester	1981
7–381	440	New Zealand	Perth	2001–02
6–369	369	Pakistan	Hobart	1999–00
7–362	359	West Indies	Georgetown	1978

Australia has also twice scored over 200 in the fourth innings of a Test, when that innings total was the highest of the match. This occurred at Durban in 1949–50, when Neil Harvey, with 151 not out, led Australia to victory (South Africa 311 and 99; Australia 75 and 5–336); and at Port Elizabeth in 1997, when Mark Waugh produced a masterly 116, perhaps his greatest Test innings, and Ian Healy ended the match with a six (South Africa 209 and 168; Australia 108 and 8–271).

10 HIGHEST INNINGS TOTALS AGAINST AUSTRALIA

Rank	Total	Inns	Versus	Venue	Series
1.	7–903d	First	England	The Oval	1938
2.	8–658d	First	England	Nottingham	1938
3.	7–657d	Third	India	Kolkata	2001
4.	636	Second	England	Sydney	1928–29
5.	5–633d	Second	India	Calcutta	1998
6.	9–627d	First	England	Manchester	1934
7.	624	Second	Pakistan	Adelaide	1983–84
8.	9–622d	First	South Africa	Durban	1970
9.	620	Third	South Africa	Johannesburg	1966–67
10.	616	Third	West Indies	Adelaide	1968–69

Australia has conceded more than 550 in the third innings of a match three times, all listed above. At Kolkata in early 2001 India had made 171 in their first innings and were made to follow on. At Johannesburg, the South Africans had been dismissed for 199 on the first day. In Adelaide, the Windies had made 276 in their first innings.

Australia has conceded more than 350 in the fourth innings of a match eight times, as follows:

Total	Chasing	Versus	Venue	Series
445	493	India	Adelaide	1977–78
7–418	418	West Indies	St John's	2003
417	463	England	Melbourne	1976–77
411	605	England	Sydney	1924–25
370	490	England	Adelaide	1920–21
363	375	England	Adelaide	1924–25
355	395	India	Brisbane	1967–68
352	735	West Indies	Sydney	1968–69

The score by the West Indies at Antigua in 2003 is a Test record for highest successful fourth-innings chase. In 1986, India were set 348 to win on the final day of the first Test, in Madras, and finished one run short, the second tie in Test history.

10 LOWEST INNINGS TOTALS BY AUSTRALIA *(Completed innings)*

Rank	Total	Inns	Versus	Venue	Series
1.	36	Second	England	Birmingham	1902
2.	42	Second	England	Sydney	1887–88
3.	44	Fourth	England	The Oval	1896
4.	53	First	England	Lord's	1896
5.	58	Fourth	England	Brisbane	1936–37
6.	60	Third	England	Lord's	1888
7.	63	First	England	The Oval	1882
8.	65	Fourth	England	The Oval	1912
9.	66	Fourth	England	Brisbane	1928–29
10.	68	Second	England	The Oval	1886

Australian paceman Ernie McCormick was ill at Brisbane in 1936–37 and did not bat. Eight years earlier, at the Brisbane Exhibition Ground, Jack Gregory was injured and Charles Kelleway ill; neither man batted.

The lowest totals in completed Test innings by Australia since World War II are 75 against South Africa in Durban in 1949–50 (a Test Lindsay

Hassett's team went on to win), 76 against the West Indies in Perth in 1984–85 and 78 against England at Lord's in 1968. The following innings ended on low totals, but were not complete:

Total	Inns	Versus	Venue	Series
7-32d	Third	England	Brisbane	1950-51
8-35	Fourth	England	Manchester	1953

Australia has twice been dismissed for less than 100 in both innings of the same Test — at Sydney in 1887–88 (42 and 82) and Manchester in 1888 (81 and 70).

10 LOWEST INNINGS TOTALS AGAINST AUSTRALIA

Rank	Total	Inns	Versus	Venue	Series
1.	36	First	South Africa	Melbourne	1931-32
2.	42	First	New Zealand	Wellington	1946
3=	45	First	England	Sydney	1886-87
3=	45	Third	South Africa	Melbourne	1931-32
5.	51	Fourth	West Indies	Port-of-Spain	1999
6.	52	First	England	The Oval	1948
7=	53	Second	England	Lord's	1888
7=	53	Third	Pakistan	Sharjah	2002
9.	54	Third	New Zealand	Wellington	1945-46
10.	58	Second	India	Brisbane	1947-48

There have been six instances of teams failing to reach 100 in either innings of a Test against Australia. Two, at Melbourne in 1931–32 and Wellington in 1946, are detailed above. The other instances occurred at Sharjah in 2002 (Pakistan 59 and 53), Lord's in 1888 (England 53 and 62), Sydney in 1894–95 (England 65 and 72, batting one man short in both innings) and Brisbane in 1947–48 (India 58 and 98).

10 NOTABLE QUOTES FROM AUSTRALIAN CRICKET HISTORY

5. 'They'll never get me like that.'

– Ian Chappell, in 1971, after learning that he was the new Australian captain, on the manner in which the selectors had sacked his immediate predecessor, Bill Lawry.

1. *Wally Grout not bowled, fifth Test v West Indies, 1960–61:* Near the end of this wonderful series, Australia needed four to win with three wickets in hand when Alf Valentine spun one past Grout and the keeper Gerry Alexander. Grout took off for a bye, but then everyone noticed that a bail had fallen to the ground. Umpires Col Egar and Col Hoy consulted, and because they had not seen the ball hit the stumps they gave the batsman the benefit of the doubt. Grout appeared to give his wicket away straight after. Australia snuck home by two wickets.

2. *Don Bradman not caught, first Test v England, Brisbane, 1946–47:* Having struggled to 28 in his comeback Test after the war, The Don sliced Voce to Jack Ikin at second slip and most observers, including all the close fieldsmen, believed he was out. But umpire George Borwick — and, interestingly, the non-striker Lindsay Hassett — thought it was a bump ball and Bradman went on to score 187. In the next Test in Sydney, with all his prewar confidence now restored, Bradman scored 234.

3. *Warwick Armstrong bowls two overs in a row, fourth Test v England, Manchester, 1921:* Armstrong bowled an over, and then the England captain, the Hon. Lionel Tennyson, declared his first innings closed. But with rain having washed out the first day, this was a two-day Test and under the two-day rules of the time you couldn't declare within 110 minutes of stumps. The home team had to keep batting, and Armstrong bowled the first over after play resumed.

4. *Michael Slater not run out, fifth Test v England, Sydney, 1998–99:* In the course of making one of the finest centuries in recent Ashes history, Slater appeared to be run out on 35, when a direct throw shattered the stumps. A 'front on' camera angle showed the ball breaking the wicket, while a side-on view showed that as the ball passed the wicket Slater was short of his ground. But bodies blocked the side-on view, so that from that angle the ball couldn't be seen directly breaking the stumps, and Slater got the benefit of the doubt.

5. *Colin McDonald not run out, fourth Test v England, Adelaide, 1958–59:* McDonald was well past his hundred when he strained a thigh muscle and had to retire hurt. Not long after he returned with Jim Burke to run for him, he appeared to be run out by around three metres, and umpire Mel McInnes quickly gave him out. However, it was then pointed out that McInnes had moved to the wrong side of the wicket to make his decision, so that he was between the runner and

the stumps; consequently he couldn't possibly have known whether Burke had made good his ground. McInnes reversed his decision, leaving McDonald to get himself out as soon as he possibly could.

6. *Keith Stackpole not run out, first Test v England, Brisbane, 1970–71:* With Australia 1–33 on the first day, Stackpole (18) survived a close run-out call, after Geoff Boycott threw down the wicket at the bowler's end. By stumps Stackpole was 175 not out, the next day he went on to 207, but by then much was being made of a photograph that seemed to show that umpire Lou Rowan had got the run-out decision wrong.

7. *Australia open the innings with an old ball, sixth Test v England, Sydney, 1978–79:* England needed just 39 to complete a 5–1 series win when the umpires ruled that the Australian spinners, Jim Higgs and Bruce Yardley, could open the innings with an old ball. The visitors protested, but despite the fact that the laws state that either team can claim a new ball at the start of an innings, the ump's ruling stood.

8. *Jim Higgs not caught behind, third Test v New Zealand, Melbourne, 1980–81:* Higgs, a career No. 11, was proving frustratingly difficult to dislodge, to the point that Kiwi medium-pacer Lance Cairns tried a bouncer. Higgs, who was wearing a helmet, gloved the ball slowly through to the keeper, but umpire Robin Bailhache called a no-ball, on the basis that the bumper was intimidatory. The rule on which Bailhache based his decision referred specifically to *fast* bowling. Non-striker Doug Walters, then on 77, went on to his 15th and final Test century.

9. *John Dyson not run out, fifth Test v England, 1982–83:* England needed to win this Test to retain the Ashes and from the last ball of the game's first over, their captain Bob Willis seemed to run out Dyson by about half a metre. But umpire Mel Johnson ruled in the local opener's favour, and at stumps on a rain-interrupted day, Australia were 2–138 with Dyson 58 not out. The next day he went on to 79, and the Test ended in a draw.

10. *WG Grace challenges the legality of Percy McDonnell's bat:* In 1884, Dr Grace had the audacity to claim that Percy Mac's bat was too wide, but seemed vindicated when the umpires inspected it and ruled it to be out of order. The Australians responded by asking for Grace's bats to be checked, and – to the Englishman's huge embarrassment and, one imagines, the Aussies' enormous pleasure – the first one measured was also deemed to be illegal.

10 HIGHEST MATCH AGGREGATES

Rank	Total	Wkts	Versus	Venue	Series	Days Played
1.	1764	39	West Indies	Adelaide	1968–69	5
2.	1753	40	England	Adelaide	1920–21	6*
3.	1723	31	England	Leeds	1948	5
4.	1661	36	West Indies	Bridgetown	1955	6
5.	1646	40	South Africa	Adelaide	1910–11	6*
6.	1644	38	West Indies	Sydney	1968–69	6
7=.	1640	24	West Indies	Bridgetown	1965	6
7=.	1640	33	Pakistan	Melbourne	1972–73	5
9.	1619	40	England	Melbourne	1924–25	7*
10.	1611	40	England	Sydney	1924–25	7*

*indicates Test played to a finish.

The highest runs aggregate Australia has achieved in a Test is 1028, when England was defeated by 562 runs at The Oval in 1934 (Australia 701 and 327, England 321 and 145). The only other occasion when Australia scored more than 1000 runs in a Test occurred against the West Indies in Sydney in 1968–69, when Bill Lawry set Garry Sobers' tourists 735 to win (Australia 619 and 8–394d, West Indies 279 and 352). No team has ever scored 1000 runs against Australia in one Test; the highest is the 7–903 (declared) Wally Hammond's team compiled in their only innings at The Oval in 1938.

10 SMALLEST MATCH AGGREGATES *(Completed Tests)*

Rank	Runs	Wickets	Versus	Venue	Series
1.	234	29	South Africa	Melbourne	1931–32
2.	291	40	England	Lord's	1888
3.	295	28	New Zealand	Wellington	1946
4.	323	30	England	Manchester	1888
5.	363	40	England	The Oval	1882
6.	374	40	England	Sydney	1887–88
7.	389	38	England	The Oval	1890
8.	392	40	England	The Oval	1896
9.	421	28	England	Sydney	1894–95
10.	422	29	Pakistan	Sharjah	2002

Other instances of match aggregates below 500 in a completed Test since 1900 are:

Runs	Wickets	Versus	Venue	Series
445	40	England	Sydney	1886–87
450	34	England	Brisbane	1950–51
451	30	England	Birmingham	1909
467	31	West Indies	Port-of-Spain	1995

The lowest match total by Australia in a completed Test is 124 (for the loss of all 20 wickets), against England at Sydney in 1887–88. Lowest match totals of fewer than 124 against Australia are:

81	20	South Africa	Melbourne	1931–32
96	20	New Zealand	Wellington	1946
112	19	Pakistan	Sharjah	2002
115	20	England	Lord's	1888

10 LONGEST TESTS

Rank	Balls	Overs	Days	Versus	Venue	Series	Result
1.	4269	711.3 x 6	7	England	Melbourne	1928–29	England by three wkts
2.	4244	707.2 x 6	8	England	Melbourne	1928–29	Australia by five wkts
3.	4174	695.4 x 6	7	England	Adelaide	1928–29	England by 12 runs
4.	3787	473.3 x 8	7	England	Melbourne	1924–25	Australia by 81 runs
5.	3652	456.4 x 8	6	South Africa	Melbourne	1952–53	South Africa by six wkts
6.	3639	454.7 x 8	7	England	Sydney	1924–25	Australia by 193 runs
7.	3597	449.5 x 8	7	England	Adelaide	1924–25	Australia by 11 runs
8.	3525	440.5 x 8	6	England	Adelaide	1946–47	Match Drawn
9.	3446	574.2 x 6	6	West Indies	Bridgetown	1955	Match Drawn
10.	3376	562.4 x 6	6	England	Sydney	1894–95	England by 10 runs

In terms of time, the longest Test involving Australia was the eight-day final Test of 1928–29, which involved 33 hours and 17 minutes, making it the longest first-class match ever played in Australia. The home team won the match, but they also faced most of the deliveries: England bowled 405.4 overs to Australia's 301.4. On what was clearly a very friendly batting track, Australia's batsmen scored at a run rate of 1.92 runs per over during this Test.

The three Tests at the top of this Top 10 were all 'timeless' matches, fought to a finish, and were played consecutively (711.3 overs in the third Test at the MCG, 694.4 in the fourth Test in Adelaide, 707.2 overs in the fifth Test, in Melbourne). The three matches from 1924–25 above were also played consecutively (Sydney, then Melbourne, then Adelaide).

10 SHORTEST TESTS *(Completed matches)*

Rank	Balls	Overs	Versus	Venue	Series	Result
1.	656	109.2 x 6	South Africa	Melbourne	1931–32	Aust by an innings and 72 runs
2.	792	198 x 4	England	The Oval	1888	Eng by an innings and 137 runs
3.	804	201 x 4	England	Manchester	1888	Eng by an innings and 21 runs
4.	872	145.2 x 6	New Zealand	Wellington	1946	Aust by an innings and 103 runs
5.	893	148.5 x 6	Pakistan	Sharjah	2002	Aust by an innings and 198 runs
6.	911	151.5 x 6	England	Sydney	1894–95	Aust by an innings and 147 runs
7.	983	163.5 x 6	West Indies	Port-of-Spain	1995	West Indies by nine wickets
8.	1034	129.2 x 8	England	Brisbane	1950–51	Australia by 70 runs
9.	1049	209.4 x 5	England	The Oval	1896	England by 66 runs
10.	1050	175 x 6	West Indies	Melbourne	1930–31	Aust by an innings and 122 runs

There have been 11 Test matches involving Australia that have been completed in two days. The shortest of these in terms of time was the Manchester Test of 1888 (England 172; Australia 81 and 70), in which 201 four-ball overs were bowled in six hours and 34 minutes. Australian bowlers sent down 117.1 of those overs. That's 469 deliveries, not many for a Test match but 140 balls more than the Australian bowlers needed to beat South Africa at the MCG in 1931–32. In that Test, which is top on the list above, the Australians bowled 23.2 six-ball overs in South Africa's first innings 36 and 31.3 overs in the second innings 45.

When Australia defeated Pakistan in Sharjah in 2002 (Australia 310, Pakistan 59 and 53), the match took one minute less than 12 hours to be completed. The Australian bowling attack of McGrath, Lee, Bichel and Warne sent down 340 deliveries in this Test.

10 NOTABLE QUOTES FROM AUSTRALIAN CRICKET HISTORY

6. 'And now here's Hollies to bowl to him from the Vauxhall End. He bowls … and Bradman goes back across his wicket and pushes the ball gently in the direction of the Houses of Parliament, which are out beyond mid-off. It doesn't go that far, it merely goes to Watkins at silly mid-off, no run, still 117 for one … Two slips, a silly mid-off and a forward short leg as Hollies pitches the ball up slowly and … he's bowled … Bradman bowled Hollies nought … bowled Hollies nought … and what do you say under those circumstances?'
– John Arlott's call of what proved to be Don Bradman's final innings in Test cricket, The Oval, 1948.

10 BIGGEST DIFFERENCES BETWEEN AUSTRALIAN INNINGS TOTALS IN ONE TEST

Rank	Diff	First	Second	Versus	Venue	Series
1.	420	586	166	England	Sydney	1894–95
2.	419	668	249	West Indies	Bridgetown	1955
3.	374	701	327	England	The Oval	1934
4.	359	118	477	England	Birmingham	1997
5.	356	198	554	South Africa	Melbourne	1931–32
6.	350	600	250	England	Melbourne	1924–25
7.	344	490	146	West Indies	Bridgetown	1999
8.	343	133	476	England	Adelaide	1911–12
9.	340	467	127	Pakistan	Colombo	2002
10.	336	419	83	India	Melbourne	1980–81

10 BIGGEST DIFFERENCES BETWEEN OPPONENT'S INNINGS TOTALS IN ONE TEST

Rank	Diff	First	Second	By	Venue	Series
1.	486	171	657-7d	India	Kolkata	2001
2.	426	506	80	South Africa	Melbourne	1910–11
3.	421	199	620	South Africa	Johannesburg	1966–67
4.	400	75	475	England	Melbourne	1894–95
5.	387	149	536-9d	West Indies	Bridgetown	1991
6.	383	547-8d	164	Sri Lanka	Colombo	1992
7.	374	574-8d	200	Pakistan	Melbourne	1972–73
8.	347	191	538	England	The Oval	1975
9.	340	276	616	West Indies	Adelaide	1968–69
10.	334	157	491	South Africa	Johannesburg	1935–36

The top-ranking instances in the two tables above — at the SCG in 1894–95 and Eden Gardens in 2001 — involved Tests in which Australia's opponents followed on.

10 NOTABLE QUOTES FROM AUSTRALIAN CRICKET HISTORY

7. 'We played badly throughout the series; we never batted for more than a day and we didn't do ourselves justice. This was the weakest Australian side I have ever played against. If we had lived up to our potential, we would have beaten them convincingly.'
   – *West Indies captain Richie Richardson's analysis of the 1995 Test series against Australia in the Caribbean, which Australia won two Tests to one.*

1. *Sammy Jones run out, Ashes Test, The Oval, 1882:* Jones was down the pitch repairing a divot when he was run out by WG Grace. According to Australian Tom Horan's version, umpire Bob Thoms' response to Grace's appeal was, 'If you claim it, sir, it is out.' The Australians were appalled, none more so than Fred Spofforth, who reputedly called Grace a 'bloody cheat' and told him that his poor form would cost England the Test. Which it did, the Demon taking 7–44 as England were bowled out for just 77, chasing 85.

2. *Clem Hill run out, first Test v England, Sydney, 1903–04:* The run out decision by Victorian umpire Bob Crockett, made after Hill attempted a *fifth* run from an overthrow, inspired something of a riot among the Sydney faithful. Most neutrals thought the umpire was probably correct, and blamed the aggrieved batsman's angry reaction to the out verdict for the turmoil that followed.

3. *Reg Simpson not run out, fourth Test v England, Leeds, 1953:* Frank Chester had been rated as the best umpire in the game, but the Australians had trouble agreeing with him after Lindsay Hassett threw in from the deep, Keith Miller broke the stumps, and Simpson seemed to be well out. Chester ruled otherwise, explaining that in the excitement he hadn't had enough time to get in a good position to make the call. This despite the fact Simpson was trying to complete a *third* run.

4. *Doug Walters caught, second Test v South Africa, Durban, 1970:* Australia were battling to avoid a heavy defeat when Walters and Ian Redpath became involved in a partnership. As the spinner John Traicos bowled, the umpire seemed to call no-ball, so Walters took advantage of the free hit and swung high into the outfield, where he was 'caught' by Graeme Pollock. But the batsman was given out, the umpire explaining that yes, he had begun to call a no-ball, but had changed his mind so despite what Walters might have heard the delivery was fair.

5. *Dean Jones run out off a no-ball, second Test v West Indies, Georgetown, 1991:* Law 38.2 states that 'if a no-ball has been called, the striker shall not be given run out unless he attempts to run'. However, this did not stop square-leg umpire Clive Cumberbatch ruling Jones out after the batsman was 'bowled' by Courtney Walsh and, believing he was dismissed, began walking disconsolately to the pavilion, in the direction of extra cover. Carl Hooper broke the stumps and Cumberbatch then made his palpably incorrect decision.

6. *Charlie McLeod run out off a no-ball, first Test v England, Sydney, 1897–98:* McLeod was deaf, and did not hear the umpire's no-ball call when 'bowled'. Unaware he'd got lucky, McLeod headed straight for the pavilion, beyond the midwicket boundary, and the English keeper, Bill Storer, impulsively ran him out.

7. *Derek Randall not caught behind, Centenary Test, Melbourne, 1977:* This is one decision that Australia — or more specifically Rod Marsh — called against itself. With many observers just starting to believe that England might even make the 463 needed for victory, Randall (on 161) edged Greg Chappell behind, and in a flurry of diving and dust Marsh came up with the ball, and the umpire said, 'Out.' However, Marsh quickly indicated that he'd gloved the chance on the half volley, and Randall was called back, to finish on 174 as Australia prevailed by 45 runs.

8. *Jack Hobbs, not run out, third Ashes Test, Leeds, 1909:* Hobbs hit Charlie Macartney through midwicket but then slipped as he set off for a run and broke his wicket with his heel. Assuming he'd been dismissed, Hobbs began to walk off, but was called back by his partner Johnny Tyldesley and ruled not out by umpire West. Some of the Australians were appalled by this decision, and one in particular was enraged directing a tirade of abuse at the not out batsman. 'The chief offender was Warwick Armstrong, who got very nasty and unsportsmanlike, refusing to accept the umpire's decision,' Hobbs remembered with some bitterness in his autobiography 26 years later.

9. *Ricky Ponting, lbw, first Test v Sri Lanka, Perth, 1995–96:* This was Ponting's Test debut, and he was set for a first-up hundred until, with his score on 96, a delivery from Chaminda Vaas appeared to strike him high up on the thigh. Umpire Khizer Hayat was one of the very few at the ground who thought the ball was going to hit the stumps.

10. *Don Bradman, caught behind, fifth Test v England, The Oval, 1930:* Bradman always maintained that he did not get a nick when given out, caught by George Duckworth, for 232. Douglas Jardine often cited Bradman's allegedly uncertain batting on a wet wicket in this innings as one of the things that led to bodyline, but The Don argued that as he was past 200 and shouldn't have been given out, he couldn't have been going too badly. What he never added was that if the decision had gone his way, he needed only 26 more runs to reach 1000 for the series, a figure no other batsman has got close to before or since.

10 LARGEST MARGINS OF VICTORY BY AN INNINGS MARGIN

Rank	Margin	Versus	Venue	Series
1.	Innings and 360 runs	South Africa	Johannesburg	2002
2.	Innings and 332 runs	England	Brisbane	1946–47
3.	Innings and 259 runs	South Africa	Port Elizabeth	1949–50
4.	Innings and 226 runs	India	Brisbane	1947–48
5.	Innings and 222 runs	New Zealand	Hobart	1993–94
6.	Innings and 217 runs	West Indies	Brisbane	1930–31
7.	Innings and 200 runs	England	Melbourne	1936–37
8.	Innings and 198 runs	Pakistan	Sharjah	2002
9.	Innings and 196 runs	South Africa	Johannesburg	1997
10.	Innings and 184 runs	South Africa	Johannesburg	1935–36

10 LARGEST MARGINS OF VICTORY BY A RUNS MARGIN

Rank	Margin	Versus	Venue	Series
1.	562 runs	England	The Oval	1934
2.	530 runs	South Africa	Melbourne	1910–11
3.	409 runs	England	Lord's	1948
4.	384 runs	England	Brisbane	2002–03
5.	382 runs	England	Adelaide	1894–95
6.	382 runs	West Indies	Sydney	1968–69
7.	377 runs	England	Sydney	1920–21
8.	365 runs	England	Melbourne	1936–37
9.	352 runs	West Indies	Melbourne	2000–01
10.	348 runs	Pakistan	Melbourne	1976–77

10 LARGEST MARGINS OF DEFEAT BY AN INNINGS MARGIN

Rank	Margin	Versus	Venue	Year
1.	Innings and 579 runs	England	The Oval	1938
2.	Innings and 230 runs	England	Adelaide	1891–92
3.	Innings and 225 runs	England	Melbourne	1911–12
4.	Innings and 219 runs	India	Kolkata	1998
5.	Innings and 217 runs	England	The Oval	1886
6.	Innings and 188 runs	Pakistan	Karachi	1988
7.	Innings and 170 runs	England	Manchester	1956
8.	Innings and 137 runs	England	The Oval	1888
9.	Innings and 129 runs	South Africa	Durban	1970
10.	Innings and 124 runs	England	Sydney	1901–02

10 LARGEST MARGINS OF DEFEAT BY A RUNS MARGIN

Rank	Margin	Versus	Venue	Year
1.	675 runs	England	Brisbane	1928–29
2.	408 runs	West Indies	Adelaide	1979–80
3.	343 runs	West Indies	Bridgetown	1991
4.	338 runs	England	Adelaide	1932–33
5.	323 runs	South Africa	Port Elizabeth	1970
6.	322 runs	England	Brisbane	1936–37
7.	307 runs	South Africa	Johannesburg	1970
8.	299 runs	England	Sydney	1970–71
9.	289 runs	England	The Oval	1926
10.	285 runs	West Indies	Melbourne	1988–89

10 NARROWEST VICTORIES BY A RUNS MARGIN

Rank	Margin	Versus	Venue	Year
1.	3 runs	England	Manchester	1902
2.	6 runs	England	Sydney	1884–85
3.	7 runs	England	The Oval	1882
4.	11 runs	England	Adelaide	1924–25
5=.	16 runs	India	Brisbane	1977–78
5=.	16 runs	Sri Lanka	Colombo	1992
7.	28 runs	England	Melbourne	1950–51
8.	38 runs	India	Adelaide	1991–92
9.	39 runs	India	Brisbane	1967–68
10.	41 runs	Pakistan	Colombo	2002

In the first ever Test match at Melbourne in 1877, Australia prevailed by 45 runs, a margin matched to the run 100 years later, when Dennis Lillee spurred Australia to victory in the Centenary Test. One difference in the two run-chases was that in 1877 England needed 154 to win; in 1977, the target was 463.

Australia has won once by one wicket, over the West Indies at the MCG in 1951–52, and three times by two wickets: v England at Sydney in 1907–08; v West Indies at Melbourne in 1960–61; and v India at Perth in 1977–78. On three occasions they have bowled the opposition out when defending less than 150 in the fourth innings — at The Oval in 1882 (England needed 85 but were dismissed for 77), at Lord's in 1888 (England set 124, all out for 62) and at Old Trafford in 1902, when England needed 124 but only scored 120 of them.

10 NARROWEST DEFEATS BY A RUNS MARGIN

Rank	Result	Versus	Venue	Year
1.	1 run	West Indies	Adelaide	1992–93
2.	3 runs	England	Melbourne	1982–83
3.	5 runs	South Africa	Sydney	1993–94
4.	10 runs	England	Sydney	1894–95
5=.	12 runs	England	Adelaide	1928–29
5=.	12 runs	England	Melbourne	1998–99
7.	13 runs	England	Sydney	1886–87
8.	18 runs	England	Leeds	1981
9.	19 runs	England	The Oval	1997
10.	29 runs	England	Birmingham	1981

Australia has lost by one wicket on four occasions: at The Oval in 1902, against England at the MCG in 1907–08, against Pakistan at Karachi in 1994, and against the West Indies at Bridgetown in 1999. On three occasions they have lost by two wickets, most recently at Chennai in 2001.

Australia has been required to score less than 150 to win a Test and failed to do so on six occasions. Two of these failures occurred on wet wickets before 1900 — at the SCG in 1886–87 when Australia was all out for 97 chasing 111, and at The Oval in 1896 when Harry Trott's side made only 44 of a target of, once again, 111.

It wasn't until 1981 that Australia fell short in this manner again, being bowled out for 83 at the MCG against India when 143 was required. Six months later at Headingley, the target was just 130, but Bob Willis took 8–43 in the first of the 'Botham's Ashes' Tests and Australia was bowled out for … 111.

In Sydney in 1993–94, Fanie De Villiers bowled South Africa to victory, Australia being all out for … 111 … after being set just 117 to win. And then at The Oval in 1997, in a low-scoring Test match, Australia needed just 124 to win the series 4–1 but were dismissed for 104.

10 NOTABLE QUOTES FROM AUSTRALIAN CRICKET HISTORY

8. 'How are you going, pal? You know you can walk straight back off whenever you like.'

– Rod Marsh to Rick McCosker, when McCosker came out to bat with a broken jaw during Australia's second innings of the Centenary Test in 1977. 'Mind your own business and go on and get a hundred,' McCosker snapped back. McCosker eventually scored 25, Marsh finished on 110 not out.

THE TOP 10 MOST DRAMATIC TEST FINISHES

(Games that ended with at least all three results — an Australian win, Australian loss or a tie — distinctly possible in the final overs)

Rank	Versus	Venue	Series	Result
1.	West Indies	Brisbane	1960-61	Tied Test
2.	England	The Oval	1882	Australia by 7 runs
3.	West Indies	Adelaide	1992-93	West Indies by 1 run
4.	India	Madras	1986	Tied Test
5.	England	Manchester	1902	Australia by 3 runs
6.	England	Melbourne	1907-08	England by 1 wicket
7.	England	Melbourne	1982-83	England by 3 runs
8.	West Indies	Bridgetown	1999	West Indies by 1 wicket
9.	West Indies	Melbourne	1951-52	Australia by 1 wicket
10.	England	Leeds	1981	England by 16 runs

The thing about the first Tied Test is that over the final 12 deliveries — from the moment Alan Davidson (80) was run out just when it seemed he and Richie Benaud's heroic seventh-wicket partnership was going to get Australia home — any of four results was possible, but rarely in the sequence of these 12 balls, especially in the final over, was one result ever clearly the most likely. And so often, within a delivery, things had changed some more. When Benaud was caught behind off a Wes Hall bumper from the second ball of the final (eight-ball) over, maybe the Windies were fractionally in front. When Meckiff blocked ball three, perhaps it was going to be a draw. Then Grout ran through for a bye to the keeper, which showed Australia wanted no part of a stalemate. From ball five, Hall ran many metres to drop a chance that square-leg Rohan Kanhai would have swallowed, and it seemed the visitors were self-destructing, only for Conrad Hunte to then radar home a famous throw from the backward square boundary to run out Grout as the Aussie keeper dived unsuccessfully for the winning third run. A Windies win was now out of the question, but with Lindsay Kline, a genuine No. 11, on strike and just two balls to go, was a home-town win the new favourite? It was later revealed that the batsmen were running on contact, which put the pressure square on Joe Solomon, the same fieldsman who had run out Davidson with a direct hit just 11 balls but a long, long time before. Back at the MCG in January 1908 (No. 6 on this Top 10), 19-year-old Gerry Hazlitt had found himself in the same situation, but threw wildly. At the Gabba, in Solomon's own words: 'I could see little more than one stump … there wasn't much time. I let it go … it hit!'

The second Tied Test has never really received the recognition it is entitled to in Australia, because it was not shown on Australian television, was played away from home, in September (footy finals time), and by an Australian team that was going through an extended 'dry' spell. Yet it featured some superb batting from David Boon, Allan Border and especially Dean Jones (not to mention Kapil Dev and Sunil Gavaskar for India), a brave effort from Greg Matthews (10–249 for the match), an inspired declaration from Border on the final morning, and a thrilling finish, which ended with Matthews getting an lbw decision from the penultimate delivery of the final over.

At The Oval in 1882 and Manchester 20 years later, England came up short chasing meagre targets. At Leeds in 1981, it was Australia's turn to lose a match they should have won. The '81 Test is ranked lower here because although Australia's target was only 130 on the final day, with time not an issue, from the time they fell from 1–56 to 8–75 they were clear outsiders. Much of the drama had been played out the previous day, when Ian Botham clubbed England back into the Test.

Three matches in Australia — Adelaide '92–93, Melbourne '82–83 and Melbourne '51–52 — provided tense, prolonged last-wicket stands, but only Doug Ring and Bill Johnston, who came together at 9–222 needing 260, managed to get Australia home.

At the Adelaide Oval, Tim May and Craig McDermott were an unlikely pair to get 41 to win in a Test that had been dominated by bowlers, but they almost did, and the effort of Allan Border and Jeff Thomson, adding 37 on the fourth evening, but only 33 more the next day when 37 were required, was just as thrilling. An estimated 18,000 people came to the MCG on that fifth morning, despite the fact that they might have only seen one delivery.

Which of these 10 famous matches provided the greatest innings? Botham at Headingley? Jones at Madras? Davidson at the Gabba? Trumper (a century before lunch on the first day) at Old Trafford? In our view, as great as this quartet was, none can be ranked higher than Lara's fourth-innings 153 not out from 256 balls at Bridgetown. On a wicket on which Australia had been bowled out in its second innings for 146, on which none of his teammates could score more than 38, Lara spectacularly got the West Indies home even though they fell to 5–105, 8–248 and 9–302 chasing 308.

The criteria we adopted for this Top 10 ruled out Tests featuring match-saving late-order partnerships, because in these instances the team daring to rescue the game was not in a position to win it. However, two such Tests involving Australian 10th-wicket stands must be acknowledged:

Duration	Partnership	Runs	Versus	Venue	Series
105 minutes	Allan Border/Terry Alderman	61	West Indies	Port-of-Spain	1984
100 minutes	Ken Mackay/Lindsay Kline	66	West Indies	Adelaide	1960–61

The thing with both these stands is that the No. 11s involved — Alderman and Kline — were by Test standards poor batsmen. Kline tells the story of being bowled so many times in the nets before he went to bat in Adelaide that he decided he was wasting his time. Yet both he and Alderman rose to the occasion. That they did so is a tribute to their commonsense approach to the task at hand, and also to the batting partners — Border and Mackay — who inspired such heroics from them. ■

10 LONGEST WINNING STREAKS

Rank	Wins	From	To	Versus	Captain(s)
1.	16	17 Oct 1999	1 Mar 2001	Z (1), P (3), I (3), NZ (3), WI (5), I (1)	S Waugh (15), Gilchrist (1)
2.	8	22 Dec 1920	5 Jul 1921	E (5), E (3)	Armstrong
3.	7	7 Oct 2002	30 Dec 2002	P (3), E (4)	S Waugh
4=	5	22 Aug 1930	14 Feb 1931	E (1), WI (4)	Woodfull
4=	5	27 Nov 1931	15 Feb 1932	SA (5)	Woodfull
4=	5	1 Jan 1948	29 Jun 1948	I (3), E (2)	Bradman
4=	5	27 Jul 1948	24 Jan 1950	E (2), SA (3)	Bradman (2), Hassett (3)
4=	5	6 Mar 1950	8 Feb 1951	SA (1), E (4)	Hassett
4=	5	28 Dec 1967	11 June 1968	I (4), E (1)	Simpson (2), Lawry (3)
4=	5	18 Dec 2001	12 Mar 2002	SA (3), SA (2)	S Waugh

The Australian team won nine Tests straight against the West Indies between 1999 and 2003 (the final Test of the 1999 series in the Caribbean, all five Tests in Australia in 2000–01, and the first three Tests of 2003). This is an Australian record for most consecutive wins against one opponent.

10 NOTABLE QUOTES FROM AUSTRALIAN CRICKET HISTORY

9. 'I don't know if you know much about horse racing, but I think Australia should be handicapped.'
   – *West Indies skipper Brian Lara to reporters after Steve Waugh's team went 2–0 up after two Tests of the 2003 Test series in the Caribbean.*

10 LONGEST SEQUENCES WITHOUT A LOSS

Rank	Tests	From	To	Wins	Draws	Captain(s)
1.	25	30 Mar 1946	8 Feb 1951	20	5	Brown (1), Bradman (15), Hassett (9)
2.	18	26 Sep 1999	1 Mar 2001	16	2	S Waugh (17), Gilchrist (1)
3.	17	23 Oct 1956	16 Dec 1959	12	5	Johnson (2), Lindwall (1), Craig (5), Benaud (9)
4.	16	22 Dec 1920	23 Jan 1925	12	4	Armstrong (10), Collins (6)
5.	14	30 Jan 1989	19 Mar 1990	7	5	Border
6.	13	16 Aug 1972	13 Mar 1974	8	5	I Chappell
7.	12	1 May 1991	6 Jan 1993	7	5	Border
8=	9	5 Jan 1898	16 Aug 1899	5	4	Trott (4), Darling (5)
8=	9	27 Aug 2001	12 Mar 2002	6	3	S Waugh
8=	9	7 Jan 1983	21 Mar 1984	3	6	G Chappell (2) Hughes (7)

Between 7 January 1937 and 8 February 1951, Australia went 14 years, 32 days — involving 32 Tests — with only one defeat (at The Oval in 1938, when England won by an innings and 579 runs).

10 LONGEST LOSING STREAKS

Rank	Losses	From	To	Versus	Captain(s)
1.	7	25 Mar 1885	15 Feb 1888	E (1), E (3), E (2), E (1)	Horan (1), Scott (3), McDonnell (3)
2.	6	4 Apr 1984	11 Dec 1984	WI (3), WI (3)	Hughes (5), Border (1)
3.	5	18 Aug 1926	8 Feb 1929	E (1), E (4)	Collins (1), Ryder (4)
4=	4	14 Aug 1888	12 Aug 1890	E (2), E (2)	McDonnell (2), Murdoch (2)
4=	4	3 Jan 1912	1 Mar 1912	E (4)	Hill
4=	4	27 Jan 1970	10 Mar 1970	SA (4)	Lawry
4=	4	11 Jan 1979	15 Mar 1979	E (3), P (1)	Yallop
8=	3	Seven occasions, most recently in the first three Tests against West Indies in Australia, 1988–89			

10 NOTABLE QUOTES FROM AUSTRALIAN CRICKET HISTORY

10. 'Truthfully, I enjoy hitting a batsman more than getting him out. It doesn't worry me in the least to see a batsman hurt, rolling around screaming and blood on the pitch.'

– Jeff Thomson during an interview with reporter Phil Wilkins for Cricketer *magazine, June 1974.*

THERE ARE 10 WAYS AN AUSTRALIAN BATSMAN CAN BE DISMISSED

The Laws of Cricket tells us that there are 10 ways you can be dismissed while batting. Here we offer examples of how each of the 10 has been applied, or might have been applied, to Australian Test cricketers.

Bowled: In what became known as 'The Kippax Incident', Australian batsman Alan Kippax was incorrectly given out bowled by square-leg umpire Dave Elder during the second Ashes Test in Sydney in 1928–29. Elder had no right to do so; the decision should have come from George Hele, the umpire at the bowler's end.

Some thought the delivery from George Geary had ricocheted off keeper George Duckworth's pads onto the wicket. Others believed it had deflected from the batsman's pads. Kippax didn't have a clue, and remained in the middle until Elder gave his controversial verdict and Jack Hobbs, England's greatest player, said to him: 'What sort of a sport are you, staying here when you're out?' Hobbs later apologised for his remark.

Caught: In the second Ashes Test at Lord's in 1884, Henry 'Tup' Scott was batting well, seemingly on the way to his maiden Test century, when WG Grace suffered a hand injury and had to leave the field. With the English 12th man preoccupied, Australian skipper Billy Murdoch — an excellent fieldsman — raced onto the field and promptly took the catch that dismissed Scott for 75.

Affie Jarvis and Charlie Turner have also caught teammates while subbing for England, but at least they weren't the captain.

Run Out: In a match against an Australian XI early on India's 1947–48 tour, the tourists' Vinoo Mankad caused a sensation when he stopped in his delivery stride and ran out Bill Brown, who was backing up too far at the non-striker's end. When this happened again in the second Test, the terms 'mankad', 'mankaded' and 'mankading' entered the cricket dictionary.

Twenty-one seasons later, the West Indies' Charlie Griffith mankaded Ian Redpath during a dramatic run chase in an Adelaide Test, and then in a rancorous match in Perth in 1978–79, Australia's Alan Hurst showed Australians could mankad with the best of them when he ran out Pakistan's No. 11 Sikander Bakht.

LBW: One of the most intriguing statistics to come out of the 1970–71 Ashes Tests, a six-match series in Australia that featured more than its share of umpiring controversies, was that the local batsmen were good enough to never once be trapped lbw. The English batsmen were not quite so clever, falling leg-before on five occasions.

By way of contrast, in the Ashes series in Australia in 2002–03 England received eight lbw decisions in its favour, and Australia got 15. And by way of even greater contrast, in the 1989 Ashes series in England (six Tests), England received nine lbw verdicts, and Australia got 30, a remarkable 19 of them to Terry Alderman.

Stumped: In the second Test of Australia's 2003 tour of the West Indies, at Port-of-Spain, Ricky Ponting had reached 206 when he tried to swing a ball away on the legside, missed, and then instinctively and somewhat bizarrely set off for a run, as if he sensed that the ball had eluded the keeper. However, Carlton Baugh had the ball in his gloves and he whipped off the bails as Ponting frantically tried to regain his ground.

A video replay showed that Ponting was probably out by a millimetre, but he had no chance of receiving the benefit of the doubt, because umpire de Silva had already fired him out, despite the fact that when Baugh broke the wicket it looked as if the ump was gazing down in the direction of the fine leg boundary.

Hit wicket: Of all the ways he could have been dismissed in the fourth Ashes Test of 1934, hit wicket could have been furthest from Bill Ponsford's mind. After all, he'd been out that way in Test matches as many times as he'd been lbw. Never! However, having reached 181 he swung Hedley Verity away on the legside and was unlucky enough to dislodge a bail with his left pad. Four weeks later, in the fifth Test, at The Oval, Ponsford ran up another big score, this time 266, before he awkwardly tried to avoid a short ball from Gubby Allen … and trod on his wicket.

Handled the ball: Alan Hurst's mankad of Sikander in Perth in 1978–79 hardly amused the Pakistanis, and left Australia needing 236 to win. The run-chase reached 0–87, when an errant throw back to the bowler's end fell at the feet of Australian opener Andrew Hilditch, who picked it up and lobbed it towards the bowler, Sarfraz Nawaz. In a cricket moment that looked plain ugly, Sarfraz ignored the gesture and instead launched an animated appeal. Umpire Tony Crafter had no alternative but to give Hilditch out handled the ball, even though the circumstances were hardly what the rulemakers had in mind when they drafted the relevant law.

In Chennai in 2001, Steve Waugh used a free hand to keep the ball away from his stumps and became the second Australian to be given out handled the ball in Test cricket.

Obstructing the Field: No one has ever been given out in this manner in a Test involving Australia but a couple of men might have been lucky. In the second Test of 1894–95, Australian batsman Charlie Turner's bat blocked a throw from Bill Lockwood as Turner struggled to make good his ground. Lockwood for one thought Turner did this deliberately and mounted a spirited appeal, but the umpire ruled in Turner's favour.

In the fourth Test of 1928–29, Wally Hammond miscued a relatively easy catch back up the wicket. All the bowler, Clarrie Grimmett, had to do was move a few paces to his right, but he found his path blocked by the non-striker, Douglas Jardine, who refused to budge and the ball dropped innocently to the ground. No one appealed against Jardine, but Grimmett later claimed that the umpire told him that if he had, *Hammond* would have been given out, obstructing the field.

Timed Out: The 'timed out' law is designed to prevent batsmen wasting too many seconds after a wicket has fallen and has never been needed in Tests, but after the infamous 'aluminium bat' incident at the WACA in 1979–80, cricket administrators might have been tempted to broaden its scope.

Dennis Lillee came out to bat with a piece of metal rather than willow, and when the umpires said he couldn't do so, the great fast bowler wasted 10 minutes arguing with captains and officials before the offending bat was thrown away and the cricket was finally allowed to continue.

Hit the Ball Twice: Again, this law has never been used in Test matches, but in a sense Steve Waugh had to hit the ball at least twice before he was dismissed in Australia's second innings of the fourth Test of 2002–03.

In one of the stranger moments in Ashes cricket history, Waugh clearly edged a Steve Harmison riser through to the keeper, James Foster. But no one appealed, at least not until 30 seconds had passed and a replay had been shown on the MCG scoreboard. Next ball, Waugh was brilliantly caught by Nasser Hussain in the covers, but that was a no-ball, and he went on to make 14 before finally edging Andy Caddick into the slip cordon.

10 LONGEST SEQUENCES WITHOUT A WIN

Rank	Tests	From	To	Losses	Draws	Ties	Captain(s)
1.	14	4 Dec 1985	28 Dec 1986	4	9	1	Border
2.	11	27 Jan 1970	13 Jun 1972	7	4	–	Lawry (9), I Chappell (2)
3=.	9	15 Jun 1926	8 Feb 1929	5	4	–	Collins (3), Bardsley (2), Ryder (4)
3=.	9	7 Mar 1984	27 Dec 1984	6	3	–	Hughes (7), Border (2)
5.	8	15 Oct 1964	11 May 1965	3	5	–	Simpson
6=.	7	29 Jan 1953	19 Aug 1953	2	5	–	Hassett
6=.	7	25 Mar 1885	15 Feb 1888	7	–	–	Horan (1), Scott (3), McDonnell (3)
6=.	7	16 Sep 1979	5 Dec 1979	2	5	–	Hughes (6), G Chappell (1)
9=.	6	15 Sep 1988	29 Dec 1988	4	2	–	Border
9=.	6	28 Mar 1892	3 Jan 1895	4	2	–	Blackham (5), Giffen (1)

In this and the previous three Top 10s, the 'From' date refers to the date when the first result of the streak occurred and the 'To' date refers to the date when the final result of the streak occurred.

The longest run of consecutive drawn Tests involving Australia is five — the three home Tests against India in 1985–86, followed by the first two Tests of the series in New Zealand that followed soon after.

10 LOWEST HIGHEST SCORES IN A COMPLETED INNINGS

Rank	Score	Batsman	Inns Total	Versus	Venue	Series
1.	10	Tom Garrett	42	England	Sydney	1887–88
2.	15	George Palmer	68	England	The Oval	1886
3.	16	Tom McKibbin	44	England	The Oval	1896
4.	17	Jack Blackham	63	England	The Oval	1882
5=.	18	Victor Trumper	36	England	Birmingham	1902
5=.	18	Graham Yallop	94	West Indies	Port-of-Spain	1978
5=.	18*	Doug Walters	83	India	Melbourne	1980–81
8.	19	Jack Lyons	91	England	The Oval	1893
9=.	20	Tom Horan	104	England	Melbourne	1876–77
9=.	20*	Jack Ferris	62	England	Lord's	1888
9=.	20	David Boon & Allan Border	114	West Indies	Melbourne	1988–89
9=.	20	Ricky Ponting	104	England	The Oval	1997

In the first Ashes Test of 1950–51, Lindsay Hassett declared Australia's second innings closed at 7–32, in order to get England back in on a sticky Brisbane wicket. Neil Harvey (12) was the only batsmen to reach double figures. In 1953, at Manchester during the following Ashes series in England, rain restricted the match to just 13 hours and 50 minutes.

Australia found themselves starting their second innings (the third innings of the Test) late on the fifth day and collapsed to 8–35, with Hassett and Jim de Courcy equal 'top' score with 8.

More positively, there are two instances in Test cricket where all 11 Australian batsmen have reached double figures. In the fifth Test against India in 1947–48, Doug Ring was the lowest scorer with 11. Don Bradman had retired hurt on 57, and last pair Len Johnson (25 not out) and Bill Johnston (23 not out) were unconquered when Bradman declared the innings closed at 8–575. In Australia's second innings total of 471 all out against Sri Lanka in Colombo in 1992, no batsman made more than David Boon's 68. Mike Whitney (10 not out) was the lowest scorer, while Ian Healy's 12 was the lowest score achieved by a dismissed batsman.

In the third Ashes Test of 2002–03, in Perth, Australia were all out for 456, Damien Martyn top scoring with 71, Justin Langer the lowest scorer of the dismissed batsmen with 19, and Glenn McGrath undefeated on 8. Eleven months earlier, Australia were dismissed for 554 in their first innings, with the lowest dismissed batsman being Ricky Ponting, run out for 14. McGrath was unbeaten on 1.

10 HIGHEST NUMBER OF PLAYERS USED BY AUSTRALIA IN A SERIES

Rank	Players	Tests	Versus	Series	Debuts	Result
1.	28	5	England	1884-85	11	L 2-3
2.	22	5	England	1894-95	9	L 2-3
3.	20	5	England	1928-29	10	L 1-4
4=	19	5	South Africa	1931-32	7	W 5-0
4=	19	5	England	1932-33	6	L 1-4
4=	19	5	India	1977-78	12	W 3-2
4=	19	5	West Indies	1984-85	4	L 1-3
4=	19	5	West Indies	1988-89	2	L 1-3
4=	19	6	England	1970-71	9	L 0-2
10=	18	3	West Indies	1979-80	1	L 0-2
10=	18	5	England	1936-37	5	W 3-2
10=	18	5	India	1947-48	5	W 4-0
10=	18	5	England	1965-66	3	D 1-1

These series were all in Australia. The most players used by Australia in a series overseas is 17, in five Tests v West Indies in 1984, when most changes were caused by injuries to senior players. The most debuts by Australian players in one series is 14, in the two Tests of 1876–77, the first two Tests ever played, when three changes were made for the rematch. The next highest number of Australian debuts in one series is 12, against India in 1977–78, when the advent of World Series Cricket led to Bob Simpson making a comeback and Wayne Clark, Paul Hibbert, Tony Mann, David Ogilvie, Steve Rixon, Peter Toohey, John Dyson, Sam Gannon, Ian Callen, Rick Darling, Graeme Wood and Bruce Yardley gaining baggy green caps.

The most consecutive Tests without a debut is 17, starting with the fifth Ashes Test of 2001 (Simon Katich having made his first Test appearance in the previous Test), and continuing until the third Ashes Test, in 2002–03 (Martin Love then made his debut in the fourth Test).

The smallest number of players used by Australia in a five-Test or six-Test series is 12, which has happened five times as follows:

Players	Tests	Versus	Series	Debuts	Result
12	6	England	1989	1	W 4–0
12	5	South Africa	1910–11	2	W 4–1
12	5	South Africa	1935–36	2	W 4–0
12	5	South Africa	1949–50	2	W 4–0
12	5	England	1964	2	W 1–0

Australia has used 13 players in a five-Test or six-Test series 12 times.

The occasion of the fewest Australian players appearing in a four-Test series came in the Caribbean in 1995 when the line-up of Slater, Taylor (c), Boon, Waugh, Waugh, Blewett, Healy, Julian, Reiffel, Warne, McGrath played in every Test. Even the Australian batting order was fundamentally unchanged through this series: the only alteration being that Taylor took the first delivery in the second innings of each of the first three Tests (Australia batted once in the deciding fourth Test).

There have been 11 occasions when the same Australian XI has played in each match of a three-Test series, including twice by the same team: at home against New Zealand in 2001–02 and then in South Africa in early 2002. The line-up that appeared in both those series — Hayden, Langer, Ponting, Waugh, Waugh, Martyn, Gilchrist, Warne, Lee, Gillespie, McGrath — actually played in nine of 11 Tests between the fifth Ashes Test of 2001 and the Test in Colombo against Pakistan in 2002. The only team changes in that time came in the Boxing Day Test against South Africa in Melbourne, when Andy Bichel replaced Jason Gillespie, and in the following match in Sydney, when Stuart MacGill came in for Bichel.

In the 1989 Ashes series, the XI of Marsh, Taylor, Boon, Border, Jones, S. Waugh, Healy, Hohns, Hughes, Lawson and Alderman remained unchanged for the final five Tests. Greg Campbell had played instead of Trevor Hohns in the first Test.

CHAPTER SEVEN

AROUND THE GROUNDS

It's quite remarkable how cricketers develop affinities with different grounds. How do you explain how Don Bradman was so phenomenal at the Melbourne Cricket Ground, but rarely at his best in Test matches in Sydney? Why is it that Allan Border was never able to get a Test hundred in Sydney, or that Merv Hughes was a bigger wicket-taker than Dennis Lillee at the WACA? Can you name the Australian bowler who took 20 Test wickets at the Gabba at the extraordinary average of 6.50? Why have the best five innings figures in a Test in Sydney been achieved by Englishmen?

We haven't set out to answer all these questions here, merely to list the top batting and bowling performances at each of the six major Australian Test grounds. As a bonus, each ABC 'ball by ball' commentator from the six Australian states has taken the time to list his Top 10 moments from 'his' ground. What we sought here were very personal lists, restricted to moments the commentators witnessed, either as young cricket fans or later as commentators. Thus, for example, you won't find Melbourne's Dan Lonergan including Charlie Bannerman's first-up century among his Top 10 Moments at the MCG, but you will find the first time he ventured to a cricket Test at the ground, as a youngster among more than 85,000 on a hot and exciting Boxing Day in the mid 1970s.

We are extremely grateful for the support of the six callers — Dan, Gerry Collins, Jim Maxwell, Glenn Mitchell, Peter Newlinds and Roger Wills. What their lists underline is the fact that just about every Australian summer, something magical occurs at one or more of Australia's Test-match venues.

ADELAIDE

TOP PERFORMANCES AT THE ADELAIDE OVAL

10 LEADING RUN-SCORERS

Rank	Batsman	Runs	Tests	Inns	NO	HS	Avge
1.	Allan Border	1415	16	29	5	205	58.96
2.	Steve Waugh	984	14	24	2	170	44.73
3.	Don Bradman	970	7	11	2	299*	107.78
4.	David Boon	920	12	23	3	135	46.00
5.	Mark Waugh	837	12	23	2	138	39.86
6.	Mark Taylor	811	11	21	1	169*	40.55
7.	Bob Simpson	805	6	11	–	225	73.18
8.	Clem Hill	714	6	11	–	160	64.91
9.	Kim Hughes	676	7	13	–	213	52.00
10.	Ian Chappell	666	9	15	–	196	44.40

10 HIGHEST SCORES BY AUSTRALIANS

Rank	Score	Batsman	Versus	Series
1.	299*	Don Bradman	South Africa	1931–32
2.	225	Bob Simpson	England	1965–66
3.	216	Dean Jones	West Indies	1988–89
4.	214*	Victor Trumper	South Africa	1910–11
5.	213	Kim Hughes	India	1980–81
6.	212	Don Bradman	England	1936–37
7.	206	Arthur Morris	England	1950–51
8.	205	Allan Border	New Zealand	1987–88
9=.	201*	Jack Ryder	England	1924–25
9=.	201	Don Bradman	India	1947–48

The only other batsman to make a double century in an Adelaide Test is South Africa's Eddie Barlow, who made 201 in 1963–64.

Arthur Morris' 206 in 1950–51, made in an innings in which no other Australian scored more than 44, was his third century in three Ashes Test innings at the Adelaide Oval, following on his double of 122 and 124 not out in 1946–47. It was also the first double century by an Australian left-hander in Test matches.

10 LEADING WICKET-TAKERS

Rank	Bowler	Wickets	Tests	Balls	Mdns	Runs	Avge	Best
1.	Dennis Lillee	45	9	2479	63	1206	26.80	6–171
2.	Craig McDermott	42	8	2325	98	1162	27.67	5–76
3.	Shane Warne	41	10	2908	134	1188	28.98	5–113
4.	Glenn McGrath	35	7	1773	87	708	20.23	4–41
5.	Clarrie Grimmett	34	4	2097	96	769	22.62	7–83
6.	Richie Benaud	27	6	2134	54	890	32.96	5–91
7=	Bill Johnston	25	4	1531	46	500	20.00	6–62
7=	Ashley Mallett	25	6	1673	55	656	26.24	8–59
9=	Jeff Thomson	24	6	864	18	504	21.00	4–68
9=	Merv Hughes	24	7	1563	56	843	35.13	5–64

10 BEST INNINGS BOWLING FIGURES BY AUSTRALIANS

Rank	Figures	Bowler	Versus	Series
1.	8–43	Albert Trott	England	1894–95
2.	8–59	Ashley Mallett	Pakistan	1972–73
3.	8–112	Geoff Lawson	West Indies	1984–85
4.	7–38	Ray Lindwall	India	1947–48
5.	7–83	Clarrie Grimmett	South Africa	1931–32
6.	7–87	Clarrie Grimmett	West Indies	1930–31
7.	7–89	Mike Whitney	West Indies	1988–89
8.	7–116	Clarrie Grimmett	South Africa	1931–32
9.	6–48	Graham McKenzie	England	1965–66
10.	6–62	Bill Johnston	West Indies	1951–52

India's Kapil Dev (8–106 in 1985–86) and England's Jack 'Farmer' White (8–126 in 1928–29) are the two overseas bowlers to take eight wickets in a Test innings at the Adelaide Oval. Two more, South Africa's Shaun Pollock (7–87 in 1997–98) and England's Derek Underwood (7–113 in 1974–75), have seven wickets in a Test innings there.

10 QUOTES ABOUT GREAT AUSTRALIAN CRICKETERS

10. If I had one ball hanging between me and death, I'd give it to Alan Davidson.'

— *Bob Simpson, quoted in Howzat (1979), by Keith Butler.*

HIGHEST AUSTRALIAN PARTNERSHIPS FOR EACH WICKET

Wkt	Runs	Batsmen	Versus	Series
1st	244	Bob Simpson/Bill Lawry	England	1965-66
2nd	275	Colin McDonald/Lindsay Hassett	South Africa	1952-53
3rd	242	Ricky Ponting/Damien Martyn	England	2002-03
4th	214	Dean Jones/Allan Border	West Indies	1988-89
5th	239	Steve Waugh/Ricky Ponting	India	1999-00
6th	171	Mark Waugh/Greg Matthews	England	1990-91
7th	168	Rod Marsh/Kerry O'Keeffe	New Zealand	1973-74
8th	243	Roger Hartigan/Clem Hill	England	1907-08
9th	114	Dean Jones/Merv Hughes	West Indies	1988-89
10th	81	Albert Trott/Syd Callaway	England	1894-95

OPINION
ROGER WILLS' 10 FAVOURITE MOMENTS FROM TEST CRICKET AT THE ADELAIDE OVAL

1. West Indies beat Australia by one run, fourth Test, 1992–93
2. Mark Waugh's debut century, first day, fourth Ashes Test, 1990–91
3. Greg Blewett's debut century, fourth day, fourth Ashes Test, 1994–95
4. Australia level the series v South Africa, final day, third Test, 1993–94
5. Dean Jones scores a century in both innings, second Test v Pakistan, 1989–90
6. Australia wins by 38 runs, fourth Test v India, 1991–92
7. Mark Waugh not given out hit wicket, final day, third Test v South Africa, 1997–98
8. Allan Border breaks Australian run-scoring record, second Test v New Zealand, 1987–88
9. Michael Bevan takes 10 wickets and scores 85, fourth Test v West Indies, 1996–97
10. Glenn McGrath catches Michael Vaughan as Australia wins the Ashes, third Test, 2002–03

The best Test finish I've witnessed occurred in Adelaide on Australia Day 1993, a one-run West Indies victory that denied Allan Border his last chance of regaining the Frank Worrell Trophy. A personal memory is of standing for 90 minutes next to the South Australian Cricket Association's match office, where I'd gone to prepare for post-match interviews after Australia fell to 8–102 needing 185. Then the drama unfolded — first the Justin Langer–Tim May partnership that took the score to 9–144, then the May–Craig McDermott stand that brought Australia to the edge of victory.

Over the final overs the crowd of around 12,000 stood and applauded every run, and when McDermott was given out they slumped and sagged, and then rose as one to applaud both teams after one of the great Test matches.

Mark Waugh's classy, stylish century on debut gave more than a hint of the pleasure he would provide in international cricket. When Greg Blewett made his maiden ton, I sat, armed with a radio mike, with his parents as he slowly worked his way through the 90s — nail-biting emotion! (The next day Devon Malcolm bowled like the wind and after England won the Barmy Army went positively barmy, swarming on to the ground to celebrate in front of the visitors' dressing room.)

The Test against South Africa in January 1994 was notable for many things. It was Hansie Cronje's first Test as captain, having taken over from the injured Kepler Wessels. It was also Allan Border's last Test in Australia, during which he scored his 11,000th Test run, and the game in which Shane Warne took his 100th Test wicket. And Steve Waugh ground out 164, and then took 4–26 to win not only the man-of-the-match award but the man-of-the-series trophy, too, despite the fact he'd missed the first two Tests through injury.

Dean Jones had to make his second century in 1989–90 on a spinning wicket to save the game, and because Imran Khan and Wasim Akram had both scored magnificent hundreds in Pakistan's second innings. Two years later, India's captain, Mohammad Azharuddin, made a superb 106, sweeping regularly against the spin of Warne (who was playing in just his second Test) before Craig McDermott took four wickets with the second new ball to give Australia a narrow victory. This was the first result I'd witnessed in a Test in Adelaide, after six draws from December 1985 to January 1991.

I was standing on the concourse at square-leg on the last day of the South Africa Test in January 1998, when Mark Waugh lost control of his bat and knocked off the bails — we all turned to wait for the video umpire Steve Davis' ultimate correct decision. Not out was the call and Waugh's uncharacteristically defensive century saved the Test. By the time of the post-match press conference Cronje had regained his composure, but earlier he'd apparently vented his frustration by belting the wall of the team's dressing room with a stump.

Border passed Greg Chappell's Australian record runs aggregate in searing heat on the way to 205 in 1987–88. That achievement was much more predictable than Michael Bevan's astonishing all-round performance against the Windies, and Glenn McGrath's brilliant catch to dismiss Michael Vaughan. Another memory that will stick with me from the 2002–03 Ashes Test is Andy Bichel's inspired spell on the Sunday evening, which included the dismissal of the England captain Nasser Hussain with a stunning yorker.

BRISBANE

TOP PERFORMANCES AT THE GABBA

10 LEADING RUN-SCORERS

Rank	Batsman	Runs	Tests	Inns	NO	HS	Avge
1.	Greg Chappell	1006	7	11	2	201	111.78
2.	Mark Taylor	912	10	18	2	164	57.00
3.	Steve Waugh	859	16	24	3	147*	40.90
4.	Allan Border	779	15	22	1	152*	37.10
5.	David Boon	750	12	20	–	143	37.50
6.	Don Bradman	736	5	7	–	226	105.14
7.	Bill Lawry	710	6	11	1	166	71.00
8=.	Ian Healy	689	11	17	4	161*	53.00
8=.	Mark Waugh	689	11	16	1	140	45.93
10.	Michael Slater	675	6	9	1	176	84.38

Don Bradman played three innings at the Exhibition Ground, for scores of 18, 1 and 223, giving him a Test aggregate in Brisbane of 978, at 97.80.

10 HIGHEST SCORES BY AUSTRALIANS

Rank	Score	Batsman	Versus	Series
1.	226	Don Bradman	South Africa	1931–32
2.	207	Keith Stackpole	England	1970–71
3.	201	Greg Chappell	Pakistan	1981–82
4.	197	Matthew Hayden	England	2002–03
5.	187	Don Bradman	England	1946–47
6.	185	Don Bradman	India	1947–48
7.	181	Norm O'Neill	West Indies	1960–61
8.	176	Michael Slater	England	1994–95
9=.	169	Brian Booth	South Africa	1963–64
9=.	169	Michael Slater	Pakistan	1999–00

Don Bradman scored 223 against the West Indies at the Brisbane Exhibition Ground in 1930–31. England's 'Patsy' Hendren scored 169 in an Ashes Test at that venue two years earlier. These were the only two Tests played in Brisbane away from the Woolloongabba Ground, better known as 'The Gabba'.

New Zealand's Martin Crowe scored 188 at the Gabba in 1985–86.

10 LEADING WICKET-TAKERS

Rank	Bowler	Wickets	Tests	Balls	Mdns	Runs	Avge	Best
1=	Glenn McGrath	51	10	2577	128	1131	22.18	6-17
1=	Shane Warne	51	8	2643	139	1071	21.00	8-71
3.	Craig McDermott	40	8	1887	69	905	22.63	6-53
4.	Dennis Lillee	31	6	1175	35	625	20.16	6-53
5.	Jeff Thomson	29	6	1396	30	697	24.03	6-46
6=	Geoff Lawson	28	6	1240	47	545	19.46	6-47
6=	Merv Hughes	28	6	1285	53	608	21.71	4-50
8.	Richie Benaud	23	5	1895	64	603	26.22	6-115
9.	Ray Lindwall	21	6	1111	30	358	17.05	5-60
10=	Ernie Toshack	20	2	455	20	130	6.50	6-29
10=	Bruce Reid	20	4	1032	36	443	22.15	5-112

Richard Hadlee took 21 wickets in three Tests in Brisbane, at 16.33.

10 BEST INNINGS BOWLING FIGURES BY AUSTRALIANS

Rank	Figures	Bowler	Versus	Series
1.	8-71	Shane Warne	England	1994-95
2.	7-23	Shane Warne	Pakistan	1995-96
3.	7-60	Keith Miller	England	1946-47
4.	6-17	Glenn McGrath	West Indies	2000-01
5.	6-29	Ernie Toshack	India	1947-48
6.	6-46	Jeff Thomson	England	1974-75
7=	6-47	Geoff Lawson	England	1982-83
7=	6-47	Terry Alderman	England	1990-91
9=	6-53	Dennis Lillee	New Zealand	1980-81
9=	6-53	Craig McDermott	England	1994-95

Richard Hadlee took 9–52 for New Zealand in 1985–86; England's Bill Voce took 6–41 in 1936–37; Harold Larwood took 6–32 for England at the Exhibition Ground in 1928–29.

10 QUOTES ABOUT GREAT AUSTRALIAN CRICKETERS

9. 'For sheer audacity, I have never seen its equal.'
   – *Jack Hobbs after the 1930 Ashes series, talking about Charlie Macartney's hundred before lunch at Leeds in 1926.*

HIGHEST AUSTRALIAN PARTNERSHIPS FOR EACH WICKET

Wkt	Runs	Batsmen	Versus	Series
1st	269	Michael Slater/Greg Blewett	Pakistan	1999-00
2nd	272	Matthew Hayden/Ricky Ponting	England	2002-03
3rd	276	Don Bradman/Lindsay Hassett	England	1946-47
4th	170	Graham Yallop/Kim Hughes	England	1978-79
5th	187	Bill Lawry/Doug Walters	England	1965-66
6th	197	Allan Border/Greg Matthews	New Zealand	1985-86
7th	142*	Steve Waugh/Shane Warne	New Zealand	1993-94
8th	135	Adam Gilchrist/Brett Lee	New Zealand	2001-02
9th	55	Doug Walters/Alan Connolly	India	1967-68
10th	86	Shane Warne/Scott Muller	Pakistan	1999-00

OPINION

GERRY COLLINS' 10 FAVOURITE MOMENTS FROM TEST CRICKET AT THE GABBA

1. Tied Test, first Test v West Indies, 1960–61
2. Doug Walters 155 on debut, third day, first Ashes Test, 1965–66
3. Ian Healy scores 161 not out and 45 not out, first Test v West Indies, 1996–97
4. Courtney Walsh's hat-trick, third day, first West Indies–Australia Test, 1988–89
5. Matthew Hayden, Justin Langer, Adam Gilchrist all score centuries, first Test v New Zealand, 2001–02
6. Matthew Hayden's 197, first and second days, first Ashes Test, 2002–03
7. Glenn McGrath's 6–17 and 4–10 match double, first Test v West Indies, 2000–01
8. Ian Healy 134, Steve Waugh 112, first and second days, first Ashes Test, 1998–99
9. Shane Warne's 8–71, final day, first Ashes Test, 1994–95
10. Steve Waugh 147 not out, Allan Border 105, third day, third Test v New Zealand, 1993–94

I did not move to Brisbane until I was transferred here with the ABC in 1987, hence the list is dominated by recent achievements. However, I've included the Tied Test and Doug Walters' debut century because they stand out deeply in my early memories of Test cricket. The Tied Test is still talked about constantly in Brisbane, to the point that I can now easily imagine being there.

I come from Raymond Terrace, a small town in the Hunter Valley not far from Dungog (where Walters was born and raised) in New South Wales, and the interest in young Doug when he first emerged was immense. There was much celebrating throughout the Hunter when he started his Test career with a century at the Gabba.

I interviewed a young Courtney Walsh after his hat-trick in 1988 and was taken by his humility and casual attitude to his achievement. Walsh's feat was spread over two innings: Tony Dodemaide with the last ball of Australia's first innings, then Michael Veletta and Graeme Wood with his first two balls, bowling first change, in the second innings two days later.

The performances of local stars, Ian Healy and Matt Hayden, in scoring centuries in front of their home crowd were special. Healy's superb unbeaten 161 in late 1996 meant that he was the first Queensland-born player to achieve a century at the Gabba. Five years later, Hayden's wonderful partnership of 224 with Justin Langer against New Zealand was magnificent for the understanding the pair had developed and the mateship that was evident as they shared each other's glory.

To have seen Glenn McGrath and Shane Warne, two of Australia's greatest ever bowlers, perform so well on the Gabba has also been a huge thrill. McGrath's 10-wicket haul for the match in 2000 and Warne's 8–71 in 1994 were both special. In the same Ashes Test that Warne bowled so well, Michael Slater and Mark Waugh scored impressive centuries and Craig McDermott, on his home ground, claimed 6–85 in the first innings.

We have been fortunate in Brisbane to host the first Test match for most seasons and the atmosphere on the first day is always very special. The Gabba, with its unique Australian name, will always have a special place in the hearts of Aussie cricket fans, including mine.

HOBART

TOP PERFORMANCES AT BELLERIVE OVAL

10 LEADING RUN-SCORERS

Rank	Batsman	Runs	Tests	Inns	NO	HS	Avge
1.	Mark Taylor	405	4	7	1	123	67.50
2.	Michael Slater	365	3	5	–	168	73.00
3=.	Justin Langer	309	2	3	–	127	103.00
3=.	Mark Waugh	309	5	8	–	111	38.63
5.	Steve Waugh	272	6	10	3	134*	38.86
6.	Greg Blewett	230	3	6	–	99	38.33
7.	Adam Gilchrist	194	2	3	1	149*	97.00
8.	David Boon	181	3	5	–	106	36.20
9.	Allan Border	169	2	3	–	85	56.33
10.	Ricky Ponting	161	3	4	1	157*	53.67

The leading aggregate by an overseas batsman at Bellerive Oval is 197 (average 49.25) by Pakistan's Inzamam-ul-Haq.

10 HIGHEST SCORES BY AUSTRALIANS

Rank	Score	Batsman	Versus	Series
1.	168	Michael Slater	New Zealand	1993–94
2.	157*	Ricky Ponting	New Zealand	2001–02
3.	149*	Adam Gilchrist	Pakistan	1999–00
4.	134*	Steve Waugh	Sri Lanka	1989–90
5.	127	Justin Langer	Pakistan	1999–00
6=.	123	Mark Taylor	Pakistan	1995–96
6=.	123	Justin Langer	New Zealand	2001–02
8.	118*	Dean Jones	Sri Lanka	1989–90
9.	114	Matthew Elliott	New Zealand	1997–98
10.	111	Mark Waugh	New Zealand	1993–94

The two batsmen to make Test centuries against Australia in Hobart are New Zealand's Matthew Horne (133 in 1997–98) and Pakistan's Inzamam-ul-Haq (118 in 1999–00).

10 LEADING WICKET-TAKERS

Rank	Bowler	Wickets	Tests	Balls	Mdns	Runs	Avge	Best
1.	Shane Warne	24	5	1074	44	461	19.21	6–31
2.	Glenn McGrath	13	3	693	39	274	21.08	5–61
3.	Paul Reiffel	11	3	449	21	195	17.73	4–38
4.	Merv Hughes	8	1	320	14	156	19.50	5–88
5.	Tim May	7	1	339	23	110	15.71	5–65
6=	Greg Campbell	5	1	336	17	143	28.60	3–102
6=	Peter Sleep	5	1	276	20	99	19.80	3–26
6=	Steve Waugh	5	6	258	12	100	20.00	3–20
9=	Craig McDermott	4	2	396	20	181	45.25	2–72
9=	Damien Fleming	4	1	323	12	143	35.75	2–54
9=	Scott Muller	4	1	174	3	131	32.75	3–68

10 BEST INNINGS BOWLING FIGURES BY AUSTRALIANS

Rank	Figures	Bowler	Versus	Series
1.	6–31	Shane Warne	New Zealand	1993–94
2.	5–61	Glenn McGrath	Pakistan	1995–96
3.	5–65	Tim May	New Zealand	1993–94
4=	5–88	Merv Hughes	Sri Lanka	1989–90
4=	5–88	Shane Warne	New Zealand	1997–98
6.	5–110	Shane Warne	Pakistan	1999–00
7.	4–38	Paul Reiffel	Pakistan	1995–96
8.	3–20	Steve Waugh	New Zealand	1997–98
9.	3–26	Peter Sleep	Sri Lanka	1989–90
10.	3–36	Shane Warne	New Zealand	1993–94

The only bowlers besides Warne to take six wickets in one Test innings at Bellerive are Pakistan's Saqlain Mushtaq, who took 6–46 against Pakistan in 1999–00, and Sri Lanka's Ravi Ratnayake, who took 6–66 in 1989–90.

10 QUOTES ABOUT GREAT AUSTRALIAN CRICKETERS

8. 'Border continues to be the backbone of nearly every Australian innings. Here he did nothing flash — he never does. His greatness lies in the frequency with which he makes vital runs for his team. His Test record is superb, and hard earned ...'

— Peter Roebuck, in his book of the 1986-87 Australia-England series,
Ashes to Ashes, writing after the second Test

HIGHEST AUSTRALIAN PARTNERSHIPS FOR EACH WICKET

Wkt	Runs	Batsmen	Versus	Series
1st	223	Justin Langer/Matthew Hayden	New Zealand	2001–02
2nd	235	Michael Slater/David Boon	New Zealand	1993–94
3rd	67	Mark Taylor/Merv Hughes	Sri Lanka	1989–90
4th	163	Mark Taylor/Allan Border	Sri Lanka	1989–90
5th	44	Mark Taylor/Greg Blewett	Pakistan	1995–96
6th	260*	Dean Jones/Steve Waugh	Sri Lanka	1989–90
7th	145	Ricky Ponting/Shane Warne	New Zealand	2001–02
8th	77	Ricky Ponting/Brett Lee	New Zealand	2001–02
9th	47	Mark Waugh/Michael Kasprowicz	New Zealand	1997–98
10th	23	Shane Warne/Glenn McGrath	Pakistan	1995–96

OPINION

PETER NEWLINDS' 10 FAVOURITE MOMENTS FROM TEST CRICKET AT BELLERIVE OVAL

1. The first Test at Hobart, second Test v Sri Lanka, 1989–90
2. Dean Jones and Steve Waugh put on 260, third and fourth days, second Test v Sri Lanka, 1989–90
3. David Boon first local to score a Test century in Hobart, first day, second Test v Sri Lanka, 1993–94
4. Mark Taylor scores 123, third day, second Test v Pakistan, 1995–96
5. Third Test v New Zealand goes down to the final ball, 1997–98
6   Waqar Younis bowls Ricky Ponting, second day, second Test v Pakistan, 1999–2000
7. Saqlain Mushtaq takes 6–17 in eight overs, second day, second Test v Pakistan, 1999–2000
8. Mark Waugh catches Inzamam-ul-Haq, fourth day, second Test v Pakistan, 1999–2000
9. Justin Langer and Adam Gilchrist add 238, fourth and fifth days, second Test v Pakistan, 1999–2000
10. Australia scores 6–411 on the first day, second Test v New Zealand, 2001–02

The Top 10 moments here are listed chronologically. No. 1 occurred on 16 December 1989, when Tasmanian cricket fans gave an emotional welcome to local legend David Boon as he walked out to bat with Mark Taylor on the first morning of Hobart's inaugural Test. This was a long awaited and extremely proud moment for Tasmanian cricket. Another highlight of the match came in Australia's second innings, when Dean

Jones and Steve Waugh added an unbroken 260 for the sixth wicket from just 346 balls. Has a pair ever run faster or better between the wickets?

Four years later, Test cricket returned to Bellerive, and this time Boon (106) became the first Tasmanian to score a Test century on home soil. Taylor had scored a century in that inaugural Test in '89–90; in 1995–96, at the height of his powers as a player and as a captain, he scored another to help set up a comfortable Australian win. In November '97, a seemingly rain-ruined Test came alive due to the captaincy of Taylor and Stephen Fleming. Set 288 to win in two sessions, New Zealand openers Matthew Horne and Nathan Astle belted 72 runs from the first 52 balls, before Shane Warne took control with a masterful display of defensive slow bowling. Australia eventually had 10.4 overs to claim the last New Zealand wicket, but Shayne O'Connor and Simon Doull hung on. One personal memory of this game is that it was played amid a pall of gloom for Australian sports fans, because on the Saturday evening Iran had knocked Australia out of soccer's World Cup finals in heartbreaking fashion at the MCG.

For a while in 1999–2000 it seemed the efforts of Saqlain and Waqar would lead to a Pakistan victory. For Waqar, it was a return to his 'salad days' of the early '90s, as he produced some stunning fast bowling in Australia's first innings, most notably when he 'Waqared' Ricky Ponting with a 90mph inswinger. This was the first of a pair of ducks for the local boy.

At a crucial stage of this enthralling Test, Inzamam, on 118, cut fiercely at Warne, and got a healthy top edge. The ball flew fast and wide of slip, but Mark Waugh, in a supreme exhibition of his spellbinding reflexes, reached high and wide with his right hand to take a stunning catch. Later in the day, Justin Langer and Adam Gilchrist formed a mighty partnership that eventually secured one of Australia's greatest Test wins. Chasing 369 to win, Australia slumped to 5–126, only for the West Australian pair to bring the home team to the brink of victory. Australia's 6–369 was then the third (now the fourth) highest fourth-innings total made to win a Test match.

The November 2001 Test against New Zealand was a drawn game, severely affected by rain, but still produced an unforgettable first day, as the home team became the first side in 70 years to score 400 runs in a day's play in Australia. Langer was on 59 at the first drinks break, with Matthew Hayden on 2, and the pair went on to add 223 in 198 minutes for the first wicket. Late in the day, Warne and Ponting continued the fun, putting on 75 runs in the closing hour, and the following morning Ponting emulated David Boon by scoring a Test century in his home state.

MELBOURNE

TOP PERFORMANCES AT THE MELBOURNE CRICKET GROUND

10 LEADING RUN-SCORERS

Rank	Batsman	Runs	Tests	Inns	NO	HS	Avge
1.	Don Bradman	1671	11	17	4	270	128.54
2.	Allan Border	1272	20	36	3	163	38.55
3.	Steve Waugh	1265	16	29	6	131	55.00
4.	Greg Chappell	1257	17	31	4	121	46.56
5.	Bill Lawry	1023	8	13	–	205	78.69
6.	Ian Chappell	948	12	19	2	165	55.76
7.	Neil Harvey	947	12	23	2	205	45.10
8.	Warwick Armstrong	918	11	20	5	133*	61.20
9.	Doug Walters	846	11	19	2	115	49.76
10.	Ian Redpath	833	9	16	–	135	52.06

Don Bradman made nine Test hundreds at the MCG, better than one every two innings. He scored at least a century in seven of his nine Melbourne Tests, and did not bat because of injury in one of the two others (v South Africa, 1931–32). Bradman made 'just' 49 and 79 in the third Ashes Test of 1946–47.

England's Jack Hobbs made five Test centuries in Melbourne (second to Bradman) in 10 appearances, and 1178 runs at 69.29.

10 HIGHEST SCORES BY AUSTRALIANS

Rank	Score	Batsman	Versus	Series
1.	307	Bob Cowper	England	1965–66
2.	270	Don Bradman	England	1936–37
3.	268	Graham Yallop	Pakistan	1983–84
4.	250	Justin Langer	England	2002–03
5=	205	Neil Harvey	South Africa	1952–53
5=	205	Bill Lawry	West Indies	1968–69
7.	188	Clem Hill	England	1897–98
8.	170	Mark Taylor	South Africa	1993–94
9.	169	Don Bradman	England	1936–37
10.	168	Gary Cosier	Pakistan	1976–77

There are three instances of overseas batsmen scoring Test double centuries at the MCG. Viv Richards made 208 for the West Indies in 1984–85, Aubrey Faulkner 204 for South Africa in 1910–11, and Wally Hammond an even 200 for England in 1928–29.

10 LEADING WICKET-TAKERS

Rank	Bowler	Wickets	Tests	Balls	Mdns	Runs	Avge	Best
1.	Dennis Lillee	82	14	3833	105	1798	21.93	7-83
2.	Hugh Trumble	46	7	1708	71	646	14.04	7-28
3.	Graham McKenzie	45	7	2370	35	1019	22.64	8-71
4.	Craig McDermott	41	10	2345	84	1201	29.29	5-42
5.	Monty Noble	39	8	1324	55	521	13.36	7-17
6.	Shane Warne	37	8	2305	99	894	24.16	7-52
7=	Bill Johnston	35	8	2247	48	852	24.34	6-152
7=	Bruce Reid	35	4	1144	53	475	13.57	7-51
9.	Alan Davidson	34	5	1646	32	643	18.91	6-53
10.	Bert Ironmonger	33	4	1104	79	283	8.58	7-23

England's Sydney Barnes took 35 wickets at 18.06 in five Tests at the MCG.

10 BEST INNINGS BOWLING FIGURES BY AUSTRALIANS

Rank	Figures	Bowler	Versus	Series
1.	9-121	Arthur Mailey	England	1920-21
2.	8-71	Graham McKenzie	West Indies	1968-69
3.	8-143	Max Walker	England	1974-75
4.	7-17	Monty Noble	England	1901-02
5.	7-23	Bert Ironmonger	West Indies	1930-31
6.	7-28	Hugh Trumble	England	1903-04
7.	7-51	Bruce Reid	England	1990-91
8.	7-52	Shane Warne	West Indies	1992-93
9.	7-55	Tom Kendall	England	1876-77
10.	7-62	Fred Spofforth	England	1878-79

In 1978–79, Pakistan's Sarfraz Nawaz took 9–86, which remain the best figures achieved in a Test at the MCG. Two English bowlers — Wilfred Rhodes (8–68) and Len Braund (8–81) — took eight wickets in a Test innings in 1903–04.

HIGHEST AUSTRALIAN PARTNERSHIPS FOR EACH WICKET

Wkt	Runs	Batsmen	Versus	Series
1st	219	Bill Lawry/Ian Redpath	South Africa	1963–64
2nd	298	Bill Lawry/Ian Chappell	West Indies	1968–69
3rd	249	Don Bradman/Stan McCabe	England	1936–37
4th	177	Allan Border/Kim Hughes	Pakistan	1978–79
5th	223*	Don Bradman/Arthur Morris	India	1947–48
6th	346	Don Bradman/Jack Fingleton	England	1936–37
7th	185	Graham Yallop/Greg Matthews	Pakistan	1983–84
8th	173	Clarence Pellew/Jack Gregory	England	1920–21
9th	100	Bert Hartkopf/Bert Oldfield	England	1924–25
10th	120	Reg Duff/Warwick Armstrong	England	1901–02

OPINION
DAN LONERGAN'S 10 FAVOURITE MOMENTS FROM TEST CRICKET AT THE MCG

1. Dennis Lillee and Max Walker rout England, second day, Centenary Test, 1977
2. Geoff Boycott bowled by Rodney Hogg for 0, second day, third Ashes Test, 1978–79
3. My first Test, first day, third Test v West Indies, 1975–76
4. Kim Hughes scores 100 not out, Lillee takes 3–3, first day, first Test v West Indies, 1981–82
5. Allan Border and Jeff Thomson almost win the fourth Ashes Test, last day, 1982–83
6. Mike Whitney withstands Richard Hadlee, last day, third Test v New Zealand, 1987–88
7. Shane Warne's first great day in Test cricket, last day, second Test v West Indies, 1992–93
8. Shane Warne takes a Test hat-trick, last day, second Ashes Test, 1994–95
9. Graham Yallop hits 268, a great day for Victoria, fourth Test v Pakistan, 1983–84
10. The Barmy Army in full voice, last day, fourth Ashes Test, 2002–03

I was eight years old during the Centenary Test, and the thing I will always remember is the amazing atmosphere as the great DK Lillee and Max Walker led the Australian fightback on the second morning after they'd been bowled out for 138 on the first day. That entire Test was a fantastic occasion. Nearly two years later, and it was the crowd again that stuck with me. World Series Cricket had weakened the Australian team and they had been dismissed early on the second day. Geoff Boycott was booed all the way to the wicket, and my mother was worried that he was 'going to bore us to death', but Rodney Hogg bowled him for a duck and the roar was deafening. Mum then said, as made his way to the pavilion, 'I feel sorry for him now.'

One thing I remember vividly about my first day of Test cricket was that it was hot … but I loved every minute of it. Lillee and Jeff Thomson bowled the Windies out 224, and Australia finished the day at 0–38, well on top, having played in front of a colossal Boxing Day crowd of 85,661. Six years later, Kim Hughes hit what was probably his best Test hundred, before Lillee went through the Windies top order before stumps, including Viv Richards off the last ball of the day. The following year, Thomson was caught in the slips by Geoff Miller after Chris Tavare couldn't hang onto a sharp chance off the bowling of Ian Botham, and Australia lost by three runs. The crowd had been let in for free, and created a tremendous atmosphere, but we were all silent at the end.

What I remember most about the maiden over Mike Whitney played out against Richard Hadlee to end the MCG Test against New Zealand in 1987–88 were Whitney's celebration after he did it. Because of his and Craig McDermott's batting efforts at the death, Australia was able to hang on to draw the Test, win the series and regain the Trans Tasman Trophy. The performances of Shane Warne — most memorably the flipper that dismissed West Indies captain Richie Richardson and announced that he'd 'arrived' in Test cricket, and the hat-trick two seasons later that ran through England's late order — and of Graham Yallop were especially notable because they were locals.

And even though the Barmy Army might be 'imports', the enthusiasm they showed, and especially the way they went berserk as Australia lost early wickets before limping home to take a 4–0 lead in the 2002–03 Ashes series, was in its own way just as outstanding.

PERTH

TOP PERFORMANCES AT THE WACA GROUND

10 LEADING RUN-SCORERS

Rank	Batsman	Runs	Tests	Inns	NO	HS	Avge
1.	Allan Border	931	16	26	3	125	40.48
2.	David Boon	846	11	19	2	200	49.76
3.	Mark Waugh	766	11	16	1	119	51.07
4.	Steve Waugh	765	14	20	2	99*	42.50
5.	Michael Slater	567	6	9	–	219	63.00
6.	Greg Chappell	497	8	13	1	117	41.42
7.	Mark Taylor	490	9	15	1	142*	35.00
8.	Dean Jones	488	5	7	1	150*	81.33
9.	Ian Healy	461	11	15	2	113*	35.46
10.	Ricky Ponting	450	7	8	–	197	56.25

David Gower scored 471 runs in five Tests for England at the WACA, at 52.33.

10 HIGHEST SCORES BY AUSTRALIANS

Rank	Score	Batsman	Versus	Series
1.	219	Michael Slater	Sri Lanka	1995–96
2.	200	David Boon	New Zealand	1989–90
3.	197	Ricky Ponting	Pakistan	1999–00
4.	176	Bob Simpson	India	1977–78
5.	171	Ian Redpath	England	1970–71
6.	159	Wayne B Phillips	Pakistan	1983–84
7.	156	Ian Chappell	West Indies	1975–76
8.	150*	Dean Jones	India	1991–92
9.	144	Justin Langer	Pakistan	1999–00
10.	142*	Mark Taylor	New Zealand	1993–94

Overseas players with scores of more than 150 at the WACA are the West Indies' Roy Fredericks (169 in 1975–76), England's Chris Broad (162, 1986–87) and New Zealand's Nathan Astle (156 not out, 2001–02).

10 LEADING WICKET-TAKERS

Rank	Bowler	Wickets	Tests	Balls	Mdns	Runs	Avge	Best
1.	Merv Hughes	39	6	1618	63	752	19.28	8-87
2=	Craig McDermott	38	8	1781	67	847	22.29	8-97
2=	Glenn McGrath	38	9	2256	104	977	25.71	4-49
4.	Dennis Lillee	30	7	1856	77	817	27.23	5-18
5.	Rodney Hogg	25	5	1240	37	502	20.08	5-57
6.	Shane Warne	23	9	1983	69	980	42.61	4-83
7.	Jeff Thomson	21	5	1097	25	571	27.19	5-93
8=	Brett Lee	20	3	702	19	444	22.20	5-61
8=	Terry Alderman	20	5	1260	62	564	28.20	6-128
10.	Jason Gillespie	19	4	814	27	428	22.53	5-88

Curtly Ambrose (West Indies) has 24 wickets from three Tests, average 12.92.

10 BEST INNINGS BOWLING FIGURES BY AUSTRALIANS

Rank	Figures	Bowler	Versus	Series
1.	8-87	Merv Hughes	West Indies	1988-89
2.	8-97	Craig McDermott	England	1990-91
3.	7-27	Mike Whitney	India	1991-92
4.	6-34	Geoff Dymock	England	1979-80
5.	6-38	Craig McDermott	England	1994-95
6.	6-84	Bruce Yardley	Pakistan	1981-82
7.	6-86	Carl Rackemann	Pakistan	1983-84
8.	6-128	Terry Alderman	West Indies	1984-85
9.	5-18	Dennis Lillee	Pakistan	1981-82
10.	5-32	Carl Rackemann	Pakistan	1983-84

10 QUOTES ABOUT GREAT AUSTRALIAN CRICKETERS

7. Writhing; grimacing; batsmen catching breath
Thought him no mortal man, but very Death;
For no man ever knew what ball would come
From that wild whirl, save one from devildom …'
–John Masefield on what confronted the England batsmen facing Fred Spofforth, from his poem of the 1882 Test at The Oval, Eighty-five to Win *(first published in the London* Times *in 1956).*

HIGHEST AUSTRALIAN PARTNERSHIPS FOR EACH WICKET

Wkt	Runs	Batsmen	Versus	Series
1st	228	Mark Taylor/Michael Slater	Sri Lanka	1995-96
2nd	259	Wayne B Phillips/Graham Yallop	Pakistan	1983-84
3rd	183	Michael Slater/Mark Waugh	England	1994-95
4th	173	Dean Jones/Tom Moody	India	1991-92
5th	327	Justin Langer/Ricky Ponting	Pakistan	1999-00
6th	219	Ian Redpath/Greg Chappell	England	1970-71
7th	116	Ian Healy/Paul Reiffel	New Zealand	1997-98
8th	78	Allan Border/Dennis Lillee	England	1979-80
9th	69	Ian Healy/Craig McDermott	New Zealand	1993-94
10th	59	Geoff Lawson/Terry Alderman	West Indies	1984-85

OPINION
GLENN MITCHELL'S 10 FAVOURITE MOMENTS FROM TEST CRICKET AT THE WACA

1. First ball in Test Cricket at the WACA, second Ashes Test, 1970–71
2. Doug Walters hits a century in a session, second day, second Ashes Test, 1974–75
3. Ross Edwards becomes the first local to score a Test century in Perth, third day, second Ashes Test, 1974–75
4. Terry Alderman injured during a ground invasion, second day, first Ashes Test, 1982–83
5. Curtly Ambrose destroys the Australians, fifth Test v West Indies, 1992–93
6. Merv Hughes' hat-trick, third day, second Test v West Indies, 1988–89
7. Glenn McGrath's hat-trick, first day, second Test v West Indies, 2000–01
8. Roy Fredericks' whirlwind century, second day, second Test v West Indies, 1975–76
9. Dennis Lillee clashes with Javed Miandad, fourth day, first Test v Pakistan, 1981–82
10. The Aluminium Bat incident, second day, first Ashes Test v England, 1979–80

Fittingly, on 11 December 1970, Western Australia's first regular Test representative, Graham McKenzie, had the honour of bowling the first ball of Perth's inaugural Test match to England's Brian Luckhurst. Four years later, another local, Ross Edwards, had the honour of scoring the first Test century by a WA batsman at the WACA, and the privilege of being at the other end as Doug Walters produced one of the great moments in Ashes cricket — clubbing Bob Willis over mid-wicket from the last ball of the day to post his century, and a century in a session. Nobody was happier than me when Ross reached three figures the next day, for he was my childhood hero. Ah, the memories.

The son of a state footballer, Terry Alderman thought he'd chosen a non-contact sport in which to make his name. But after being struck on the head by a ground intruder, he decided to pursue the chap and tackle him to the ground. Alas for the swing king, he badly dislocated his shoulder and spent the next 12 months recuperating. A demolition job of a different kind came a decade later, when Curtly Ambrose produced one of the game's most devastating spells. In the space of 32 deliveries, he captured seven wickets while conceding just a solitary run, and Australia went from 2–85 to all out 119. The West Indies won the match shortly before lunch on the third day, and the curator was fired!

Big Merv Hughes produced one of Test cricket's more unusual hat-tricks. He finished off the West Indian first innings by claiming Curtly Ambrose with the last ball of his 36th over and Patrick Patterson from the first ball of his 37th, and then trapped Gordon Greenidge leg before with the first ball of the Windies' second innings. Glenn McGrath's hat-trick also included his 300th Test wicket, but unfortunately hundreds of fans were denied viewing history as they were stuck outside the ground an hour after play commenced because of problems getting the patrons through the turnstiles.

Roy Fredericks' innings, against a rampant Lillee and Thomson, was one the most exhilarating hundreds ever seen. He cut and hooked his way to a century off just 71 balls, before finally being out for 169. In total contrast, at 3pm on 16 November 1981, Lillee and Javed Miandad became involved in one of the game's more unsavoury moments. After pushing Lillee in an endeavour to reach his ground at the non-striker's end, Miandad was given a light kick on the leg by the Australian fast bowler, and responded by lifting his bat and threatening to swing it at him. Two seasons earlier, Lillee turned his aluminium bat into a javelin and hurled it across the outfield. What looked like a good idea at the time turned into a marketing disaster.

SYDNEY

TOP PERFORMANCES AT THE SYDNEY CRICKET GROUND

10 LEADING RUN-SCORERS

Rank	Batsman	Runs	Tests	Inns	NO	HS	Avge
1.	Allan Border	1177	17	29	8	89	56.05
2.	Greg Chappell	1150	12	22	4	204	63.89
3.	David Boon	1127	11	21	3	184*	62.61
4.	Steve Waugh	903	15	22	1	103	43.00
5.	Doug Walters	900	11	19	2	242	52.94
6.	Clem Hill	824	12	22	–	191	37.45
7.	Victor Trumper	809	10	19	2	185*	47.59
8.	Don Bradman	703	8	12	–	234	58.58
9.	Syd Gregory	690	10	19	2	201	40.59
10.	Mark Waugh	683	11	18	–	121	37.94

Allan Border made 11 Test fifties at the SCG without ever scoring a century.

In five Tests in Sydney before World War II, Don Bradman scored a meagre (by his standards) 381 runs at an average of 47.63. In contrast, England's Wally Hammond made five Test-match appearances in Sydney, scoring 808 runs at 161.60, including two double centuries and two centuries.

10 HIGHEST SCORES BY AUSTRALIANS

Rank	Score	Batsman	Versus	Series
1.	242	Doug Walters	West Indies	1968–69
2=	234	Sid Barnes	England	1946–47
2=	234	Don Bradman	England	1946–47
4.	223	Justin Langer	India	1999–00
5.	204	Greg Chappell	India	1980–81
6.	201	Syd Gregory	England	1894–95
7.	191	Clem Hill	South Africa	1910–11
8.	190	Neil Harvey	South Africa	1952–53
9.	187*	Stan McCabe	England	1932–33
10.	185*	Victor Trumper	England	1903–04

The three highest scores made in Test matches at the SCG have been made against Australia: 287 by England's Reginald Foster in 1903–04, 277 by the

West Indies' Brian Lara in 1992–93 and 251 by England's Wally Hammond in 1928–29. In all, 11 Test double centuries have been made in Sydney, five of them by visiting batsmen. Hammond made 231 not out in 1936–37 and India's Ravi Shastri made 206 (and became Shane Warne's first Test wicket) in 1991–92.

10 LEADING WICKET-TAKERS

Rank	Bowler	Wickets	Tests	Balls	Mdns	Runs	Avge	Best
1.	Shane Warne	49	10	3120	143	1291	26.35	7–56
2.	Charlie Turner	45	6	2106	209	602	13.38	7–43
3.	Dennis Lillee	43	8	2191	61	1036	24.09	4–40
4.	Ray Lindwall	42	8	1968	41	726	17.29	7–63
5.	Richie Benaud	36	10	3136	95	1022	28.39	5–83
6.	Glenn McGrath	34	8	1777	73	796	23.41	5–48
7.	George Giffen	33	7	1427	82	593	17.97	7–117
8.	Fred Spofforth	32	5	1194	122	482	15.06	7–44
9=.	Clarrie Grimmett	31	6	1728	75	673	21.71	6–37
9=.	Stuart MacGill	31	4	1546	59	699	22.55	7–50

England's George Lohmann took 35 wickets at an average of 9.46 in four Tests at the SCG between 1887 and 1892.

10 BEST INNINGS BOWLING FIGURES BY AUSTRALIANS

Rank	Figures	Bowler	Versus	Series
1.	7–43	Charlie Turner	England	1887–88
2.	7–44	Fred Spofforth	England	1882–83
3.	7–46	Allan Border	West Indies	1988–89
4.	7–50	Stuart MacGill	England	1998–99
5.	7–56	Shane Warne	South Africa	1993–94
6.	7–63	Ray Lindwall	England	1946–47
7.	7–68	George Palmer	England	1881–82
8.	7–90	Herbert Hordern	England	1911–12
9.	7–98	Bruce Yardley	West Indies	1981–82
10.	7–100	Monty Noble	England	1903–04

The best five bowling figures returned in a Sydney Test were achieved by overseas bowlers: George Lohmann took 8–35 in 1886–87 and 8–58 five seasons later; Tom Richardson, 8–94 in 1897–98; Dick Barlow, 7–40 in 1882–83; John Snow 7–40 in 1970–71.

Other instances of Australians taking seven wickets in a Test innings in Sydney are MacGill (7–104 v West Indies, 2000–01), Neil Hawke (7–105 v England 1965–66) and George Giffen (7–117 v England 1884–85).

HIGHEST AUSTRALIAN PARTNERSHIPS FOR EACH WICKET

Wkt	Runs	Batsmen	Versus	Series
1st	219	Justin Langer/Matthew Hayden	South Africa	2001–02
2nd	224	Warren Bardsley/Clem Hill	South Africa	1910–11
3rd	193	Joe Darling/Jack Worrall	England	1897–98
4th	336	Bill Lawry/Doug Walters	West Indies	1968–69
5th	405	Sid Barnes/Don Bradman	England	1946–47
6th	187	Warwick Armstrong/Charles Kelleway	England	1920–21
7th	160	Richie Benaud/Graham McKenzie	SouthAfrica	1963–64
8th	154	George Bonnor/Sammy Jones	England	1884–85
9th	154	Syd Gregory/Jack Blackham	England	1894–95
10th	127	Johnny Taylor/Arthur Mailey	England	1924–25

OPINION
JIM MAXWELL'S 10 FAVOURITE MOMENTS FROM TEST CRICKET AT THE SCG

1. Steve Waugh's century, second day, fifth Ashes Test, 2002–03
2. Bob Barber's 185 for England, first day, third Ashes Test, 1965–66
3. Shane Warne's 300th Test wicket, fourth day, second Test v South Africa, 1997–98
4. John Dyson's catch, fourth day, second Test v West Indies, 1981–82
5. Courtney Walsh's reaction to Colin Miller's hair, fifth Test v West Indies, 2000–01
6. Greg Chappell's 182, third day, fifth Test v Pakistan, 1983–84
7. Brian Lara's 277, third and fourth days, third Test v West Indies, 1992–93
8. Bob Massie and John Watkins' ninth-wicket stand, fourth day, third Test v Pakistan, 1972–73
9. Darren Gough's hat-trick, first day, fifth Ashes Test, 1998–99
10. Clive Lloyd's last Test innings, fourth day, fifth Test v West Indies, 1984–85

Steve Waugh reached his hundred, perhaps the most important — on a personal level at least — that he's ever made, by cover driving offspinner Richard Dawson for four from the last ball of the day. It was the climax to an enthralling and dramatic afternoon. The left-handed Bob Barber produced excitement of a different kind, a brilliant innings that lasted for 272 deliveries, on a day in which England reached 1–303 more than an hour before stumps before Neil Hawke was able to dismiss him.

Shane Warne's 300th wicket was Jacques Kallis, bowled by a top-spinner delivered from around the wicket late in the day with the floodlights on. John Dyson's catch in front of The Hill to dismiss Sylvester Clarke was probably the best outfield catch I've seen taken in Sydney, while — if Courtney Walsh's paroxysms of laughter were any indication — Colin Miller's blue rinse was certainly the most outrageous hairstyle.

Greg Chappell's 182 in his final Test innings, during which he went past Sir Donald Bradman's Australian record Test aggregate and also past 7000 runs, was a memorable day, though Brian Lara's 277, the highest Test score on the ground since 1903, was just as stylish. Neither Bob Massie nor Johnny Watkins would put themselves in the batsmanship league of Chappell or Lara, but their partnership of 83 against Pakistan did set up an unlikely win. Darren Gough's hat trick — Ian Healy, Stuart MacGill and Colin Miller — came at the end of a fabulous day's cricket that had already featured a superb century by Mark Waugh and a 96 from Steve Waugh. Clive Lloyd's final innings in Test cricket might not have been a century — he made 78 — but the Sydney crowd made it a memorable one by the manner in which they acknowledged the West Indies captain's enormous contribution to the game.

The quality of this top 10 is best demonstrated by the individual efforts left out: Graeme Pollock's 122 for South Africa in 1963–64; 18-year-old Sachin Tendulkar's 148 for India in 1991–92; Michael Slater's 123 out of 184 scored in Australia's second innings in 1998–99; Doug Walters' then unique double of 242 and 103 against the Windies in 1968–69; the Test debut of 'Peter Who' (Peter Taylor), who responded to his shock selection in 1986–87 by taking six wickets the first time he bowled in Test cricket. There are the close finishes: South Africa by 5 runs in 1993–94, Australia over England in the second-last over in 1986–87, Australia with 35 balls to spare in 1974–75. And the great controversies, most memorably the England walk-off in 1970–71 after Ray Illingworth and John Snow had clashed with umpire Lou Rowan, and Snow had been shoved by a drunken fan in front of the old Paddo hill.

The most popular scores — between 80 and 99 — for dismissals of Australian batsmen are as follows:

Rank	Outs	Score
1=.	22	80
1=.	22	85
3.	20	88
4=.	18	83
4=.	18	89
6=.	17	81
6=.	17	96
6=.	17	99
9=.	16	84
9=.	16	92

Thus, Australian batsmen have been dismissed in Tests for 80 and 85 on more occasions (each 22 times) than for any other score between and including 80 and 99. Next most frequent score is 88 (20 times), then 83, 89 and so on.

Legend has it that an Australian cricketer should be nervous if his score hits 87, but this Top 10 rather strongly suggests otherwise. There are plenty of other scores to worry about. Eighty seven has proved the 'devil's number' for an Australian batsman 12 times in Test cricket, which would put it equal 14th with 98 if we had listed here all the scores from 80 to 99. Only 94 (11 dismissals), 86 and 97 (nine dismissals each), 93 (eight dismissals) and 95 (six dismissals) offer safer havens for a batsman trying to reaching his hundred.

For the record, the Australian batsmen to be dismissed for 87 in Test cricket are: George Bonnor (1882–83), Sammy Jones (1886), Clem Hill (1901–02), Hill again (1907–08), Victor Trumper (1910–11), Jack Ryder (1928–29), Jack Moroney (1949–50), Brian Booth (1963–64), Keith Stackpole (1970–71), John Dyson (1982), Peter Taylor (1990) and Adam Gilchrist (2000–01). Bill Lawry (1963–64) and Michael Bevan (1996–97) have remained 87 not out.

The only Australian to be dismissed for 187 was Don Bradman in the first Ashes Test after World War II. Of course, Stan McCabe's great innings against the bodyline attack in the first Ashes Test of 1932–33 saw him unconquered on 187 not out.

CHAPTER EIGHT

AROUND THE WORLD

Here we focus on Australian performances against the six Test-playing nations against whom Australia has played the most Tests. There are no specific Top 10s relating to Test matches against Sri Lanka, Zimbabwe or Bangladesh, but please don't think that this is a sledge on these countries; there just haven't been sufficient Tests to generate meaningful Top 10s.

Australia played 13 Test matches against Sri Lanka between 1983 and 1999. Ian Healy, with 11, was the Australian with the most appearances in these matches. Four Australians have scored more than 500 runs in these Tests against Sri Lanka, as follows:

Rank	Batsman	Tests	Inns	NO	HS	Runs	Avge
1.	Steve Waugh	8	11	3	170	701	87.63
2.	Mark Taylor	8	15	1	164	611	43.64
3.	Allan Border	7	11	1	106	543	54.30
4.	Dean Jones	6	11	2	118*	537	59.67

No batsman besides Waugh, Border and Jones has played 10 Test innings and averaged 50 or more per innings in these Tests against Sri Lanka.

To the end of that 1999 series, three Australians had bowled in 10 Test innings against Sri Lanka. They were the three leading wicket-takers in Australia–Sri Lanka matches:

Rank	Bowler	Tests	Balls	Mdns	Runs	Wkts	Avge	Best
1=.	Craig McDermott	7	1534	60	735	27	27.22	4-53
1=.	Glenn McGrath	6	1342	54	652	27	24.15	5-40
3.	Shane Warne	8	1554	71	706	23	30.70	5-52

As at 10 September 2003, Australia's only Test against Zimbabwe was the game played at Harare in October 1999, Healy's final Test, an encounter Steve Waugh's team won by 10 wickets. The captain scored 151 not out in Australia's first innings, and received strong support from his twin Mark (90) and No. 9 Damien Fleming (65). Glenn McGrath (6–90 for the match) and Shane Warne (6–147) were the Australians' leading wicket-takers.

The first Tests between Australia and Bangladesh were staged in July 2003, in Darwin and then Cairns, and Australia won both decisively, by an innings. Steve Waugh (100 not out and 156 not out) scored centuries in both matches, making him the only player to achieve an innings of 150 or more against all nine Test-playing nations, and the first man to score Test centuries on seven different grounds in Australia (his highest Test score in Perth being 99 not out). However, Darren Lehmann, with innings of 110 and 177, outscored Waugh to become the leading Australian runscorer in Tests against Bangladesh. The leading wicket-taker for the series was Stuart MacGill, who took 7–86 for the match at Darwin and 10–133 at Cairns.

In the 'leading averages' Top 10s in this chapter, we have set the qualification at 10 innings.

10 LEADING RUN-SCORERS AGAINST ENGLAND

Rank	Batsman	Tests	Inns	NO	Runs	HS	Avge
1.	Don Bradman	37	63	7	5028	334	89.79
2.	Allan Border	47	82	19	3548	200*	56.32
3.	Steve Waugh	46	73	18	3200	177*	58.18
4.	Clem Hill	41	76	1	2660	188	35.47
5.	Greg Chappell	35	65	8	2619	144	45.95
6.	Mark Taylor	33	61	2	2496	219	42.31
7.	Neil Harvey	37	68	5	2416	167	38.35
8.	Victor Trumper	40	74	5	2263	185*	32.80
9.	David Boon	31	57	8	2237	184*	45.65
10.	Bill Lawry	29	51	5	2233	166	48.54

10 LEADING BATTING AVERAGES AGAINST ENGLAND

Rank	Batsman	Tests	Inns	NO	Runs	HS	Avge
1.	Don Bradman	37	63	7	5028	334	89.79
2.	Sid Barnes	9	14	2	846	234	70.50
3.	Adam Gilchrist	10	13	2	673	152	61.18
4.	Steve Waugh	46	73	18	3200	177*	58.18
5.	Justin Langer	11	19	2	961	250	56.53
6.	Allan Border	47	82	19	3548	200*	56.32
7.	Matthew Elliott	6	10	–	556	199	55.60
8.	Damien Martyn	10	15	2	702	118	54.00
9.	Greg Matthews	10	16	5	589	128	53.55
10.	Dean Jones	17	28	2	1320	184*	50.77

10 LEADING WICKET-TAKERS AGAINST ENGLAND

Rank	Bowler	Tests	Balls	Mdns	Runs	Wkts	Avge	Best
1.	Dennis Lillee	29	8516	361	3507	167	21.00	7–89
2.	Hugh Trumble	31	7895	448	2945	141	20.89	8–65
3.	Shane Warne	26	7792	408	3040	132	23.03	8–71
4.	Glenn McGrath	22	5221	244	2344	117	20.03	8–38
5.	Monty Noble	39	6895	353	2860	115	24.87	7–17
6.	Ray Lindwall	29	6728	216	2559	114	22.45	7–63
7.	Clarrie Grimmett	22	9164	427	3439	106	32.44	6–37
8.	George Giffen	31	6391	435	2791	103	27.10	7–117
9.	Bill O'Reilly	19	7864	439	2587	102	25.36	7–54
10.	Charlie Turner	17	5179	457	1670	101	16.53	7–43

10 LEADING BOWLING AVERAGES AGAINST ENGLAND

Rank	Bowler	Tests	Balls	Mdns	Runs	Wkts	Avge	Best
1.	Jack Ferris	8	2030	224	684	48	14.25	5–26
2.	Charlie Turner	17	5179	457	1670	101	16.53	7–43
3.	Rodney Hogg	11	2629	94	952	56	17.00	6–74
4.	Fred Spofforth	18	4185	416	1731	94	18.41	7–44
5=.	Harry Boyle	12	1743	175	641	32	20.03	6–42
5=.	Glenn McGrath	22	5221	244	2344	117	20.03	8–38
7.	Bruce Reid	9	2273	93	959	47	20.40	7–51
8.	Hugh Trumble	31	7895	448	2945	141	20.89	8–65
9.	Dennis Lillee	29	8516	361	3507	167	21.00	7–89
10.	Terry Alderman	17	4717	192	2117	100	21.17	6–47

10 LEADING RUN-SCORERS AGAINST INDIA

Rank	Batsman	Tests	Inns	NO	Runs	HS	Avge
1.	Allan Border	20	35	5	1567	163	52.23
2.	David Boon	11	20	3	1204	135	70.82
3.	Bob Simpson	11	21	–	1125	176	53.57
4.	Kim Hughes	11	21	2	988	213	52.00
5.	Bill Lawry	12	23	4	892	100	46.95
6.	Steve Waugh	14	24	4	823	150	41.15
7.	Neil Harvey	10	13	–	775	153	59.62
8.	Doug Walters	10	17	5	756	102	63.00
9.	Don Bradman	5	6	2	715	201	178.75
10.	Mark Waugh	14	24	3	698	153*	33.24

10 LEADING BATTING AVERAGES AGAINST INDIA

Rank	Batsman	Tests	Inns	NO	Runs	HS	Avge
1.	David Boon	11	20	3	1204	135	70.82
2.	Doug Walters	10	17	5	756	102	63.00
3.	Dean Jones	8	13	2	681	210	61.91
4.	Bob Cowper	6	11	1	604	165	60.40
5.	Neil Harvey	10	13	–	775	153	59.62
6.	Bob Simpson	11	21	–	1125	176	53.57
7.	Allan Border	20	35	5	1567	163	52.23
8.	Kim Hughes	11	21	2	988	213	52.00
9.	Bill Lawry	12	23	4	892	100	46.95
10.	Graham Yallop	7	14	1	568	167	43.69

10 LEADING WICKET-TAKERS AGAINST INDIA

Rank	Bowler	Tests	Balls	Mdns	Runs	Wkts	Avge	Best
1.	Richie Benaud	8	2953	198	956	52	18.38	7–72
2.	Graham McKenzie	10	2563	106	967	47	20.57	7–66
3.	Glenn McGrath	7	1712	106	595	37	16.08	5–48
4.	Ray Lindwall	10	2085	91	725	36	20.14	7–38
5.	Craig McDermott	9	2150	98	980	34	28.82	5–54
6.	Alan Connolly	10	2169	100	765	31	24.68	4–31
7.	Alan Davidson	6	1607	95	473	30	15.77	7–93
8.	Shane Warne	11	3085	112	1608	29	55.45	4–47
9=	Wayne Clark	5	1585	27	701	28	25.04	4–46
9=	Ashley Mallett	5	1792	129	535	28	19.11	6–64

10 LEADING BOWLING AVERAGES AGAINST INDIA

Rank	Bowler	Tests	Balls	Mdns	Runs	Wkts	Avge	Best
1.	Alan Davidson	6	1607	95	473	30	15.77	7-93
2.	Glenn McGrath	7	1712	106	595	37	16.08	5-48
3.	Ian Johnson	6	1044	43	339	19	17.84	4-35
4.	Richie Benaud	8	2953	198	956	52	18.38	7-72
5.	Ashley Mallett	5	1792	129	535	28	19.11	6-64
6.	Ray Lindwall	10	2085	91	725	36	20.14	7-38
7.	Graham McKenzie	10	2563	106	967	47	20.57	7-66
8.	Alan Connolly	10	2169	100	765	31	24.68	4-31
9.	Ken Mackay	8	678	47	176	7	25.14	3-27
10.	Bob Simpson	11	1624	60	647	23	28.13	5-59

10 LEADING RUN-SCORERS AGAINST NEW ZEALAND

Rank	Batsman	Tests	Inns	NO	Runs	HS	Avge
1.	Allan Border	23	32	3	1500	205	51.72
2.	David Boon	17	27	2	1187	200	47.48
3.	Steve Waugh	23	34	5	1117	151*	38.52
4.	Greg Chappell	14	22	3	1076	247*	56.63
5.	Doug Walters	11	16	2	901	250	64.36
6.	Mark Waugh	14	20	2	766	111	42.56
7.	Justin Langer	9	15	2	695	123	53.46
8.	Mark Taylor	11	16	2	666	142*	47.57
9=	Ian Chappell	6	10	–	486	145	48.60
9=	Rod Marsh	14	18	–	486	132	27.00

10 LEADING BATTING AVERAGES AGAINST NEW ZEALAND

Rank	Batsman	Tests	Inns	NO	Runs	HS	Avge
1.	Doug Walters	11	16	2	901	250	64.36
2.	Greg Chappell	14	22	3	1076	247*	56.63
3.	Justin Langer	9	15	2	695	123	53.46
4.	Allan Border	23	32	3	1500	205	51.72
5.	Adam Gilchrist	6	10	2	404	118	50.50
6.	Ian Chappell	6	10	–	486	145	48.60
7.	Michael Slater	6	10	–	482	168	48.20
8.	Mark Taylor	11	16	2	666	142*	47.57
9.	David Boon	17	27	2	1187	200	47.48
10.	Mark Waugh	14	20	2	766	111	42.56

10 LEADING WICKET-TAKERS AGAINST NEW ZEALAND

Rank	Bowler	Tests	Balls	Mdns	Runs	Wkts	Avge	Best
1.	Shane Warne	15	4409	210	1881	75	25.08	6–31
2.	Craig McDermott	13	3214	130	1460	48	30.42	5–97
3.	Dennis Lillee	8	1770	63	740	38	19.47	6–53
4.	Brett Lee	6	1209	45	666	32	20.81	5–67
5.	Glenn McGrath	9	2266	115	977	30	32.57	5–32
6.	Max Walker	6	1854	61	599	28	21.39	4–39
7.	Merv Hughes	5	1340	65	589	25	23.56	4–51
8.	Kerry O'Keeffe	8	1609	59	505	21	24.05	5–101
9.	Ashley Mallett	6	1462	41	525	19	27.63	4–22
10.	Gary Gilmour	5	992	11	510	17	30.00	5–64

10 LEADING BOWLING AVERAGES AGAINST NEW ZEALAND

Rank	Bowler	Tests	Balls	Mdns	Runs	Wkts	Avge	Best
1.	Dennis Lillee	8	1770	63	740	38	19.47	6–53
2.	Brett Lee	6	1209	45	666	32	20.81	5–67
3.	Max Walker	6	1854	61	599	28	21.39	4–39
4.	Merv Hughes	5	1340	65	589	25	23.56	4–51
5.	Kerry O'Keeffe	8	1609	59	505	21	24.05	5–101
6.	Shane Warne	15	4409	210	1881	75	25.08	6–31
7.	Doug Walters	11	494	8	245	9	27.22	4–39
8.	Ashley Mallett	6	1462	41	525	19	27.63	4–22
9.	Gary Gilmour	5	992	11	510	17	30.00	5–64
10.	Craig McDermott	13	3214	130	1460	48	30.42	5–97

10 LEADING RUN-SCORERS AGAINST PAKISTAN

Rank	Batsman	Tests	Inns	NO	Runs	HS	Avge
1.	Allan Border	22	36	8	1666	153	59.50
2.	Greg Chappell	17	27	2	1581	235	63.24
3.	Mark Taylor	12	20	3	1347	334*	79.24
4.	Kim Hughes	16	25	–	1016	106	40.64
5.	Michael Slater	12	20	1	946	169	49.79
6.	Steve Waugh	20	30	3	934	157	34.59
7.	Mark Waugh	15	22	–	933	117	42.41
8.	Graham Yallop	10	15	–	882	268	58.80
9.	Justin Langer	10	14	–	749	144	53.50
10.	Rod Marsh	20	33	3	724	118	24.13

10 LEADING BATTING AVERAGES AGAINST PAKISTAN

Rank	Batsman	Tests	Inns	NO	Runs	HS	Avge
1.	Mark Taylor	12	20	3	1347	334*	79.24
2.	Ricky Ponting	7	10	1	658	197	73.11
3.	Greg Chappell	17	27	2	1581	235	63.24
4.	Allan Border	22	36	8	1666	153	59.50
5.	Graham Yallop	10	15	–	882	268	58.80
6.	Justin Langer	10	14	–	749	144	53.50
7.	Michael Slater	12	20	1	946	169	49.79
8.	Mark Waugh	15	22	–	933	117	42.41
9.	Kim Hughes	16	25	–	1016	106	40.64
10.	Steve Waugh	20	30	3	934	157	34.59

10 LEADING WICKET-TAKERS AGAINST PAKISTAN

Rank	Bowler	Tests	Balls	Mdns	Runs	Wkts	Avge	Best
1.	Shane Warne	12	3304	168	1414	76	18.61	7-23
2.	Dennis Lillee	17	4433	127	2161	71	30.44	6-82
3.	Glenn McGrath	14	3193	138	1476	62	23.81	5-61
4.	Geoff Lawson	8	1815	61	882	33	26.73	5-49
5.	Damien Fleming	6	1535	47	742	29	25.59	5-59
6.	Carl Rackemann	5	1151	53	434	26	16.69	6-86
7.	Terry Alderman	6	1302	49	606	23	26.35	5-65
8.	Bruce Yardley	6	1327	40	702	21	33.43	7-187
9.	Tim May	5	1493	66	644	20	32.20	4-97
10=.	Richie Benaud	4	1446	99	416	19	21.89	5-93
10=.	Rodney Hogg	6	1303	27	640	19	33.68	4-49

10 LEADING BOWLING AVERAGES AGAINST PAKISTAN

Rank	Bowler	Tests	Balls	Mdns	Runs	Wkts	Avge	Best
1.	Shane Warne	12	3304	168	1414	76	18.61	7-23
2.	Glenn McGrath	14	3193	138	1476	62	23.81	5-61
3.	Damien Fleming	6	1535	47	742	29	25.59	5-59
4.	Terry Alderman	6	1302	49	606	23	26.35	5-65
5.	Geoff Lawson	8	1815	61	882	33	26.73	5-49
6.	Dennis Lillee	17	4433	127	2161	71	30.44	6-82
7.	Rodney Hogg	6	1303	27	640	19	33.68	4-49
8.	Greg Chappell	17	1082	37	418	12	34.83	5-61
9.	Craig McDermott	5	1143	36	628	18	34.89	5-49
10.	Allan Border	22	540	26	208	5	41.60	2-35

10 LEADING RUN-SCORERS AGAINST SOUTH AFRICA

Rank	Batsman	Tests	Inns	NO	Runs	HS	Avge
1.	Neil Harvey	14	23	3	1625	205	81.25
2.	Steve Waugh	16	25	2	1147	164	49.87
3.	Mark Waugh	18	29	2	1135	116	42.04
4.	Bill Lawry	14	28	1	985	157	36.48
5.	Warren Bardsley	11	17	1	982	164	61.38
6.	Bob Simpson	15	27	2	980	153	39.20
7.	Victor Trumper	8	15	3	900	214*	75.00
8.	Matthew Hayden	10	18	2	822	138	51.38
9.	Don Bradman	5	5	1	806	299*	201.50
10.	Arthur Morris	10	17	–	792	157	46.59

10 LEADING BATTING AVERAGES AGAINST SOUTH AFRICA

Rank	Batsman	Tests	Inns	NO	Runs	HS	Avge
1.	Neil Harvey	14	23	3	1625	205	81.25
2.	Victor Trumper	8	15	3	900	214*	75.00
3.	Clem Hill	8	13	1	752	191	62.67
4.	Warren Bardsley	11	17	1	982	164	61.38
5.	Warwick Armstrong	8	13	1	691	159*	57.58
6.	Stan McCabe	10	13	2	621	189*	56.45
7.	Charles Kelleway	8	12	2	548	114	54.80
8.	Lindsay Hassett	10	14	–	748	167	53.43
9.	Damien Martyn	8	12	2	518	118	51.80
10.	Justin Langer	6	11	1	517	126	51.70

10 LEADING WICKET-TAKERS AGAINST SOUTH AFRICA

Rank	Bowler	Tests	Balls	Mdns	Runs	Wkts	Avge	Best
1.	Shane Warne	18	6130	303	2257	101	22.35	7–56
2.	Clarrie Grimmett	10	3913	248	1199	77	15.57	7–40
3.	Richie Benaud	13	4136	116	1413	52	27.17	5–49
4.	Bill Whitty	8	2055	89	875	50	17.50	6–17
5.	Glenn McGrath	14	3284	174	1233	49	25.16	6–86
6.	Bill Johnston	10	3420	90	1129	44	25.66	6–44
7.	Graham McKenzie	13	3745	105	1646	41	40.15	5–46
8.	Bill O'Reilly	7	2046	140	634	34	18.65	5–20
9=.	Bert Ironmonger	4	1331	112	296	31	9.55	6–18
9=.	Ray Lindwall	8	1835	31	631	31	20.35	5–32

10 LEADING BOWLING AVERAGES AGAINST SOUTH AFRICA

Rank	Bowler	Tests	Balls	Mdns	Runs	Wkts	Avge	Best
1.	Clarrie Grimmett	10	3913	248	1199	77	15.57	7–40
2.	Steve Waugh	16	866	50	270	17	15.88	5–28
3.	Bill Whitty	8	2055	89	875	50	17.50	6–17
4.	Bill O'Reilly	7	2046	140	634	34	18.65	5–20
5.	Ray Lindwall	8	1835	31	631	31	20.35	5–32
6.	Keith Miller	9	1801	34	631	30	21.03	5–40
7.	Shane Warne	18	6130	303	2257	101	22.35	7–56
8.	Glenn McGrath	14	3284	174	1233	49	25.16	6–86
9.	Bill Johnston	10	3420	90	1129	44	25.66	6–44
10.	Richie Benaud	13	4136	116	1413	52	27.17	5–49

10 LEADING RUN-SCORERS AGAINST WEST INDIES

Rank	Batsman	Tests	Inns	NO	Runs	HS	Avge
1.	Steve Waugh	32	51	7	2192	200	49.82
2.	Allan Border	31	59	7	2052	126	39.46
3.	Mark Waugh	28	48	3	1858	139*	41.29
4.	Ian Chappell	17	31	4	1545	165	57.22
5.	David Boon	22	40	4	1437	149	39.92
6.	Greg Chappell	17	31	6	1400	182*	56.00
7.	Ian Redpath	16	29	1	1247	132	44.54
8.	Doug Walters	9	14	1	1196	242	92.00
9.	Justin Langer	17	31	1	1093	146	36.43
10.	Graeme Wood	17	33	1	1077	126	33.66

10 LEADING BATTING AVERAGES AGAINST WEST INDIES

Rank	Batsman	Tests	Inns	NO	Runs	HS	Avge
1.	Doug Walters	9	14	1	1196	242	92.00
2.	Bill Lawry	10	17	2	1035	210	69.00
3.	Ricky Ponting	12	21	4	1043	206	61.35
4.	Adam Gilchrist	9	11	2	523	101*	58.11
5.	Ian Chappell	17	31	4	1545	165	57.22
6.	Greg Chappell	17	31	6	1400	182*	56.00
7.	Keith Miller	10	16	1	801	147	53.40
8.	Steve Waugh	32	51	7	2192	200	49.82
9.	Norm O'Neill	9	17	1	788	181	49.25
10.	Colin McDonald	11	20	1	880	127	46.32

10 LEADING WICKET-TAKERS AGAINST WEST INDIES

Rank	Bowler	Tests	Balls	Mdns	Runs	Wkts	Avge	Best
1.	Glenn McGrath	20	4701	248	1847	97	19.04	6–17
2.	Jeff Thomson	14	2774	56	1817	62	29.31	6–50
3.	Craig McDermott	14	3036	84	1703	59	28.86	5–80
4.	Dennis Lillee	12	2677	62	1526	55	27.74	7–83
5.	Merv Hughes	14	2886	104	1524	53	28.75	8–87
6.	Jason Gillespie	13	2706	138	1056	50	21.12	6–40
7.	Shane Warne	16	3284	132	1581	49	32.27	7–52
8.	Stuart MacGill	12	2878	115	1532	48	31.92	7–104
9.	Graham McKenzie	10	3185	83	1435	47	30.53	8–71
10.	Richie Benaud	11	3289	103	1278	42	30.43	5–96

10 LEADING BOWLING AVERAGES AGAINST WEST INDIES

Rank	Bowler	Tests	Balls	Mdns	Runs	Wkts	Avge	Best
1.	Clarrie Grimmett	5	1436	61	593	33	17.97	7–87
2.	Glenn McGrath	20	4701	248	1847	97	19.04	6–17
3.	Paul Reiffel	7	1205	53	568	27	21.04	5–73
4.	Jason Gillespie	13	2706	138	1056	50	21.12	6–40
5.	Neil Hawke	5	1312	52	524	24	21.83	6–72
6.	Max Walker	8	2262	97	859	37	23.22	6–114
7.	Bruce Yardley	8	1776	78	823	35	23.51	7–98
8.	Brett Lee	6	1222	54	667	28	23.82	5–61
9.	Keith Miller	10	2157	53	1039	40	25.98	6–107
10.	Ray Lindwall	10	2288	44	1121	41	27.34	6–95

10 QUOTES ABOUT GREAT AUSTRALIAN CRICKETERS

6. 'In my office at Parliament House in Canberra, an office in which files and conferences and more files take their turn hour after hour, there are two pictures which half a dozen times a day at least refresh me. One is a small glowing landscape by Tom Roberts, who was one of the great founders of Australian *plein-air* impressionist painting; one of the immortals of Australian art. The other picture is a simple photograph of Keith Miller finishing a cover drive ...'

– *Australian Prime Minister Robert Menzies, in the foreword to Miller and RS Whitington's 1953 book, Bumper*

CHAPTER NINE

YOUNGEST AND OLDEST

Here's an idea for a game of different kind involving Australian Test cricketers: the 'Under 20s' v the 'Over 40s'. To qualify for the teenage XI you need to have played a Test before your 20th birthday; for the old boys, you need to have played for Australia after your 40th …

A team of Australian teenage Test players, in batting order, might read like this: Archie Jackson, Ian Craig, Clem Hill, Neil Harvey, Stan McCabe, Doug Walters, Ron Archer, Tibby Cotter, Craig McDermott, Graham McKenzie and Jack Ferris. We concede that this combination is top heavy with opening bowlers; perhaps Tom Garrett, who bowled medium-paced off-cutters, should play instead of one of the last four. Craig, easily Australia's youngest Test captain, would be the skipper. Hill, who made his debut for South Australia as a keeper/batsman just nine days after his 16th birthday and has a first-class stumping to his credit, would be the wicketkeeper.

Unlike the young 'uns, the over 40s team has no problems finding a keeper, with no less than Hanson Carter, Bert Oldfield and Jack Blackham all available. A team of mature Australian Test players might be, in batting order: Warren Bardsley, Bob Simpson, Charlie Macartney, Syd Gregory, Vic Richardson, Warwick Armstrong, Charles Kelleway, Hanson Carter, Clarrie Grimmett, Don Blackie and Bert Ironmonger. All of Bardsley, Simpson, Gregory, Richardson and Armstrong captained Australia after their 40th birthday (as did Blackham), but as Bardsley was the oldest to do so he gets the job here.

The clash with our teenage XI would be interesting, if for no other reason than the two teams' very different bowling attacks. While the teenage side is loaded with exuberant pace bowlers, the veterans' line-up is dominated by spinners — Macartney and Kelleway will have to open the bowling, with Grimmett, Blackie, Ironmonger, Armstrong and Simpson all ready to bowl some slow stuff.

❖ ❖ ❖

10 YOUNGEST AUSTRALIAN TEST CRICKETERS

Rank	Age (years, days)	Player	Test debut
1.	17, 239	Ian Craig	Fifth Test v South Africa, 1952–53
2.	18, 232	Tom Garrett	First Test v England, 1876–77
3.	19, 85	Albert Cotter	Fourth Test v England, 1903–04
4.	19, 96	Clem Hill	First Test v England, 1896
5.	19, 100	Gerry Hazlitt	First Test v England, 1907–08
6.	19, 104	Ron Archer	Fifth Test v South Africa, 1952–53
7.	19, 107	Neil Harvey	Fourth Test v India, 1947–48
8.	19, 149	Archie Jackson	Fourth Test v England, 1928–29
9.	19, 173	John Cottam	Second Test v England, 1886–87
10=	19, 252	Jack Ferris	First Test v England, 1886–87
10=	19, 252	Craig McDermott	Fourth Test v West Indies, 1984–85

The ages listed here refer to the players' ages on their first day as Test cricketers. Besides these 11 players, there have been three other instances of teenagers playing Test cricket for Australia: Stan McCabe (19 years, 332 days on debut), Doug Walters (19, 354) and Graham McKenzie (19, 363).

Ron Archer and Neil Harvey, each with four, played the most Tests before their respective 20th birthdays; Hill and McCabe each played three Tests as teenagers; Cotter, Hazlitt, Jackson, Ferris, McDermott and Garrett each played two.

Australia's youngest Test wicketkeeper was Fred Burton, who was 21 years 115 days when he made his debut in the second Test of 1886–87. This was the same match in which John Cottam played his only Test. Cottam had only made his first-class debut the previous week, after Burton dropped out of the New South Wales XI to play Alfred Shaw's English tourists. He scored 29 and 14 not out, and then — after a host of interstate players, including George Giffen, Jack Blackham, Bill Bruce, George Palmer and John Trumble, all refused or were unable to come to Sydney, and Alec Bannerman and the Demon Spofforth were controversially ignored — was named as 12th man for the Test. Then Sammy Jones dropped out of the Australian team at the last moment, and Cottam was a Test cricketer. He scored 1 and 3, didn't bowl, and by never playing another first-class match became the only Australian to appear in a Test before but never after his 20th birthday.

10 OLDEST AUSTRALIAN TEST CRICKETERS

Rank	Age (years, days)	Player	Final Test
1.	50, 327	Bert Ironmonger	Fifth Test v England, 1932–33
2.	46, 309	Don Blackie	Fourth Test v England, 1928–29
3.	44, 69	Clarrie Grimmett	Fifth Test v South Africa, 1935–36
4.	43, 259	Hanson Carter	Third Test v South Africa, 1921
5.	43, 255	Warren Bardsley	Fifth Test v England, 1926
6.	42, 224	Charles Kelleway	First Test v England, 1928–29
7.	42, 175	Bert Oldfield	Fifth Test v England, 1936–37
8.	42, 130	Syd Gregory	Third Test v England, 1912
9.	42, 89	Bob Simpson	Fifth Test v West Indies, 1978
10.	42, 86	Warwick Armstrong	Fifth Test v England, 1921

The years and days refer to the players' ages on the final day of their final Tests. Grimmett, with 16, is the Australian to appear in the most Tests after his 40th birthday. Ironmonger (14 Tests) and Armstrong, Oldfield and Simpson (each with 10) also played 10 or most Tests after they turned 40.

There are five other Australians besides the 10 above who played Test cricket into their forties: Vic Richardson (who was 41) and Arthur Mailey, Jack Blackham, Ron Oxenham and Charlie Macartney (who were all 40).

10 OLDEST PLAYERS ON DEBUT

Rank	Age (years, days)	Player	First Test
1.	46, 253	Don Blackie	Second Test v England, 1928–29
2.	46, 237	Bert Ironmonger	First Test v England, 1928–29
3.	38, 35	Bob Holland	Second Test v West Indies, 1984–85
4=	37, 290	Ned Gregory	First Test v England, 1876–77
4=	37, 290	Nat Thomson	First Test v England, 1876–77
6.	37, 184	Hammy Love	Fourth Test v England, 1932–33
7.	37, 163	Jack Harry	Third Test v England, 1894–95
8.	37, 154	Ron Oxenham	Third Test v England, 1928–29
9.	36, 148	Arthur Richardson	First Test v England, 1924–25
10.	35, 127	Jack Iverson	First Test v England, 1950–51

The years and days refer to the players' ages on the opening days of their debut Tests. Four other Australians made their Test debuts after their 35th birthdays: Ken Eastwood (35 years, 81 days), Jack Wilson (35, 67) Albert Hartkopf (35, 4) and Trevor Hohns (35, 3).

On of the more bizarre pieces of trivia to come out of Australian cricket history is that the two oldest debutants — Blackie and Ironmonger — were born two days apart (Blackie being the older), played for the same club, state and country, and made their debuts in the same series, in successive Tests. Even more intriguing is the fact that Ned Gregory and Nat Thomson were born on the same day, 29 May 1839, in the Sydney suburbs of Waverley and Surry Hills respectively (around eight kilometres apart). Thomson was the first man out in Test cricket, and Gregory the first man out for a duck.

For many years, Nathaniel Frampton Davis Thomson was referred to by statisticians as Nathaniel Thompson, born at Birmingham in England in 1838. However, due to the work of cricket historian Alf James in the early 1990s, Thomson's middle names, the correct spelling of his surname, and his true place and date of birth have now been confirmed.

10 YOUNGEST CENTURIONS

Rank	Age (years, days)	Batsman	Score	Versus	Venue	Series
1.	19, 122	Neil Harvey	153	India	Melbourne	1947–48
2.	19, 152	Archie Jackson	164	England	Adelaide	1928–29
3.	19, 357	Doug Walters	155	England	Brisbane	1965–66
4.	20, 129	Don Bradman	112	England	Melbourne	1928–29
5.	20, 240	Jim Burke	101*	England	Adelaide	1950–51
6.	20, 317	Clem Hill	188	England	Melbourne	1897–98
7.	21, 149	Graeme Wood	126	West Indies	Georgetown	1978
8.	21, 226	Victor Trumper	135	England	Lord's	1899
9.	21, 233	Ron Archer	128	West Indies	Kingston	1955
10.	21, 327	Bill Brown	105	England	Lord's	1934

The years and days refer to the players' ages on the day they scored their maiden ton. Harvey and Walters both scored two Test centuries before their 21st birthdays. Hill, who was born in Adelaide while cricket's first Test players were enjoying a rest day during the inaugural Test match at Melbourne, holds the record for the highest score by an Australian batsman aged under 21 with his 188. Don Bradman is the youngest Australian to score a Test double century; he was two months short of his 22nd birthday when he hit 254 at Lord's in 1930. Two weeks later at Leeds Bradman was 21 years 318 days when he became the youngest to score a triple century (334).

WHAT'S IN A NAME?

For the purpose of this Top 10, a cricketer's first name is the one by which he is or was known. Thus, Kevin Douglas Walters is a Douglas, Hedley Brian Taber a Brian. Getting slightly more complicated, if a player was known by a derivative of his given name, he is considered in this Top 10 by his given name, not the derivative. Thus, Jack Fingleton (christened John Henry Webb Fingleton) is a John. Jack Gregory, who was christened Jack Morrison Gregory, is a Jack, but 'Jack' Badcock — christened Clayvel Lindsay Badcock but known by friends, fans and family by his nickname — is Clayvel.

Names spelt in different ways have been separated. Thus, there has only been one Allan (Border), but seven Alans (Connolly, Davidson, Fairfax, Hurst, Kippax, Thomson and Turner) have played Test cricket for Australia.

The most popular first names of Australian Test cricketers are:

Rank	Name	Players	Total Tests	Player with Most Tests
1.	John	32	267	Jack Blackham (35)
2.	William	17	307	Bill Lawry (67)
3.	Thomas	11	115	Tom Veivers (21)
4.	David	9	163	David Boon (107)
5=.	Ian	8	350	Ian Healy (119)
5=.	Peter	8	103	Peter Burge (42)
7=.	Alan	7	135	Alan Davidson (44)
7=.	George	7	72	George Giffen (31)
7=.	Henry	7	62	Harry Trott (24)
10=.	Gregory	6	206	Greg Chappell (87)
10=.	Michael	6	130	Michael Slater (74)
10=.	Robert	6	114	Bob Simpson (62)
10=.	Arthur	6	102	Arthur Morris (46)
10=.	Charles	6	100	Charles Kelleway (26)

There have been eight players with the name Graham (McKenzie, Yallop), Graeme (Beard, Hole, Watson, Wood) or Grahame (Corling, Thomas) for a total of 192 Tests; and seven with the name Geoffrey (Dymock, Lawson, Marsh), Jeffrey (Hammond, Moss, Thomson) or Geffery (Noblet) for 177 Tests. Three names with few representatives but large numbers of Test appearances are Mark (Waugh 128 Tests, Taylor 104), Stephen or Steven (Stephen Waugh 162 Tests, Stephen Rixon 13, Steven Smith 3) and Rodney (Marsh 96, Hogg 38).

continued over

So what does this all mean for a budding parent, hoping that his or her newborn son will play Test cricket? We will use as a sample the 10 most popular names chosen in New South Wales in 2002. These were (number of Australian Test players in brackets): Joshua (0), Lachlan (0), Jack (1), Thomas (11), Ethan (0), James (5), Daniel (0), Nicholas (0), William (17) and Benjamin (1). Among the next 10 most popular names were Liam, Luke, Jacob, Dylan, Ryan, Jayden and Jordan, none of whom have ever played for Australia. Do all these zeroes indicate that the Test teams of the future might be in trouble? Does Australian cricket need a rapid re-emergence of names such as John, George, Alan, Ian and Arthur, before it's too late?

Probably not. The current Australian team carries precious few first names that were popular in days of old. There has been only one Ricky play Test cricket for Australia, one Justin, one Glenn, one Jason, one Brett, one Stuart, one Darren, and they're all playing at the moment. And there's only ever been one Shane wear the baggy green. In 20 years' time, it could very well be that Joshua and Ethan will be opening the batting, with Lachlan at first wicket, Jayden and Jordan opening the bowling, Liam behind the stumps, and Dylan bowling the leg-breaks.

10 Test Cricketers Who Were Better Known by Their Nickname

1. Harry Houston 'Bull' Alexander
2. Clayvel Lindsay 'Jack' Badcock
3. William 'Barlow' Carkeek
4. Hanson 'Sammy' Carter
5. Albert 'Tibby' Cotter
6. Leslie O'Brien 'Chuck' Fleetwood-Smith
7. John Bryant 'Sam' Gannon
8. Holmesdale Carl 'Slinger' Nitschke
9. Clarence Everard 'Nip' Pellew
10. Thomas Welbourn 'Tim' Wall

Slinger Nitschke made his debut in the first Test against South Africa in 1931–32, and scored 6. Alan Kippax had to pull out of the Australian side for the second Test, as he was still suffering the effects of being struck on the head by the Queensland quick Eddie Gilbert in a Sheffield Shield match, and Keith Rigg replaced him. Slinger hit 47 in the second Test, adding 85 with Stan McCabe, but Rigg scored 112, so when Kippax returned for the third Test it was Slinger who made way. He never played another Test. Forty-one years later, Slinger Nitschke was back in the sporting headlines as the owner of Dayana, which won four derbies, including the Victoria Derby, during the 1972–73 racing season.

10 OLDEST CENTURIONS

Rank	Age (years, days)	Batsman	Score	Versus	Venue	Series
1.	43, 202	Warren Bardsley	193*	England	Lord's	1926
2.	41, 360	Bob Simpson	100	India	Adelaide	1977–78
3.	41, 268	Warwick Armstrong	123*	England	Melbourne	1920–21
4.	40, 29	Charlie Macartney	109	England	Manchester	1926
5.	39, 335	Don Bradman	173*	England	Leeds	1948
6.	39, 301	Lindsay Hassett	104	England	Lord's	1953
7.	39, 143	Jack Ryder	112	England	Melbourne	1928–29
8.	38, 131	Allan Border	105	New Zealand	Brisbane	1993–94
9.	38, 55	Steve Waugh	156*	Bangladesh	Cairns	2003
10.	37, 353	Arthur Richardson	100	England	Leeds	1926

The years and days refer to the players' ages on the day they reached three figures. Macartney and Armstrong both scored three Test centuries after their 40th birthdays, and Simpson scored two. The oldest Australian to score a double century in a Test is Don Bradman, who was 39 years 149 days when he made 201 not out against India at Adelaide in January 1948. The oldest to make a triple century is Mark Taylor, who was 33 years 354 days when he scored 334 not out at Peshawar in October 1998.

10 YOUNGEST AUSTRALIANS TO TAKE FIVE WICKETS IN AN INNINGS

Rank	Age	Bowler	Analysis	Versus	Series	Before 23rd
1.	19, 95	Albert Cotter	6–40	England	1903–04	2
2.	19, 253	Jack Ferris	5–76	England	1886–87	3
3.	20, 2	Graham McKenzie	5–37	England	1961	3
4.	20, 75	Craig McDermott	6–70	England	1985	3
5.	21, 183	Steve Waugh	5–69	England	1986–87	1
6.	21, 196	Dennis Lillee	5–84	England	1970–71	2
7.	21, 329	Jason Gillespie	5–54	South Africa	1997	2
8.	21, 343	Albert Trott	8–43	England	1894–95	1
9.	22, 269	Gary Gilmour	5–64	New Zealand	1974	1
10.	22, 304	Ron Archer	5–53	England	1956	1

'Age' refers to years and days, and to the bowler's age on the day he first took five wickets in an innings. Thus, Albert 'Tibby' Cotter was 19 years and 95 days when he took 6–40 in the fifth Ashes Test of 1903–04, and (as the far right column indicates) took five or more wickets in an innings twice before his 23rd birthday.

The only other Australians to take a Test five-for before they turned 23 were Ian Meckiff (22 years, 352 days in South Africa in 1957–58) and George Palmer (22 years, 360 days England in 1881–82). The youngest Australian bowler to take seven wickets in a Test innings was Craig McDermott, who was 20 years 111 days when he took 8–141 at Old Trafford in 1985.

10 OLDEST AUSTRALIANS TO TAKE FIVE WICKETS IN AN INNINGS

Rank	Age (y,d)	Bowler	Analysis	Versus	Series	After 36th
1.	49, 314	Bert Ironmonger	6–18	South Africa	1931–32	4
2.	46, 272	Don Blackie	6–94	England	1928–29	1
3.	44, 69	Clarrie Grimmett	6–73	South Africa	1935–36	18
4.	40, 223	Arthur Mailey	6–138	England	1926	2
5.	40, 99	Bill O'Reilly	5–14	New Zealand	1946	1
6.	39, 231	Frank Laver	8–31	England	1909	1
7.	39, 34	Bob Holland	6–106	New Zealand	1985–86	3
8.	37, 141	Ian Johnson	7–44	West Indies	1955	1
9.	36, 316	Colin Miller	5–32	West Indies	2000–01	3
10.	36, 301	Hugh Trumble	7–28	England	1903–04	2

'Age' refers to years and days, and to the bowler's age on the day he last took five wickets in an innings. Thus, Bert Ironmonger was just 51 days from his 50th birthday when he took five wickets in a Test innings for the fourth and final time in his Test career. Ironmonger actually took all of his Test five-fors after his 48th birthday. He was 48 years, 312 days when he took 7–23 against the West Indies at the MCG in 1930–31. All of Bob Holland's Test five fors were taken after he turned 38, while Clarrie Grimmett took the first of his 21 Test five-fors when he was 33 (5–45 and 6–37 on his Test debut in 1924–25) and 10 of them after he turned 40. While we remain unconvinced that Grimmett was as great a bowler as some historians suggest, there is no doubt that for his age he was a marvel.

The two Australian bowlers to take a Test five-for after they turned 36, other than those listed above, were Harry Boyle (36 years, 213 days when he took 6–42 in 1884) and Keith Miller (36 years, 211 days at the start of the 1956 Lord's Test in which he took 5–72 and 5–80). Don Blackie's 6–94 was the only instance of him taking five wickets in a Test innings. It was his second Test, having taken 4–148 from 59 six-ball overs on his Test debut two weeks earlier.

10 YOUNGEST CAPTAINS

Rank	Age (years, days)	Captain	First Test as Captain
1.	22, 194	Ian Craig	First Test v South Africa, 1957–58
2.	25, 57	Kim Hughes	Second Test v Pakistan, 1978–79
3.	25, 324	Billy Murdoch	Only Test v England, 1880
4.	26, 55	Graham Yallop	First Test v England, 1978–79
5.	27, 113	Greg Chappell	First Test v West Indies, 1975–76
6.	27, 139	Ian Chappell	Seventh Test v England, 1970–71
7.	27, 191	Henry Scott	First Test v England, 1886
8.	27, 332	Bob Simpson	Second Test v South Africa, 1963–64
9.	28, 60	Richie Benaud	First Test v England, 1958–59
10.	28, 76	Percy McDonnell	First Test v England, 1886–87

The years and days refer to the captains' ages on the opening days of their first Tests as leaders.

Ian Craig's only Tests as captain were the five in South Africa in 1957–58. At series end he was 22 years, 265 days old. Thus, even in what proved to be his final Test as a player or captain, he was two years and five months younger than any other Australian captain. Struck down by hepatitis before the start of the 1958–59 Australian summer, Craig reluctantly pulled out of that season's Ashes series and never recovered his Test place. He eventually retired from first-class cricket, without fanfare, in 1962, aged just 26, having been described the previous year by the West Indies' great fast bowler Wes Hall as being the hardest batsman to dismiss in Australia.

10 OLDEST CAPTAINS

Rank	Age (years, days)	Captain ·	Final Test as Captain
1.	43, 233	Warren Bardsley	Fourth Test v England, 1926
2.	42, 130	Syd Gregory	Third Test v England, 1912
3.	42, 89	Bob Simpson	Fifth Test v West Indies, 1978
4.	42, 86	Warwick Armstrong	Fifth Test v England, 1921
5.	41, 178	Vic Richardson	Fifth Test v South Africa, 1935–36
6.	40, 223	Jack Blackham	First Test v England, 1894–95
7.	39, 357	Don Bradman	Fifth Test v England, 1948
8.	39, 356	Lindsay Hassett	Fifth Test v England, 1953
9.	39, 220	Jack Ryder	Fifth Test v England, 1928–29
10.	38, 334	Ian Johnson	Third Test v India, 1956

The years and days refer to the players' ages on the final day of their farewell Test in charge.

The 14 years, 124 days between Bob Simpson's first Test as Test captain and his last is an Australian record, though of course he did have almost 10 years out of the job between 1967 and 1977. Next longest span, from first game as leader to last, is Don Bradman's 11 years and 258 days, but his tenure was interrupted by World War II, and also, technically, by Bill Brown's one Test in charge in New Zealand in March 1946. Bradman had been 28 years, 99 days when he first led Australia, against England in Brisbane in 1936–37. Allan Border's nine years, 110 days represents the longest uninterrupted reign as Australian captain. Border was 38 years, 245 days old when his Test career ended in South Africa in 1994.

CHAPTER TEN

EXTRAS

On 10 April 2003, in Georgetown, Guyana, Steve Waugh became Australia's 'most capped' Test cricketer. Since 6 September 1880, only six men have held this title of having appeared in more Tests than any other Australian. Waugh has played down the significance of the record, arguing that as it is a measure of longevity it is a mark that is made to be broken, but clearly he is now a member of a very exclusive club — as it was with the men who preceded him to the honour, his achievement in playing at the top level for so long is a great tribute to his class, spirit and persistence.

Following the two Tests against Bangladesh in 2003, Waugh has played in 162 of Australia's most recent 183 Tests. He had been dropped for 13 matches between January 1991 and September 1992, and between December 1993 and August 2001 missed a further eight through injury. In his first 44 Tests before his omission in 1991, Waugh scored 2097 runs at an average of 37.44, hitting three hundreds and 13 fifties. Since he returned to the side for the first Test against the West Indies in 1992–93, Waugh has played in a further 118 Tests, and scored 8424 runs at 56.16, with one double century, 28 single centuries and 46 fifties. Not every cricketer gets a second chance the way Steve Waugh did; no one has ever taken better advantage of a recall than he has.

Waugh has had 67 Test teammates. Seventeen of these came from NSW, 15 from Western Australia, 12 from Queensland, nine each from Victoria and South Australia, four from Tasmania, plus Colin Miller who was a representative of both Tasmania and then Victoria. The Top 10 of the cricketers he has played the most Tests with looks this way:

Rank	Teammate	Tests Together
1.	Mark Waugh	108
2.	Ian Healy	101
3.	Shane Warne	96
4.	Glenn McGrath	89
5.	Mark Taylor	85
6.	David Boon	79
7.	Michael Slater	67
8.	Allan Border	65
9.	Ricky Ponting	64
10.	Justin Langer	63

The list continues this way: 44 Greg Blewett; 43 Craig McDermott; 42 Merv Hughes; 43 Adam Gilchrist; 42 Matthew Hayden, Jason Gillespie; 40 Geoff Marsh; 37 Dean Jones; 33 Paul Reiffel; 32 Brett Lee; 29 Damien Martyn; 24 Stuart MacGill; 23 Bruce Reid; 21 Tim May; 20 Damien Fleming; 19 Matthew Elliott; 17 Greg Matthews, Terry Alderman, Colin Miller; 16 Michael Bevan; 15 Michael Kasprowicz, Andy Bichel; 13 Darren Lehmann; 11 Greg Ritchie; 10, Tim Zoehrer, Geoff Lawson, Peter Sleep, Peter Taylor; 8 Mike Veletta, Tony Dodemaide; 7 Ray Bright, Trevor Hohns, Carl Rackemann; 6 Greg Dyer, Graeme Wood, Brendon Julian; 5 Dave Gilbert, Wayne B Phillips, Martin Love; 4 Greg Campbell, Tom Moody, Jo Angel; 3 Chris Matthews, Mike Whitney, Brad Hogg, Gavin Robertson; 2 Peter McIntyre, Simon Cook, Scott Muller; 1 David Hookes, Bob Holland, Simon Davis, Dirk Wellham, Shaun Young, Paul Wilson, Matthew Nicholson, Adam Dale.

Which leads us to a trivia question: Since Steve Waugh made his Test debut, four men have played Test cricket for Australia but have not played in the same Test XI as Steve Waugh. Who are they?

The answer: Wayne N Phillips (fifth Test v India, 1991–92), Phil Emery (third Test v Pakistan, 1994), Stuart Law (first Test v Sri Lanka, 1995–96) and Simon Katich (fourth Ashes Test, 2001).

10 QUOTES ABOUT GREAT AUSTRALIAN CRICKETERS

5. 'It is difficult to bracket him alongside any other player I have seen, but Viv Richards would be the closest to him for freedom and expression of skills and the pure essence of what batting is all about.'
  – *Steve Waugh on Adam Gilchrist, after Gilchrist had scored 204 not out and 138 in the first two Tests in South Africa in 2002*

10 AUSTRALIANS WITH MOST TEST APPEARANCES

Rank	Player	Career	Tests	Runs	Avge	Wkts	Avge
1.	Steve Waugh	1985–	162	10521	51.07	91	36.48
2.	Allan Border	1978–1994	156	11174	50.56	39	39.10
3.	Mark Waugh	1991–2002	128	8029	41.82	59	41.17
4.	Ian Healy	1988–1999	119	4356	27.40	–	–
5.	David Boon	1984–1996	107	7422	43.66	0	–
6.	Shane Warne	1992–	107	2238	16.83	491	25.71
7.	Mark Taylor	1989–1999	104	7525	43.50	1	26.00
8.	Rod Marsh	1970–1984	96	3633	26.52	0	–
9.	Glenn McGrath	1993–	95	450	6.62	430	21.72
10.	Greg Chappell	1970–1984	87	7110	53.86	47	40.70

Others with 70 or more appearances are Neil Harvey (79), Ian Chappell (75), Doug Walters (74), Michael Slater (74), Craig McDermott (71), Dennis Lillee (70) and Kim Hughes (70). Ricky Ponting, after the Tests against Bangladesh in 2003, had 69.

Of the 11 men in the first ever Australian Test XI, eight returned for the second Test of that 1876–77 summer. When the third Test was played nearly two years later, only four of that eight played, and only one of that quartet — Jack Blackham — was selected for the fourth ever Test, the first in England, at The Oval in 1880. Blackham would go on to play in all of the first 17 Tests, and in 35 in total (the last of which was the opening Ashes Test of 1894–95), an appearance record that stood until Syd Gregory played in his 36th Test, in South Africa in October 1902.

Gregory played his 58th and final Test in England in 1912. This remained the Australian record until Neil Harvey went to 59 in Pakistan in 1959–60.

Harvey retired after the 1962–63 Ashes series with 79 Test appearances, and this was the Australian appearance record until Rod Marsh played in his 80th Test, against the West Indies at the Adelaide Oval in 1981–82. Marsh's final Test, the fifth v Pakistan in 1983–84, was his 96th, a record that was broken by Allan Border in Pakistan in 1988.

Border reached 100 Tests against the Windies at the Melbourne Cricket Ground in the following Australian season, and retired after the 1994 tour of South Africa with a world record 156 appearances.

Steve Waugh equalled this mark in the final Ashes Test of 2002–03, and past it when he led Australia in the opening match of the series in the Caribbean that followed soon after.

Occupation	Cricketer
Jackaroo	Jack Iverson
Bee farmer	Bill Howell
Sheep shearing machinery repairer	Tom McKibbin
Stonemason	Tommy Andrews
Undertaker	Hanson Carter
Police roundsman	Richie Benaud
Horse racing handicapper	Clem Hill
Speaker in the South Australian Parliament	Gil Langley
Theatre manager	Harry Musgrove
Head of the NSW Treasury	Dave Gregory

These days, all Australian Test cricketers are full-time professionals. Many complement their cricket with work in the media, where they sit alongside a number of retired players who have entered the fourth estate. However, not all ex-players have simply joined the *cricket* media: among Mike Whitney's many successful television roles was a stint as referee in the *Gladiators* series, while Brendon Julian is now a presenter on the Nine Network's *Getaway*. A few years back, Mark Taylor was studying to be a surveyor, Geoff Lawson an optometrist, Steve Waugh even spent a few hours at teachers' college, but now it seems the only tertiary education budding stars need is provided by the Australian Cricket Academy.

It wasn't always this way. For the purpose of this Top 10, we've looked for three jobs held by men *before* they became Test players, three performed *during* Test careers and three achieved *after* cricket retirement. And then we've nominated one more, arguably the highest office outside cricket held by an Australian Test cricketer.

Few men took a more unusual route to Test cricket than Jack Iverson, who was a jackaroo on a station in country Victoria in the mid to late 1930s, before he served in World War II and well before he spun through the Englishmen in 1950–51. 'Farmer Bill' Howell worked among the bee hives at Penrith, west of Sydney, before he came to the big city with a team of country cricketers to win a place in the Australian XI in 1897–98 with his medium-pace cutters and occasionally successful big hitting. Three years earlier, Tom McKibbin had taken time off from his job at Bathurst, 300km west of Sydney, repairing the shearer's equipment, to replace Charlie Turner for the crucial fifth Ashes Test.

Tommy Andrews' family owned a number of funeral parlours, and Andrews himself made the headstones for both Victor Trumper and Archie Jackson. Trumper's funeral was directed by Walter Carter, Hanson's father; the Test wicketkeeper had once been a partner with Victor in a sporting goods store before joining his family in the undertaking business. Richie Benaud is a journalist by profession, who following the 1956 Ashes tour approached his editor at the Sydney *Sun* and asked to write for general news rather than the back pages. He was given the opportunity to work under the legendary crime reporter Noel Bailey.

Clem Hill worked as chief handicapper for the South Australian Jockey Club, the Victoria Amateur Turf Club (who stage the Caulfield Cup) and the Geelong Racing Club. Gil Langley was one of four Test cricketers to enter state parliaments, Charles Eady and Joe Darling (both Tasmania) and Sam Loxton (Victoria) being the others. (Another Test cricketer, Jack Fingleton, briefly worked as press secretary to Billy Hughes, a former prime minister.)

Harry Musgrove was an intriguing figure — Test cricketer for one match in 1884–85 (scoring 4 and 9), manager of the 1896 team that toured England, and also manager of an ill-fated tour to the USA by an Australian representative baseball team in 1897. That team, made up of ball players from Melbourne and Adelaide and captained by future Test bowler Frank Laver, had little luck, and Musgrove was accused by team members of absconding with the tour funds (some of the players had to work as stokers on the boat home, to pay their way). Away from cricket and baseball, Musgrove ran the Princess Theatre and the Theatre Royal in Melbourne, working in the entertainment business for much of the last 40 years of his life. His brother George was one of the leading theatrical entrepreneurs in Australia, and an original partner in JC Williamson's business empire.

While Harry Musgrove's integrity might have been questioned, this was never so with Dave Gregory, Australia's first Test captain. Gregory and Tom Garrett, his teammate in the Tests of 1877 and 1879, climbed to the very top of the New South Wales Public Service — Gregory as the Paymaster of the Treasury, Garrett as the senior public servant at the Supreme Court. When the Commonwealth of Australia was formed in 1901, Gregory was invited to take the job as head of the Federal Treasury. He was also offered a knighthood, but the appointment would have meant him moving from Sydney to Melbourne, so he declined.

10 TOP INSTANCES OF PLAYERS MAKING CONSECUTIVE APPEARANCES

Rank	Tests	Player	From	To
1.	153	Allan Border	First Test v Pakistan, 1978–79	Third Test v South Africa, 1994
2.	107	Mark Waugh	First Test v England, 1993	Third Test v Pakistan, 2002
3.	71	Ian Chappell	Fourth Test v England, 1965–66	Sixth Test v West Indies, 1975–76
4.	64	Ian Healy	First Test v Pakistan, 1988	Second Test v Pakistan, 1994
5.	60	David Boon	Only Test v New Zealand, 1990	Third Test v Sri Lanka, 1995–96
6.	55	Ian Healy	First Test v England, 1994–95	Only Test v Zimbabwe, 1999
7.	54	Glenn McGrath	First Test v Pakistan, 1998	Fourth Test v England, 2002–03
8.	53	Kim Hughes	First Test v England, 1978–79	Fifth Test v England, 1982–83
9.	52	Rod Marsh	First Test v England, 1970–71	Fifth Test v England, 1977
10.	52	Mark Taylor	Second Test v South Africa, 1994	Fifth Test v England, 1998–99

The only other Australian to play 50 consecutive Tests is Greg Chappell, whose Test life began one match after Rod Marsh made his debut. Like Marsh, Chappell's career continued uninterrupted until the final Ashes Test of 1977, when they, like many of their teammates, put their official Test careers on hold to join World Series Cricket.

In the two years of World Series Cricket, Rod Marsh was one of only two Australians (Ray Bright being the other) to not miss even one of his team's 13 'SuperTests'. Then, when all players again became available for Tests, at the beginning of the 1979–80 Australian season, Marsh was immediately reinstalled as his country's keeper. And he did not miss a Test until he was unavailable for the short tour to Sri Lanka in 1983, a run of 39 Tests.

10 PLAYERS WHO HAVE APPEARED IN MOST TEST WINS

Rank	Wins	Player	Tests	Win %
1.	83	Steve Waugh	162	51.23
2.	72	Mark Waugh	128	56.25
3=	62	Shane Warne	107	57.94
3=	62	Glenn McGrath	95	65.26
5.	55	Ian Healy	119	46.22
6.	52	Mark Taylor	104	50.00
7.	50	Allan Border	156	32.05
8.	48	Ricky Ponting	69	69.57
9.	44	Michael Slater	74	59.46
10.	42	Justin Langer	65	64.62

'Win %' indicates wins as a percentage of total appearances.

The first Australian cricketer to be a part of 30 winning Test sides was Don Bradman — his final Test, the fifth Ashes Test of 1948, was his 30th victory. The first to 40 was Neil Harvey, who completed his career with 41 Test victories (as, 33 years later, did David Boon). First to 50 was Allan Border, whose last win was the second Test in South Africa in 1994. Steve Waugh was first to 60, 70 and 80, but it is interesting to note that when Mark Waugh retired at the beginning of the 2002–03 Ashes series, he was just two Test wins behind Steve, despite the fact that when the younger twin began his Test career, the elder had already played in 42 Tests (for 12 wins).

Australian cricketers besides those featured in this Top 10 who played in at least 40 Tests and at least half of them were wins include Warwick Armstrong (28 wins in 50 Tests), Greg Blewett (27 in 46), Don Bradman (30 in 52), Adam Gilchrist (36 in 45), Jason Gillespie (30 in 45), Neil Harvey (41 in 79), Lindsay Hassett (26 in 43), Mathew Hayden (31 in 44), Clem Hill (25 in 49), Ian Johnson (28 in 45), Bill Johnston (25 in 40), Ray Lindwall (33 in 61), Keith Miller (31 in 55), Arthur Morris (27 in 46), Monty Noble (21 in 42) and Bert Oldfield (29 in 54).

Colin McCool has played the most Tests without experiencing a loss. Australia's massive defeat at The Oval in 1938, by an innings and 579 runs, would prove to be the only Test loss for Sid Barnes and Chuck Fleetwood-Smith. This was Barnes' debut Test, and Fleetwood-Smith's last.

10 AUSTRALIANS WITH THE BEST WINNING RECORDS
(Based on a percentage, wins as a proportion of total appearances; qualification 10 Tests)

Rank	Win %	Player	Tests	Wins	Draws	Losses	Ties
1.	83.33	Sam Loxton	12	10	2	–	–
2.	80.00	Adam Gilchrist	45	36	3	6	–
3.	78.79	Brett Lee	33	26	3	4	–
4.	78.57	Darren Lehmann	14	11	1	2	–
5.	76.92	Sid Barnes	13	10	2	1	–
6.	75.00	Ernie Toshack	12	9	3	–	–
7.	73.33	Andy Bichel	15	11	1	3	–
8=.	71.43	Don Tallon	21	15	5	1	–
8=.	71.43	Colin McCool	14	10	4	–	–
10.	70.45	Matthew Hayden	44	31	3	10	–

Adam Gilchrist started his Test career with 15 straight wins, beginning with the first Test against Pakistan in 1999–2000 and continuing until the Australians were defeated in Kolkata in 2001.

10 AUSTRALIANS WITH THE POOREST WINNING RECORDS

(Based on a percentage, wins as a proportion of total appearances; qualification 10 Tests)

Rank	Win %	Player	Tests	Wins	Draws	Losses	Ties
1.	8.00	Ray Bright	25	2	13	9	1
2.	10.00	Kevin Wright	10	1	4	5	–
3.	10.00	Tim Zoehrer	10	1	5	3	1
4.	10.00	Tony Dodemaide	10	1	6	3	–
5.	13.33	Greg Ritchie	30	4	12	13	1
6.	14.29	Jack Lyons	14	2	2	10	–
7.	14.81	Wayne B Phillips	27	4	12	11	–
8.	16.67	Andrew Hilditch	18	3	7	8	–
9.	17.24	Brian Booth	29	5	18	6	–
10.	18.18	Greg Matthews	33	6	19	7	1

Geoff Marsh's Test career ran to 50 matches, and featured 16 wins, 23 draws, 10 losses and a tie. However, he didn't enjoy his first victory until his 14th Test, the longest run an Australian cricketer has had to endure before being on the winning side in a Test. Marsh made his first Test appearance in the opening Test against India in 1985–86, the same match in which Bruce Reid debuted. Steve Waugh wore the baggy green for the first time in the following Test. From that Test against India in Adelaide until (but not including) the fifth Ashes Test of 1986–87, which Australia won by 55 runs, Australia played 13 Tests for no wins, one tie, three losses and nine draws. Marsh played in all 13 of these matches, Waugh in all but the first, Reid in all but the second Test in India in 1986. Marsh was actually appointed Australia's vice-captain for his 14th Test, having never played in a winning Test team.

The preponderance of players from the mid-1980s in this Top 10 reflects just what a disheartening time that was for Australian cricket. No wonder that on his retirement, Allan Border (the captain through much of these hard times) implored another senior player, David Boon, to 'never, ever let the younger blokes know what it's like to get their backsides kicked week in, week out'.

One amazing aspect of the Australian XI that played in the Tied Test in Madras in 1986 is the fact that the side was just so not used to winning. Between them, the players had been part of 33 Test victories: Allan Border had played in 21 wins, David Boon and Greg Ritchie in three, Greg Matthews, Craig McDermott and Ray Bright in two. Five players — Marsh, Waugh, Reid, Zoehrer and Dean Jones — were yet to experience a Test-match triumph. By way of comparison, after the Test against Bangladesh at Cairns in July 2003 the Australian XI team members had, between them, 388 individual wins to their credit.

10 AUSTRALIANS WHO HAVE PLAYED IN MOST DRAWS

Rank	Draws	Player	Tests	Draw%
1.	59	Allan Border	156	37.82
2.	43	Steve Waugh	162	26.54
3.	40	David Boon	107	37.38
4.	35	Ian Healy	119	29.41
5.	33	Rod Marsh	96	34.38
6.	32	Mark Taylor	104	30.77
7.	30	Greg Chappell	87	34.49
8.	29	Bill Lawry	67	43.28
9.	29	Mark Waugh	128	22.66
10.	28	Doug Walters	74	37.84

'Draw%' indicates wins as a percentage of total appearances.

Four players appeared in at least 10 Tests and never played in a draw: Sammy Jones (12 Tests, 5 wins, 7 losses), Affie Jarvis (11, 4, 7), Bert Ironmonger (14, 8, 6) and Wayne Clark (10, 4, 6).

Nine players have appeared in at least 10 Tests and more than half of the Tests they participated in were draws: Brian Booth (29, 18, 62.07 draw percentage), Tom Veivers (21, 13, 61.90), Tony Dodemaide (10, 6, 60.00), Bruce Reid (27, 16, 59.26), Greg Matthews (33, 19, 57.58), Frank Laver (15 Tests, 8 draws, 53.33), Peter Burge (42, 22, 52.38), Ray Bright (25, 13, 52.00) and Neil Hawke (27, 14, 51.85).

The 'draw percentages' of some of the high-profile members of the 2002–03 Australian team are low, in some cases remarkably low, reflecting the fact that in 46 Tests since the 1999 tour of Sri Lanka, Australia has only drawn three Tests, in consecutive matches against New Zealand in 2001–02:

Draws	Player	Tests	Draw %
3	Adam Gilchrist	45	6.67
3	Jason Gillespie	45	6.67
3	Matthew Hayden	44	6.82
3	Brett Lee	33	9.09
10	Ricky Ponting	69	14.49
14	Glenn McGrath	95	14.74
10	Justin Langer	65	15.38
4	Stuart MacGill	25	16.00
21	Shane Warne	107	19.63

Although Steve Waugh has played in the second-highest number of draws, he has played in only five in his last 55 Tests.

10 AUSTRALIANS WHO HAVE PLAYED IN MOST LOSSES

Rank	Losses	Player	Tests	Loss%
1.	46	Allan Border	156	29.49
2.	35	Steve Waugh	162	21.60
3.	30	Graeme Wood	59	50.85
4=.	29	Kim Hughes	70	41.43
4=.	29	Ian Healy	119	24.37
6.	27	Mark Waugh	128	21.09
7=.	25	Rod Marsh	96	26.04
7=.	25	David Boon	107	23.36
9.	24	Shane Warne	107	22.43
10.	20	Mark Taylor	104	19.23

'Losses %' indicates wins as a percentage of total appearances.

Five Australian cricketers have played in 10 or more Tests and never been in a losing Australian side. Three of them — Sam Loxton (12 Tests, 10 wins, two draws), Colin McCool (14, 10, 4) and Ernie Toshack (12, 9, 3) played in Tests immediately after World War II, when Australia had a run of 25 Tests without defeat (only Test v New Zealand, March 1946 to fourth Test v England, February 1951). The other two — Ted McDonald (11 Tests, seven wins, four draws) and 'Nip' Pellew (10, 8, 2) — played their Tests immediately after World War I, when Australia went 14 Tests without defeat.

The Australian to play in the most Tests and all of them wins is Ken Archer, whose three Tests against England in 1950–51 and two against the West Indies the following season all ended in hometown victories. Archer's contribution to these successes was modest; he opened the batting nine times, but never once reached 50.

A number of Australian cricketers who finished their Test careers before 1900 played in losing teams in over 50 per cent of their matches. However, since 1900 only three men with 10 or more Test appearances have done so: Graeme Wood as above, Wayne Clark (six losses in 10 Tests) and Peter Toohey (nine losses in 15 Tests). Seven other cricketers lost exactly half their Test matches: Brian Taber (16 Test appearances), Alan Hurst (12), Craig Serjeant (12), John Dyson (30), Rick Darling (14), Jim Higgs (22) and Kevin Wright (10).

Alan Thomson, who appeared in four Tests in 1970–71 which all ended in draws, is the only Australian to appear in more than three Tests and never experience a Test victory.

THE TOP 10 AUSTRALIAN FOOTBALLERS TO PLAY TEST CRICKET

Rank	Footballer	Rank	Footballer
1.	Laurie Nash	6.	Eric Freeman
2.	George Coulthard	7.	Roy Park
3.	Jack Reedman	8.	Charles Eady
4.	Jack Worrall	9.	Keith Miller
5.	Neil Hawke	10.	Keith Slater

Our objective here is to nominate the best footballers to play Test cricket, not the other way around. Not surprisingly then, the top four players on our Top 10 are the only Test cricketers to be recognised for their football prowess by the official Australian Football Hall of Fame.

Laurie Nash was a somewhat controversial fast-medium bowler who could also bat a bit, and also one of the greatest players in the Victorian Football League (VFL) in the 1930s. During the bodyline series, there was a thought about that if Australia was to retaliate, Nash was the man to lead that counterattack, but though he had played in the fifth Test against South Africa the season before, he was not called up again until the final Ashes Test of 1936–37, when some wondered if Bradman had picked him as 'insurance', in case England decided to bowl short again. From his two Tests, Nash finished with a Test bowling average of 12.60 (10 wickets for 126 runs).

Nash had been the best footballer in Tasmania in 1931 and 1932 before joining South Melbourne in the VFL in 1933, where he won a premiership in his first year, a star at centre halfback. Later he moved with enormous success to centre half forward. An often told story has it that when asked who was the best player in the game, he humbly replied, 'I look at him in the mirror every morning.' He might have been right.

George Coulthard was called the 'grandest player of his day' by *The Australasian*'s football writer back in 1879, when he was a key man for Carlton in the Victorian Football Association (the forerunner to the VFL). Coulthard played one Test for Australia, batting at No. 11 (for 6 not out) and not bowling in 1881–82. Reedman captained South Australia at football and cricket, but while his football career in Adelaide was long and much celebrated, featuring eight premierships as player and coach, he appeared in only one cricket Test, the first of 1894–95, when he scored 17 and 4 and took 1–24 from 9.3 overs. Jack Worrall was a rover for Fitzroy in the VFA between 1883 and 1893, a Test cricketer in 11 matches between 1885 and 1899, the first official coach of a VFL team (taking charge of Carlton in 1902) and a long-time writer on football and cricket for *The Australasian*.

Neil Hawke and Eric Freeman both played Test cricket in the 1960s, club football for Port Adelaide in the SANFL and interstate footy for South Australia. Hawke had made his debut with Port in 1957, kicking 15 goals in his third game, before moving to Perth, where he won back-to-back premierships with East Perth. When he returned to Adelaide for the 1961 season, he linked up with West Torrens with some success, though injuries and cricket impeded what might have been one of the great football careers. Freeman was outstanding enough to top the SANFL goalkicking list in 1966, and to go straight into the club's top team for the 1968 finals, after he returned from that year's Ashes tour.

Within a week of returning from England, Port Adelaide coach Fos Williams put Freeman on the bench for the second semi-final against Sturt. Eight minutes into the final quarter, Freeman was on, and with his first touch he dragged down a mark and goaled; with his second touch he marked on his chest and goaled again, this time from 45 metres. Unfortunately, the fightback ended with Port 13 points adrift. Freeman was again a reserve for the preliminary final against North Adelaide, which Port won, and for the Grand Final. In his report on the premiership decider for *the Advertiser*, Keith Butler wrote of Freeman's dramatic entrance:

> *Williams, halfway through the third quarter, amid great excitement, sent Eric Freeman, his big gun, into the action ...*

The Test cricketer would end the game as Port's leading scorer, kicking 2.2, but Sturt won the flag by 27 points.

Roy Park (one Test in 1920–21) would have been an even better footballer but for his medical studies, but he was still good enough to finish second in the VFL's goalkicking list for 1915. Jack Worrall always said that Tasmania's Charles Eady (two Tests, one on the 1896 Ashes tour, one in 1901–02) was the best footballer he ever saw. Keith Miller played football for St Kilda and Victoria. Keith Slater (one Test in 1958–59), who rounds out our Top 10, captained Western Australia.

Of course, the list of prominent footballers/Test cricketers does not end here. Especially in the seasons before World War I, it was common for the country's best athletes to participate and sometimes excel in summer *and* winter. In his book *Everything You Ever Wanted to Know About Australian Rules Football But Couldn't Be Bothered Asking* (1982), Graeme Atkinson noted that all of the following allrounders had played top-grade Australian football and Test cricket:

Victoria: Frank Allan, Warwick Armstrong, Jack Barrett, Jack Blackham, Harry Boyle, Barlow Carkeek, Harry Graham, Albert Hartkopf, Tom Horan, Tom Kendall, Sam Loxton, Jimmy Matthews, Ted McDonald, John McIlwraith, George McShane, Harry Musgrove, Simon O'Donnell, George Palmer, James Slight, George Tribe, Max Walker and Graeme Watson.

South Australia: Joe Darling, Algy Gehrs, George Giffen, Clem Hill, Ernie Jones, Gil Langley, 'Nip' Pellew, Vic Richardson and Mervyn Waite.

Western Australia: Mick Malone and John Inverarity.

Tasmania: Kenny Burn.

No one has ever been able to complete the double of playing Tests in rugby league and cricket. Jack Scott, a Test umpire immediately after World War II and a pace bowler good enough to play Sheffield Shield cricket between 1908 and 1929, was the man who scored the first ever try in Sydney premiership rugby league. Playing in the centres for Newtown on Easter Monday, 20 April 1908, Scott snared an early intercept and careered away. Three seasons later, Herbert Collins, later an Australian cricket captain, was five-eighth in the Eastern Suburbs team that won the premiership. In the 1940s, Ray Lindwall was an excellent winger and fullback who played in two losing grand finals with St George before he became a Test fast bowler.

Two men have represented Australia in rugby union Tests and Test cricket. Otto Nothling came into the Australian cricket team for the second Test of 1928–29, the new allrounder in the side following the forced retirement through injury of Jack Gregory, scored 8 and 44, took 0–60 and 0–12, and never played again. Nothling's career in rugby was more successful. He had been a stalwart of the NSW team through the early 1920s, winning 19 caps between 1921 and 1924. In two matches in 1922 against the New Zealand Maoris, he was joined in the NSW XV by Johnny Taylor, a clever goalkicking centre and five-eighth who was already an accomplished Test cricketer.

These rugby matches were not recognised as official Tests until 1986, when the Australian Rugby Union gave Test status to all the international games NSW played while the Queensland Rugby Union was defunct between 1919 and 1929. Until that retrospective decision, the closest anyone had come to doing the Test double was Alan Walker, who toured South Africa in 1949–50 (but did not play in a Test), having made his Test debut for the Wallabies in 1947.

10 LONGEST TEST CAREERS
(From first day of debut to last day of last Test)

Rank	Age (years, days)	Player	Career Span
1.	22, 32	Syd Gregory	1890 – 1912
2.	20, 131	Bob Simpson	1957-58 – 1978
3.	19, 263	Don Bradman	1928-29 – 1948
4.	19, 227	Warwick Armstrong	1901-02 – 1921
5.	18, 248	Charlie Macartney	1907-08 – 1926
6.	17, 362	Charles Kelleway	1910-11 – 1928-29
7.	17, 280	Jack Blackham	1876-77 – 1894-95
8.	17, 214	Steve Waugh	1985-86 – 2003
9.	17, 83	Warren Bardsley	1909 – 1926
10.	16, 75	Bert Oldfield	1920-21 – 1936-37

Steve Waugh's figures are as at the end of the second Test v Bangladesh, which ended on 28 July 2003. To beat Gregory's career span, Waugh would have to keep playing until well into the 2007–08 season. Indeed, if, as has occurred in recent years, the final Test of the 2007–08 Australian summer was the Sydney New Year's Test, Waugh would have to continue on into Australia's next series after that to create a new record.

The Test careers of Allan Border, Ian Chappell, Clem Hill, Neil Harvey, Doug Walters and Lindsay Hassett each spanned 15 years.

10 LONGEST GAPS IN A TEST CAREER *(By time)*

Rank	Years	Days	Player	Interval	Tests Missed
1.	9	305	Bob Simpson	1967-68–1977-78	71
2.	6	218	Steve Rixon	1978–1984-85	66
3.	6	179	Brad Hogg	1996–2003	86
4.	6	137	Affie Jarvis	1888–1894-95	11
5.	6	133	Jack Worrall	1888–1894-95	10
6.	6	117	Mike Whitney	1981–1987-88	58
7.	6	65	Damien Martyn	1993-94–2000	68
8.	5	217	Billy Murdoch	1884-85–1890	13
9=.	5	140	William Bruce	1886–1891-92	8
9=.	5	140	George Giffen	1886–1891-92	8

This Top 10 does not include the six men who played for Australia either side of World War I (Hanson Carter, Warwick Armstrong, Edgar Mayne, Charlie Macartney, Warren Bardsley and Charles Kelleway) or the five who played either side of World War II (Don Bradman, Bill O'Reilly, Bill

Brown, Lindsay Hassett and Sid Barnes). It also doesn't include Sammy Woods and Kepler Wessels, who played for Australia and then, after a substantial break, played for another country (Woods for England, Wessels for South Africa).

10 AUSTRALIANS WHO HAVE BEEN MOST TIMES 12TH MAN
(In Australia)

Rank	Times 12th man	Player	Career as 12th man
1.	15	Andy Bichel	1997-98–2003
2=	7	Terry Jenner	1970-71–1975-76
2=	7	Paul Reiffel	1991-92–1996-97
4=	6	Tommy Andrews	1920-21–1928-29
4=	6	Ashley Mallett	1968-69–1980-81
4=	6	Glenn McGrath	1993-94–1994-95
4=	6	Michael Kasprowicz	1995-96–1999-00
8=	5	Keith Rigg	1930-31–1931-32
8=	5	Jim Burke	1950-51–1954-55
8=	5	Max Walker	1973-74–1976-77
8=	5	Ray Bright	1976-77–1986-87
8=	5	Geoff Lawson	1981-82–1986-87
8=	5	Carl Rackemann	1982-83–1990-91
8=	5	Tim May	1987-88–1995-96
8=	5	Colin Miller	1998-99–2000-01

Definitively identifying the Australia Test team's 12th man is often difficult, especially on overseas tours when on occasions no official 12th man is ever announced. Consequently, we have restricted this study to Tests in Australia, when in most instances the selectors will choose a squad of 12 or perhaps 13 and then identify the official 12th man when the final XI is announced.

There have been occasions when a XII has been picked and then, on the morning of the game, the man omitted has been cleared to return to play for his state, but in such instances that man, rather than the local cricketer who has filled the role of substitute, is the man we have considered to be the 12th man. For nine of the first 22 Test matches played in Australia, there was no official 12th man. Thus, this Top 10 is based on 311 Tests. In them, 158 players have been 12th man, 11 of whom never got the chance to actually be part of a Test XI: Leslie Poidevin (1901–02), Leslie Hill (1907–08), Colin McKenzie (1907–08), Edgar Waddy (1907–08), Syd Hird (1932–33), Bert Tobin (1932–33), Ian McLachlan (1962–63), Jack Potter

(1963–64), Geoff Davies (1968–69), Shaun Graf (1980–81) and Brad Williams (2001–02).

Terry Jenner, Tommy Andrews, Ashley Mallett, Ray Bright and Tim May were 12th man after they played their final Test matches.

10 AUSTRALIANS WHO HAVE BEEN MOST TIMES MAN OF THE MATCH *(1979 to 2003)*

Rank	Player	Awards
1=.	Shane Warne	14
1=.	Steve Waugh	14
3.	Allan Border	12
4.	Glenn McGrath	9
5=.	Geoff Lawson	6
5=.	Dean Jones	6
5=.	Mark Taylor	6
5=.	Michael Slater	6
5=.	Justin Langer	6
5=.	Ricky Ponting	6

The practice of naming an official man of the match for Tests in Australia was introduced for the much-hyped 1975–76 Australia–West Indies series and was commonplace across the cricket world by 1979–80. Consequently, this Top 10 is restricted to Test cricket from that first Australian season post-World Series Cricket (1979–80) to the Bangladesh series in 2003. The only Tests involving Australia since then that did not offer official man of the match awards were the three played in India in 1986, so we'll hand out our own prizes. Dean Jones gets the award in the first Test for his monumental 210, in the second rain-ruined match we'll go for Tim Zoehrer for his 52 not out, and in the third Dilip Vengsarkar's unbeaten 164 gets the gong.

Our sample involves 248 Tests. In seven of these, the awards were shared by two players; for our purposes both players get a 'full' award. Of these 255, 156 went to Australians, 99 to opponents.

---

10 QUOTES ABOUT GREAT AUSTRALIAN CRICKETERS

4. 'Is Vic here?'
   – Australian captain Joe Darling 'roll call' before his team departed their hotel for a day's play on the 1902 Ashes tour. When assured Trumper was aboard, Darling would say, 'All right driver, we can get going now. Don't worry about the others.'

THE TOP 10 CONTROVERSIES

Rank	Controversy	Immediate Consequence
1.	World Series Cricket, 1977–79	Most of Australia's best players miss two years of Test cricket.
2.	The Bodyline Series, 1932–33	'Unsportsmanlike' England put British Empire at risk.
3.	Players v Cricket Board dispute, 1911–12	Six of Australia's best players miss 1912 tour of England.
4.	Aussie bowlers accused of throwing, 1958–59	World 'cleanup' ends with Ian Meckiff 'thrown' out of Tests in 1963.
5.	South Africa's Australian tour cancelled, 1971	South Africa out of Test cricket until 1992.
6.	Australia rebels tour South Africa, 1985–87	Fifteen Australian players banned from Test matches.
7.	Australian team pay dispute, 1884–85	Australian needs new team for second Ashes Test.
8.	Match-fixing allegations, 1995 to 1998	Australian players admit to taking bookies' money for information.
9.	Pakistan tour nearly abandoned 1988	Australian team continues tour after protests over umpiring.
10.	Melbourne pitch illegally watered, 1954–55	MCG admits nothing; Test goes on with England clearly advantaged.

Of course, with most of these controversies, the consequences were actually much more far-reaching that what is outlined above. World Series Cricket — which came about because of a dispute between the Australian Cricket Board and media mogul Kerry Packer over TV rights, and because the Board failed to appreciate the extent of the players' entrenched belief that they were being shortchanged when revenues were distributed — changed the game immeasurably, in a manner that remains important and obvious even today. Think about the rises in players' salaries, the one-day international cricket boom, the way media coverage has been revolutionised. Bodyline might have matched WSC for the depth of feeling it generated, and some of those animosities persisted for lifetimes, but it hardly changed the game as emphatically as WSC did.

Most of the controversies we have selected revolved around one of two issues: money or politics (cricket or otherwise). The South Africa issue simmered in one shape or form for much of the two decades the Springboks were banned from 1971. The rebel tours of 1985–86 and 1986–87 clearly hurt the Australian team in the short term, but might also have resulted in inexperienced players such as Steve Waugh, Dean Jones, David Boon, Geoff

Marsh and Merv Hughes having extended runs in the Test team. The dispute that prevented captain Clem Hill, Warwick Armstrong, Hanson Carter, Tibby Cotter, Vernon Ransford and Victor Trumper from going to England in 1912 was about more than just the players' cut from the tour; the players resented not so much the concept of a Board of Control running the game but the methods and perceived biases of the officials who were taking control. World War I might have limited the long-term impact of this dispute, to the Board's advantage, but for many involved the bitterness cut deep, and Armstrong's short reign as Australian captain after the war featured a number of skirmishes with prominent officials.

Many, we imagine, would rank the match-fixing controversy higher. It is true that the fact that Mark Waugh and Shane Warne admitted to taking money from 'John the bookmaker' in return for providing to him what they saw as harmless information (and that the Australian Cricket Board agreed to keep this fact quiet for three years) was the most *sensational* Australian event of the match-fixing scandal. But compared to others in this saga, Warne and Waugh were hardly major players — and as the story evolved the Australian team, and Australian cricket, seemed always on the periphery of an outrage that eventually claimed the careers of three high-profile overseas Test captains. ◾

10 GROUNDS WHERE AUSTRALIA HAS BEEN MOST SUCCESSFUL *(Qualification: five Tests played)*

Rank	Win %	Ground (first used)	Tests	W	D	T	L
1.	88.88	Cape Town (1902)	9	8	0	0	1
2.	66.66	Hobart (1989–90)	6	4	2	0	0
3.	60.00	Port Elizabeth (1949–50)	5	3	0	0	2
4.	57.77	The Gabba (1931–32)	45	26	10	1	8
5.	57.14	Georgetown (1955)	7	4	1	0	2
6.	56.66	Perth (1970–71)	30	17	6	0	7
7.	54.73	Melbourne (1876–77)	95	52	15	0	28
8.	51.68	Sydney (1881–82)	89	46	16	0	27
9.	50.00	Auckland (1974)	6	3	0	0	3
10.	49.18	Adelaide (1884–85)	61	30	16	0	15

The ground on which Australia has played the most Tests while remaining undefeated at that ground is Bellerive Oval in Hobart. The ground on which Australia has played the most Tests and kept a perfect winning record at that ground is Corporation (Nehru) Stadium in Madras (now Chennai), where three Australia v India Tests were played between 1956 and 1964.

Australia's 'least successful' ground has been the National Stadium in Karachi, where there have been eight Australia v Pakistan Tests played since 1956 for three draws and five home team victories. Next worst for Australia, of those where Australia has played at least five Tests, is The Oval in London, which has seen only six Australian victories (plus 12 draws and 15 losses) in 33 Tests since 1880.

Australia's victories at The Oval came in 1882, 1930, 1934, 1948, 1972 and 2001.

The only ground at which Australia has never even drawn is Centurion Park in Pretoria, South Africa, where Mark Taylor's team was beaten in 1997. That remains the only Australia v South Africa Test played at that venue.

THE FIRST 10 GROUNDS ON WHICH AUSTRALIA PLAYED TEST CRICKET *(All against England)*

Order	Ground	City	Season of First Test
1.	Melbourne Cricket Ground	Melbourne	1876–77
2.	The Oval	London	1880
3.	Sydney Cricket Ground	Sydney	1881–82
4.	Old Trafford	Manchester	1884
5.	Lord's	London	1884
6.	Adelaide Oval	Adelaide	1884–85
7.	Trent Bridge	Nottingham	1899
8.	Headingley	Leeds	1899
9.	Edgbaston	Birmingham	1902
10.	Bramall Lane	Sheffield	1902

10 GROUNDS ON WHICH AUSTRALIA MOST RECENTLY PLAYED TEST CRICKET FOR THE FIRST TIME

Order	Ground	City	Season of First Test	Opponent
1.	Bundaberg Rum Stadium	Cairns	2003	Bangladesh
2.	Marrara Oval	Darwin	2003	Bangladesh
3.	Sharjah Stadium	Sharjah	2002	Pakistan
4.	P. Saravanamuttu	Colombo	2002	Pakistan
5.	Seddon Park	Hamilton	2000	New Zealand
6.	Harare Sports Club	Harare	1999	Zimbabwe
7.	Galle International Stadium	Galle	1999	Sri Lanka
8.	Arbab Niaz Stadium	Peshawar	1998	Pakistan
9.	Centurion Park	Verwoerdburg	1997	South Africa
10.	Rawalpindi Cricket Stadium	Rawalpindi	1994	Pakistan

THE TOP 10 AUSTRALIAN CRICKET SONGS

1. **C'mon Aussie C'mon**, words and music by Allan Johnston and Alan Morris (1978)
2. **Under the Southern Cross I Stand** — performed by various victorious Australian cricket teams since the 1970s, led by men such as Rod Marsh, Allan Border, David Boon, Ian Healy and Ricky Ponting
3. **Our Don Bradman** — written by Jack O'Hagan, performed by Art Leonard with novelty accompaniment (1930)
4. **Here Come the Aussies** — written by Daniel Boone and Rod McQueen, performed by the 1972 Australian Ashes touring team.
5. **Our Eleven** — written by Jack Lumsdaine, performed by Art Leonard with novelty accompaniment (1930)
6. **Bradman** — written and performed by Paul Kelly (1987)
7. **The Tiger and The Don** — written and performed by Ted Egan (1988)
8. **Old Fashioned Locket/Our Bungalow of Dreams** — Don Bradman at the piano (1930)
9. **Can't Bowl, Can't Throw** — performed by Six and Out (2000)
10. **Howzat** — written by Garth Porter and Tony Mitchell, performed by Sherbet (1976)

In the same way World Series Cricket changed the face of Australian cricket, so too the marketing strategy that supported the cricket revolutionised the way the game was promoted in this country. At the head of this campaign was the song *C'mon Aussie C'mon*, the lyrics of which featured the biggest names in the Australian team and which became something of an anthem, especially for the young fans who grew to accept the 'rebel' sport in big numbers. Today, 25 years on from WSC, many cricket fans can remember those lyrics … of Lillee 'pounding down like a machine' … of Hookesy 'clearing pickets' … of 'Dougie chewing gum' … and 'Gilmour wielding the willow like an axe'.

It was the Australian team of the 1970s that established the tradition of chanting *Under the Southern Cross I Stand* in the dressing room after Test match wins. The role of leading the team in song was seen within the team as an important one, filled by a player who embodied the pride in the baggy green cap that all in the team felt. David Boon, who took over from Allan Border after Border became Australian captain in 1984, was so proud of his time in this role that he insisted on his autobiography being called *Under the Southern Cross*.

A book released nine years before Boon's life story was entitled *Our Don Bradman*. It took its name from a very successful record that had been first released in 1930. The old '78' with *Our Don Bradman* on one side and *Our Eleven* on the other remains a prized collectable, and features lyrics such as:

Who is it that all Australia raves about?
Who has won our very highest praise?
Now is it Amy Johnson, or little Mickey Mouse?
No! it's just a country lad who's bringing down the house.
And he's ...

Our Don Bradman ...

Jack Lumsdaine, the writer of *Our Eleven*, also wrote the words for a song entitled *Every Day is a Rainbow for Me*, which was composed by none other than Don Bradman. The song was definitely performed in public, and there are reports of Bradman speaking on stage about his role in its composition.

Paul Kelly's tribute to The Don first appeared on his 1987 album, *Under the Sun*. Many years earlier, Bradman's *Old Fashioned Locket* was released at the height of his fame following the 1930 Ashes tour. As the story goes, Columbia Records were more than a little surprised when The Don announced he wanted to record a musical piece; when they signed the world's greatest batsman they had anticipated committing a talk on cricket to vinyl.

The final two positions in this table are something of a 'long bow'. Six and Out are hardly U2, but they do uniquely feature two Test cricketers in Brett Lee (guitar) and Gavin Robertson (drums), and their song is based loosely on the famously unflattering description of another Test bowler, Scott Muller, by the mysterious Joe the Cameraman. Sherbet's biggest hit came about, according to songwriters Garth Porter and Tony Mitchell, after the band discussed the idea of recording a 'cricket song', but other than the title and a couple of catchy phrases the song has little to do with the game. Still, it became a No. 1 hit in Australia, reached No. 4 in the UK, and charted highly in South Africa, as well as several mainland European and Asian countries. *Howzat* actually reached No. 2 in Thailand, of all places, but whether that was because of its cricket connection has never been determined.

10 HIGHEST ATTENDANCES AT TESTS IN AUSTRALIA

(In Australia)

Rank	Crowd	Ground	Test & Day's Play	Date
1.	90,800	MCG	1960–61 v West Indies, 5th Test, 2nd day	11 February
2.	87,798	MCG	1936–37 v England, 3rd Test, 3rd day	4 January
3.	85,661	MCG	1975–76 v West Indies, 3rd Test, 1st day	26 December
4.	79,630	MCG	1936–37 v England, 3rd Test, 1st day	1 January
5.	77,181	MCG	1936–37 v England, 5th Test, 2nd day	27 February
6.	77,167	MCG	1974–75 v England, 3rd Test, 1st day	26 December
7.	73,812	MCG	1997–98 v South Africa, 1st Test, 1st day	26 December
8.	73,233	MCG	2000–01 v West Indies, 4th Test, 1st day	26 December
9.	72,891	MCG	1996–97 v West Indies, 3rd Test, 1st day	26 December
10.	72,022	MCG	1946–47 v England, 3rd Test, 4th day	4 January

The top 36 attendances in Australian Test history have been at the Melbourne Cricket Ground (MCG). This figure of 36 includes the 61,850 people who turned up on Boxing Day 1998 for the opening day of the fourth Ashes Test but didn't see a ball bowled as the day's play was washed out. The record highs at other venues in Australia are as follows:

Ground	Crowd	Test & Day's Play	Date
Sydney Cricket Ground	58,446	1928–29 v England, 2nd Test, 2nd day	15 December
Adelaide Oval	50,962	1932–33 v England, 3rd Test, 2nd day	14 January
Exhibition Ground, Brisbane	24,422	1928–29 v England, 1st Test, 2nd day	1 December
The Gabba, Brisbane	30,598	1936–37 v England, 1st Test, 2nd day	5 December
The WACA Ground, Perth	24,151	1974–75 v England, 2nd Test, 3rd day	15 December
Bellerive Oval, Hobart	9,015	1989–90 v Sri Lanka, 1st Test, 1st day	16 December
Marrara Cricket Ground, Darwin	6,238	2003 v Bangladesh, 1st Test, 1st day	18 July
Bundaberg Rum Stadium, Cairns	5,248	2003 v Bangladesh, 2nd Test, 1st day	25 July

The biggest attendance at a day's play of an overseas Test involving Australia was most likely the estimated 90,000 plus that came to the fifth day's play of the second Test at Eden Gardens in Kolkata in 2001. No official attendance figure for that exciting day in Indian cricket history — when the home team defeated Steve Waugh's Australians despite having to follow on — was ever published.

Webster and Miller, in *First-Class Cricket in Australia (Volume 1)*, record that the lowest total attendance for a Test in Australia is 1973, for the only Ashes Test of 1887–88. On the first day 1173 people came to the SCG, and there was no play on days two and three. On day four, the 'crowd' was 700 and on day five 100 were there to see Australia lose its last five wickets.

10 AUSTRALIAN UMPIRES WITH MOST TEST APPEARANCES

Rank	Tests	Umpire	Years	Home	Away
1.	48	Darrell Hair	1991-92–2003	21	27
2.	36	Steve Randell	1984-85–1997-98	26	10
3=.	33	Tony Crafter	1978-79–1991-92	33	0
3=.	33	Daryl Harper	1998-99–2003	7	26
5.	32	Bob Crockett	1901-02–1924-25	32	0
6=.	29	Jim Phillips	1884-85–1905-06	13	16
6=.	29	Col Egar	1960-61–1968-69	29	0
8.	27	Robin Bailhache	1974-75–1988-89	27	0
9.	25	Lou Rowan	1962-63–1970-71	25	0
10.	24	George Borwick	1930-31–1947-48	24	0

'Home' indicates Tests umpired in Australia; 'Away' indicates Tests umpired outside Australia.

To create a Top 10 of umpires with most appearances in Australia, Daryl Harper and Jim Phillips would be replaced by Tom Brooks (23 Tests) and Peter McDonnell (22 Tests), and Mel Johnson would join Darrell Hair in equal 10th place with 21 Tests.

The Australian umpires with the most appearances in consecutive Tests are George Borwick, who officiated in 22 straight between 1931–32 and 1947–48, and Col Egar, 22 straight between 1962–63 and 1968–69. The third Ashes Test of 1962–63 was the only Test in Australia in the 1960s that Egar was not a part of.

Egar and Lou Rowan umpired 19 Tests as a partnership, easily an Australian record. Borwick and George Hele (10) and Borwick and Jack Scott (10) are the only other pairs with 10 Tests. Twelve of Egar and Rowan's Tests were in succession, from 1965–66 to 1968–69. All of Borwick and Hele's and Borwick and Scott's Tests as pairs were in a row.

In 1994 the ICC established a panel of 'international' umpires, and ruled that each Test would feature one home umpire and one 'independent' umpire. This provided Australian umps with the chance to stand in Tests overseas, hence the appearance numbers of men such as Darrell Hair, Steve Randell and Daryl Harper. Previously, only two Australians had umpired in overseas Tests — Jim Phillips, in England and South Africa between 1893 and 1906, and the former Test allrounder Arthur Richardson, who worked in two Tests in the West Indies in 1935. In 2002, the ICC took their initiative a major step further, by establishing a panel of elite umpires and deciding that in future Tests would be controlled by two independent umpires. Thus, the highest position to which an Australian umpire can now aspire for Tests in Australia is to be the 'third' or 'TV' umpire. The first Australian to umpire in a Test outside Australia under the ICC banner was Hair, in the fourth Test between England and the West Indies, in Barbados, in 1994. The first Australian umpires to work as a pair in a Test outside Australia were Harper and Simon Taufel in the first Sri-Lanka-New Zealand Test, in Colombo, in 2003.

The most Test appearances by an independent umpire in Australia is 10, by Steve Bucknor of the West Indies. Srinivas Venkataraghavan (India), David Shepherd (England) and Rudi Koertzen (South Africa) have all umpired in six Tests in Australia.

10 MOST PROLIFIC BIRTHPLACES FOR AUSTRALIAN TEST CRICKETERS *(State, Territory, overseas country)*

Rank	No.	Birthplace
1.	130	New South Wales
2.	105	Victoria
3.	42	South Australia
4.	39	Western Australia
5.	36	Queensland
6.	12	Tasmania
7.	9	England
8.	3	New Zealand
9=	2	Ireland
9=	2	India

Five birthplaces are responsible for one Australian Test cricketer: Archie Jackson was born in Rutherglen, Scotland; Dav Whatmore in Colombo, Ceylon (now Sri Lanka); Kepler Wessels in Bloemfontein, South Africa; Damien Martyn in Darwin in the Northern Territory; and Michael Bevan in Belconnen in the Australian Capital Territory.

As for the title of most fantastic birthplace for an Australian Test cricketer, some might like to suggest Dacca, in what was then India (Bransby Cooper in 1844), or perhaps Caversham, near Dunedin, New Zealand (Clarrie Grimmett, on Christmas Day 1891), but we believe it is hard to go past where Sydney Edward Gregory was born. Syd's father, Ned, played for Australia in the first ever Test match, by which time he was also ensconced as the head groundsman at what was then known as the 'Association Ground', soon to become the Sydney Cricket Ground. Philip Derriman, in his history of the SCG, *The Grand Old Ground*, writes: 'He [Ned] was in charge of raising and levelling the playing area, and he laid the new wickets. Later, he designed the SCG's first mechanical scoreboard.

He lived on the ground in the caretaker's cottage, raised his children there and died there [in 1899]. If it were ever discovered that the SCG had a ghost, the chances are it would be Ned Gregory.'

Derriman believes that Ned Gregory was most likely living in the stone cottage that was situated besides the cricket ground from the late 1860s. Syd Gregory — a future Australian captain — was born on 14 April 1870, reputedly in that cottage, just a lofted drive from the centre of what would become Sydney's premier cricket ground.

10 SHORTEST LIVED AUSTRALIAN TEST PLAYERS

Rank	Age at death (years, days)	Player	Life span
1.	23, 164	Archie Jackson	1909–1933
2.	26, 102	Ross Gregory	1916–1942
3.	27, 56	Gerry Hazlitt	1888–1915
4.	27, 82	George Coulthard	1856–1883
5.	29, 147	John Cottam	1867–1897
6.	32, 332	Albert Cotter	1884–1917
7.	33, 118	Reg Duff	1878–1911
8.	33, 184	Jack Ferris	1867–1900
9.	34, 328	Jack McLaren	1886–1921
10.	37, 238	Victor Trumper	1877–1915

Three other Australian Test players died before what would have been their 40th birthday. Percy McDonnell, who was 37 years, 316 days when his heart failed him in 1896, remains the shortest-lived Australian captain. Bob McLeod and Billy Midwinter both died in their 40th year.

The causes of death of the men in this table are varied. Jack Ferris (during the Boer War), Tibby Cotter (at Beersheba in Palestine) and Ross Gregory (in India) all died at war. Victor Trumper also died during wartime, but in Sydney, from kidney failure; the manner in which his death stunned and hurt a nation conditioned to tragedy by the battles in Europe reflects the universal regard his public had for him. George Coulthard, the champion footballer, succumbed to tuberculosis within two years of his only Test, while Reggie Duff died destitute, effectively of alcoholism, a little more than six years after he proudly returned from the 1905 Ashes tour having scored a stirring 146 in the final Test at The Oval.

However, it is Jackson's death, which occurred after a long battle with tuberculosis and on the day England regained the Ashes in Brisbane in February 1933, that offers the cruellest case of 'what might have been'. At the Adelaide Oval four years before he had crafted one of the greatest debut innings in Test history, an innings that drew comparisons with the style and panache of the immortal Trumper, and though the 18 months that followed proved that Bradman was clearly the more ruthless rungetter, few thought Jackson less skilful. The Don himself called him a 'batting genius'. Harold Larwood, the man Jackson cover drove for four to reach his hundred in Adelaide, reckoned he was 'born to be great'. Jackson played only eight Tests, some when he was ill (in the 1930 Ashes series, he scored exactly 900 runs less than Bradman) and all before his 22nd birthday, but Arthur Mailey in the 1960s still picked him in his all-time Australian XI. Had he been more robust, every indication is that this Scottish-born boy from Balmain would have been at least the equal of Stan McCabe.

His funeral was one of the biggest Sydney has seen, with crowds four and five deep lining the streets for six kilometres from the family home in Drummoyne to the Field of Mars Cemetery at North Ryde. Among his pallbearers were some of the greats of Australian cricket: captain Bill Woodfull, Don Bradman, Bill Ponsford, Bert Oldfield, Vic Richardson. Alan Kippax stepped in to replace a distraught McCabe at the graveside. This might have been in the middle of the Depression, but the paperboys who worked outside the SCG still garnered enough precious shillings to send a wreath for their fallen hero. A week later, a memorial service at an overcrowded church in Balmain was broadcast by two radio stations, including the national broadcaster. In September 1933, the NSW Premier, Mr Stevens, was on hand when an elaborate headstone was placed over Jackson's grave. Inscribed on it was the epitaph …

'He played the game.'

10 QUOTES ABOUT GREAT AUSTRALIAN CRICKETERS

3. 'We picked Warne as a surprise packet, but we never thought he'd turn out quite so surprising.'

– Allan Border at The Oval in 1993, after Shane Warne had taken 34 wickets in his first Ashes series.

2. 'I've been criticised as a captain for overbowling Dennis Lillee. My answer is: have you tried to take a bone off a Doberman? That's what it was like trying to get the ball off Dennis Lillee.'

– Ian Chappell, interviewed in 2001 for ESPN's Legends of Cricket.

1. 'It was as though D'Artagnan had been detected in the act of taking out a life insurance policy.'

– Neville Cardus, in his report of the second day's play of the first Ashes Test of 1938, writing about Don Bradman being forced to defend on a turning pitch.

FURTHER CRICKET READING

BIOGRAPHY

Richie Benaud, *On Reflection*; Collins, Sydney, 1984

Richie Benaud, *Anything But ... An Autobiography*; Hodder & Stoughton, London, 1998

David Boon, *Under the Southern Cross*; HarperSports, Sydney, 1996

Mihir Bose, *Keith Miller: A Cricketing Biography*; George Allen & Unwin, North Sydney, 1979

Don Bradman, *Farewell to Cricket*; Hodder & Stoughton, London, 1950

Richard Cashman, *The Demon Spofforth*; NSW University Press, Sydney, 1990

Ian Chappell, *Chappelli*; Hutchinson, Melbourne, 1976

Alan Davidson, *Fifteen Paces*; Souvenir Press, London, 1963

Marc Fiddian, *Ponsford and Woodfull: A Premier Partnership*; The Five Mile Press, Fitzroy, 1988

Jack Fingleton, *The Immortal Victor Trumper*; Collins, London, 1981

Jack Fingleton, *Batting From Memory*; Collins, London, 1981

WG Grace, *WG: Cricketing Reminiscences & Personal Recollections*; The Hambledon Press, London, 1980 (first published in 1899)

Gideon Haigh, *Mystery Spinner*; Text Publishing, Melbourne, 2000

Gideon Haigh, *The Big Ship*; Text Publishing, Melbourne, 2001

Ian Healy, *Hands & Heals*; HarperSports, Sydney, 2000

Sir Jack Hobbs, *My Life Story*; The Hambledon Press, London, 1978 (first published in 1935)

Patrick Keane, *Merv: The Full Story*; HarperSports, Sydney, 1997

James Knight, *Lee To The Power of Two*; HarperSports, Sydney, 2001
Jack McHarg, *Bill O'Reilly: A Cricketing Life*; Millennium, Sydney, 1990
Keith Miller, *Cricket Crossfire*; Oldbourne Press, London, 1956
MA Noble, *The Game's The Thing*; Cassell & Company, Sydney, 1926
Michael Richardson, *RN Harvey: His Record Innings by Innings*; Association of Cricket Statisticians, Nottingham, 1998
Simon Rae, *WG Grace*; Faber & Faber, London, 1998
John Ringwood, *Ray Lindwall: Cricket Legend*; Kangaroo Press, Sydney, 1995
Irving Rosenwater, *Sir Donald Bradman*; BT Batsford Limited, London, 1978
Peter Sharpham, *Trumper: The Definitive Biography*; Hodder & Stoughton; Sydney, 1985
Steven Sheen, *FR Spofforth: His Record Innings by Innings*; Association of Cricket Statisticians, Nottingham, 1994
Mark Taylor with Ian Heads, *Time to Declare*; Ironbark, Sydney, 1999
Doug Walters, *Looking For Runs*; Pelham Books, London, 1971
RS Whitington, *Time of the Tiger*; Hutchinson, Melbourne, 1970
RS Whitington & George Hele, *Bodyline Umpire*; Rigby, Adelaide, 1974
RS Whitington, *Keith Miller: The Golden Nugget*; Rigby, Adelaide, 1981
Charles Williams, *Bradman*; Little Brown & Company, London, 1996

HISTORY AND TOUR BOOKS

Geoff Armstrong, *ESPN's Legends of Cricket*; Allen & Unwin, Sydney, 2002
Warwick Armstrong, *The Art of Cricket*; Methuen & Co. Ltd, London, 1922
Ralph Barker & Irving Rosenwater, *Test Cricket: England v Australia*; Batsford Ltd, London, 1969
Peter Baxter & Peter Hayter, *The Ashes: Highlights Since 1948*; BBC Books, London, 1989
Richie Benaud, *A Tale of Two Tests*; Hodder & Stoughton, London, 1962
Lionel H Brown, *Victor Trumper and the 1902 Australians*; Secker & Warburg, London, 1981
Keith Butler, *Howzat*; Collins, Sydney, 1979
Neville Cardus, *Cardus on Cricket*; Souvenir Press, London, 1977 (first published in 1949)
Neville Cardus, *Cardus in the Covers*; Souvenir Press, London, 1978
Neville Cardus, *Play Resumed With Cardus*; Souvenir Press, London, 1979
Neville Cardus, *A Fourth Innings With Cardus*; Souvenir Press, London, 1981
Greg Chappell, *The 100th Summer*; Garry Sparke & Associates, Melbourne, 1977
Ian Chappell, *Passing Tests*; Lynton Publications; Adelaide, 1973

Philip Derriman, *The Grand Old Ground*; Cassell, Sydney, 1981
Philip Derriman, *True to the Blue*; Richard Smart Publishing, Sydney, 1985
Philip Derriman, *The Top 100 & The 1st XI*; The Fairfax Library, Sydney, 1987
Jack Fingleton, *Brightly Fades The Don*; Collins, London, 1949
David Frith, *England Versus Australia*; Rigby, Adelaide, 1977
David Frith, *Bodyline Autopsy*; ABC Books, Sydney, 2002
Benny Green (compiler), *The Wisden Book of Cricketers' Lives*; Macdonald Queen Anne Press, London, 1988
Gideon Haigh, *The Summer Game*; Text Publishing, Melbourne, 1977
Ronald Mason, *Warwick Armstrong's Australians*; Epworth Press, London, 1971
Christopher Martin-Jenkins, *The Complete Who's Who of Test Cricketers*; Rigby, Sydney, 1981
AG Moyes, *A Century of Cricketers*; Harrap, London, 1950
AG Moyes, *Australian Bowlers*; Angus & Robertson, Sydney, 1953
AG Moyes, *Australian Batsmen*; Angus & Robertson, Sydney, 1954
AG Moyes, *Australian Cricket: A History*; Angus & Robertson, Sydney, 1959
Jack Pollard, *Cricket the Australian Way*; Lansdowne Press, Melbourne, 1968 (first published in 1961)
Jack Pollard, *Australian Cricket: The Game and the Players*; Hodder and Stoughton, Sydney, 1982
Ray Robinson, *On Top Down Under*; Cassell Australia, Sydney, 1976
Peter Roebuck, *Ashes to Ashes*; Kingswood Press, London, 1987
Sir Pelham Warner, *Cricket Between Two Wars*; Chatto & Windus, London, 1942
RS Whitington, *Captains Outrageous?*; Hutchinson, Melbourne, 1972
Peter Wynne-Thomas, *The Complete History of Cricket Tours*; Hamlyn, London, 1989

SCORECARDS AND STATISTICS
ABC Australian Cricket Almanacs (1990–1994)
Philip Bailey (ed), *ACS International Cricket Year Book 17th Edition 2002*; published by the Association of Cricket Statisticians and Historians, West Bridgford, Nottingham, 2002 (and earlier editions)
David Clark (ed), *ABC Australian Sports Almanac 2003*; Hardie Grant Books, Melbourne, 2002
David Clark (ed), *ABC Australian Sports Almanac 2002*; Hardie Grant Books, Melbourne, 2001
The Cricket Statistician (Quarterly Journal), published by the Association of Cricket Statisticians and Historians, West Bridgford, Nottingham

Graham Dawson & Charlie Wat, *Test Cricket Lists*; The Five Mile Press, Melbourne, 1998

Bill Frindall, *The Wisden Book of Test Cricket Volume 1 1877–1970*; Headline, London 2000

Bill Frindall, *The Wisden Book of Test Cricket Volume 2 1970–1996*; Headline, London 2000

Bill Frindall, *The Wisden Book of Test Cricket Volume 3 1996–2000*; Headline, London 2000

Allan Miller, *Allan's Cricket Annual 14th edition 2001*; published by Allan Miller, Busselton, 2001 (and earlier editions)

The Sydney Morning Herald Australian Cricket Almanac, 1995

Ray Webster & Allan Miller, *First-Class Cricket in Australia (Volume 1, 1850–51 to 1941–42)*; published by Ray Webster, Glen Waverley, 1991

Ray Webster, *First-Class Cricket in Australia (Volume 2, 1945-46 to 1976-77)*; published by Ray Webster, Glen Waverley, 1997

Wisden Cricketers' Almanack 140th edition 2003; John Wisden & Co. Ltd, Alton, Hampshire 2003 (and earlier editions)

Wisden Cricketers' Almanack Australia fifth edition 2002-03; Hardie Grant Books, Melbourne, 2002 (and earlier editions)

WEBSITES, NEWSPAPERS AND MAGAZINES

Among those consulted were *howstat.com.au* and *cricinfo.com*, *The Advertiser* (Adelaide), *The Age* (Melbourne), *The Australasian* (Melbourne), *The Australian*, *The Daily Telegraph* (Sydney), *The Referee* (Sydney), *The Sydney Morning Herald*, *The Sun-Herald* (Sydney), *The Times* (London), various ABC Cricket Books, Cricketer magazines, *Australian Cricket* magazines, Wisden Cricket Monthly magazines.